Contents

Contents

Acknowledgments

Early drafts of various parts of this book had their beginnings in lectures at Regent College, Vancouver; Wycliffe Hall, Oxford University in England; and Laity Lodge in Texas. "Isaiah of Jerusalem," now much revised, originated as a lecture at Regent College and was published in *Subversive Spirituality* (Vancouver, British Columbia: Regent College Publishing, 1997). Fragments of the chapter on Elijah are from the "Introduction to the Prophets" in *The Message* (Colorado Springs: NavPress, 2002). The material on Herod, Caiaphas, and Josephus was delivered as lectures at McCormick Theological Seminary/Lutheran School of Theology in 2003, at George Truett Seminary at Baylor University in 2005 (as the Parchman Lectures), and at the Christian Century Forum, Washington Island, Wisconsin, 2005.

Friends and colleagues have provided encouragement and correction. Fifteen years of conversation with Jon Stine are evident between the lines on most of these pages. Old Testament scholar Dr. Elmer Joy was generous with his time and attention. David Wood, Alan Reynolds, Virginia Stem Owens, Walt Wright, Luci Shaw, Paul Stevens, Marva Dawn, Arthur Paul Boers, and my pastor, Wayne Pris, helped, often when they didn't know they were helping, as did many, many others in sanctuaries and classrooms and homes. Jan, my wife, is a prayerful presence.

The Jesus Way is dedicated to Michael and Nancy Crowe. Their lives and friendship are daily confirmations of wise discernments practiced on the Way.

"The Purification of Means"

This is a conversation on the spirituality of the ways we go about following Jesus, the Way. The ways Jesus goes about loving and saving the world are personal: nothing disembodied, nothing abstract, nothing impersonal. Incarnate, flesh and blood, relational, particular, local.

The ways employed in our North American culture are conspicuously impersonal: programs, organizations, techniques, general guidelines, information detached from place. In matters of ways and means, the vocabulary of numbers is preferred over names, ideologies crowd out ideas, the gray fog of abstraction absorbs the sharp particularities of the recognizable face and the familiar street.

My concern is provoked by the observation that so many who understand themselves to be followers of Jesus, without hesitation, and apparently without thinking, embrace the ways and means of the culture as they go about their daily living "in Jesus' name." But the ways that dominate our culture have been developed either in ignorance or in defiance of the ways that Jesus uses to lead us as we walk the streets and alleys, hike the trails, and drive the roads in this God-created, God-saved, God-blessed, God-ruled world in which we find ourselves. They seem to suppose that "getting on in the world" means getting on in the world on the world's terms, and that the ways of Jesus are useful only in a compartmentalized area of life labeled "religious."

This is wrong thinking, and wrong living. Jesus is an alternative to the dominant ways of the world, not a supplement to them. We cannot use impersonal means to do or say a personal thing — and the gospel is personal or it is nothing.

In this matter of ways, the *how* of following Jesus and taking up with the world cannot be depersonalized by reduction into a how-to formula. We are involved in a highly personal, interrelational, dynamic way of life consisting of many elements — emotions and ideas, weather and work, friends and enemies, seductions and illusions, legislation and elections — that are constantly being rearranged, always in flux, and always in relation to our very personal and holy God and our very personal (but not so holy!) brothers and sisters.

Ways and means permeate everything that we *are* in worship and community. But none of the ways and means can be compartmentalized into functions or isolated as concepts apart from this comprehensive biblical and Trinitarian world in which we follow Jesus. They permeate everything we are and do. If any of the *means* we use to follow Jesus are extraneous to who we are in Jesus — detached "things" or role "models" — they detract from the *end* of following Jesus. Do our ways derive from "the world, the flesh, and the devil" of which we have been well warned for such a long time? Or do they serve life in the kingdom of God and the following of Jesus in which we have been given, historically and liturgically, a long apprenticeship?

$$* \quad * \quad *$$

The prevailing ways and means curricula in which we are all immersed in North America[1] are designed to help us get ahead in whatever field of work we find ourselves: sales and marketing, politics, business, church, school and university, construction, manufacturing, farming,

---

1. I refer to "North America" because this is the culture in which I have lived and worked, and the culture I know best. But from what friends from other countries tell me, a similar ways and means curriculum has infiltrated most of the Western world. Christians living in other cultures will need to make adjustments as you read, adapting the language to your conditions.

laboratory, hospital, home, playground, sports. The courses first instruct us in skills and principles that we are told are foundational and then motivate us to use these skills so that we can get what we want out of this shrunken, dessicated "world, flesh, and devil" field. And of course it works wonderfully as long as we are working in that particular field, the field in which getting *things* done is the "end."

When it comes to *persons*, these ways of the world are terribly destructive. They are highly effective in getting ahead in a God-indifferent world, but not in the community of Jesus, not in the kingdom of God. When we uncritically accept these curricula as our primary orientation in how to get on in the world, we naively embrace the very temptations of the devil that Jesus so definitively vetoed and rebuked.

Warnings are frequently and prominently posted by our sages and prophets to let us know that these purely pragmatic ways and means of the world weaken and enervate the community of the baptized. The whole North American ways and means culture, from assumptions to tactics, is counter to the rich and textured narrative laid out for us in our Scriptures regarding walking in the way of righteousness, running in the way of the commandments, following Jesus. In matters of ways and means, the world gives scant attention to what it means to *live,* to really live, to live eternal life in ordinary time: God is not worshiped, Jesus is not followed, the Spirit is not given a voice.

To take a person trained in ways and means that are custom-formulated to fit into the world's ways and then place that person in the worshiping, evangelizing, witnessing, reconciling, peace-making, justice-advocating people of God is equivalent to putting an adolescent whose sole qualifications consist of a fascination with speed, the ability to step on the accelerator, and expertise in operating the radio, behind the wheel of a brand-new Porsche.

Jacques Maritain, one of our more prescient and incisive prophetic voices from the twentieth century, continues to call on all of us who have taken up membership in the Christian community to be vigilant and active in what he called "the Purification of Means." He saw this as urgent work, about which we should not procrastinate if we are to follow Jesus in the freedom where he leads us, and if we are not to end up as slaves of a de-souled culture.[2]

The American Way

Here is a text, words spoken by Jesus, that keeps this in clear focus: "I am the way, and the truth, and the life" (John 14:6). The Jesus way wedded to the Jesus truth brings about the Jesus life. We can't proclaim the Jesus truth but then do it any old way we like. Nor can we follow the Jesus way without speaking the Jesus truth.

But Jesus as the truth gets far more attention than Jesus as the way. Jesus as the way is the most frequently evaded metaphor among the Christians with whom I have worked for fifty years as a North American pastor. In the text that Jesus sets before us so clearly and definitively, way comes first. We cannot skip the way of Jesus in our hurry to get the truth of Jesus as he is worshiped and proclaimed. The way of Jesus is the way that we practice and come to understand the truth of Jesus, living Jesus in our homes and workplaces, with our friends and family.

A Christian congregation, the church in your neighborhood, has always been the primary location for getting this *way* and *truth* and *life* of Jesus believed and embodied in the places and among the people with whom we most have to do day in and day out. There is more to the church than this local congregation. There is the church continuous through the centuries, our fathers and mothers who continue to influence and teach us. There is the church spread out throughout the world, communities that we are in touch with through prayer and suffering and mission. There is the church invisible, dimensions and instances of the Spirit's work that we know nothing about. There is the church triumphant, that "great cloud of witnesses" who continue to surround us (Heb. 12:1). But the local congregation is the place where

2. Jacques Maritain, *Freedom in the Modern World* (New York: Charles Scribner and Sons, 1936), p. 133.

we get all of this integrated and practiced in the immediate circumstances and among the men, women, and children we live with. This is where it becomes *local* and *personal*.

The local congregation is the place and community for listening to and obeying Christ's commands, for inviting people to consider and respond to Jesus' invitation, "Follow me," a place and community for worshiping God. It is the place and community where we are baptized into a Trinitarian identity and go on to mature "to the measure of the full stature of Christ" (Eph. 4:13), where we can be taught the Scriptures and learn to discern the ways that we follow Jesus, the Way.

The local congregation is the primary place for dealing with the particulars and people we live with. As created and sustained by the Holy Spirit, it is insistently local and personal. Unfortunately, the more popular American church strategies in respect to congregation are not friendly to the local and the personal. The American way with its penchant for catchy slogans and stirring visions denigrates the local, and its programmatic ways of dealing with people erode the personal, replacing intimacies with functions. The North American church at present is conspicuous for replacing the Jesus way with the American way. For Christians who are serious about following Jesus by understanding and pursuing the ways that Jesus is the Way, this deconstruction of the Christian congregation is particularly distressing and a looming distraction from the way of Jesus.

A Christian congregation is a company of praying men and women who gather, usually on Sundays, for worship, who then go into the world as salt and light. God's Holy Spirit calls and forms this people. God means to do something with us, and he means to do it in community. We are in on what God is doing, and we are in on it together.

And here is how we are in on it: we become present to what God intends to do with and for us through worship, become present to the God who is present to us. The operating biblical metaphor regarding worship is sacrifice — we bring ourselves to the altar and let God do with us what he will. We bring ourselves to the eucharistic table and enter into that grand fourfold shape of the liturgy that shapes us: taking, blessing, breaking, and giving — the life of Jesus taken and blessed, broken and distributed. That eucharistic life now shapes our lives as we give ourselves, Christ in us, to be taken, blessed, broken, and distributed in lives of witness and service, justice and healing.[3]

But that is not the American way. The great American innovation in congregation is to turn it into a consumer enterprise. We Americans have developed a culture of acquisition, an economy that is dependent on wanting more, *requiring* more. We have a huge advertising industry designed to stir up appetites we didn't even know we had. We are insatiable.

It didn't take long for some of our Christian brothers and sisters to develop consumer congregations. If we have a nation of consumers, obviously the quickest and most effective way to get them into our congregations is to identify what they want and offer it to them, satisfy their fantasies, promise them the moon, recast the gospel in consumer terms: entertainment, satisfaction, excitement, adventure, problem-solving, whatever. This is the language we Americans grow up on, the language we understand. We are the world's champion consumers, so why shouldn't we have state-of-the-art consumer churches?

Given the conditions prevailing in our culture, this is the best and most effective way that has ever been devised for gathering large and prosperous congregations. Americans lead the world in showing how to do it. There is only one thing wrong: this is not the way in which God brings us into conformity with the life of Jesus and sets us on the way of Jesus' salvation. This is not the way in which we become less and Jesus becomes more. This is not the way in which our sacrificed lives become available to others in justice and service. The cultivation of consumer spirituality is the antithesis of a sacrificial, "deny yourself" congregation. A consumer church is an antichrist church.

We can't gather a God-fearing, God-worshiping congregation by cultivating a consumer-pleasing, commodity-oriented congregation. When we do, the wheels start falling off the wagon. And they *are* falling off the wagon. We can't suppress the Jesus way in order to sell the Jesus

---

3. I elaborate this "shape" in considerable detail in my *Christ Plays in Ten Thousand Places* (Grand Rapids: Eerdmans, 2005), pp. 206-11.

truth. The Jesus way and the Jesus truth must be congruent. Only when the Jesus way is organically joined with the Jesus truth do we get the Jesus life.

Ends and Means

Men and women who take time to think and write about these things spend substantial energy considering matters of ends and means. Across the centuries, the consensus has been that if the nature of the means has been compromised and is in contradiction to the nature of the end, the end is desecrated, poisoned, and becomes a thing of horror.[4]

Ends: goals, destinations, purposes, the "what" of life, its ultimate meaning. *Means:* the way we get to the goal, the language we use, the work we do, the character we develop, the families and friends we form, the "how" of life.

The end, for Christians, is God's work of salvation. This is a salvation understood as comprehensive, intricate, patiently personal, embracingly social, insistently political. Salvation is the work of God that restores the world and us to wholeness. God's work complete. Glory. Eternal life. And we are in on it, in on the redemption of the world. Whoever I am, and wherever I find myself in history, in geography, in "sickness or in health," in whatever circumstance, I am in the middle of it, God's work of salvation. "Kingdom of God" is Jesus' term for it. This is what is going on.

And the means? In one word, Jesus. Jesus, pure and simple. If we want to *participate* (and not just go off in a corner and do our own thing), participate in the end, the salvation, the kingdom of God, we must do it in the way that is appropriate to that end. We follow Jesus. "For in him all the fullness of God was pleased to dwell, and through him God was pleased to reconcile to himself all things, whether on

4. The premier philosopher of our time engaged in this work is Albert Borgmann. See especially his *Technology and the Character of Contemporary Life* (Chicago: University of Chicago Press, 1984).

earth or in heaven, by making peace through the blood of his cross" (Col. 1:19-20). We cannot pick and choose ways and means that are more to our liking. The popularized acronym WWJD ("What would Jesus do?") is not quite accurate. The question must be "*How* does Jesus do it?" The old Puritan preacher Joseph Hall had it right: "God loveth adverbs; and careth not how good, but how well."[5] Adverbs modify and give clarity to the verb *follow*, giving daily and detailed texture to the *way* we follow Jesus.

So, Jesus. I am interested in the ways Jesus leads because they are necessarily the ways by which I follow. I cannot follow Jesus any which way I like. My following must be consonant with his leading. The way Jesus leads and the way that I follow Jesus are symbiotic. And this symbiosis is not treated with sufficient seriousness and depth in the Christian community of North America.

More often than not I find my Christian brothers and sisters uncritically embracing the ways and means practiced by the high-profile men and women who lead large corporations, congregations, nations, and causes, people who show us how to make money, win wars, manage people, sell products, manipulate emotions, and who then write books or give lectures telling us how we can do what they are doing. But these ways and means more often than not violate the ways of Jesus. North American Christians are conspicuous for going along with whatever the culture decides is charismatic, successful, influential — whatever gets things done, whatever can gather a crowd of followers — hardly noticing that these ways and means are at odds with the clearly marked way that Jesus walked and called us to follow. Doesn't anybody notice that the ways and means taken up, often enthusiastically, are blasphemously at odds with the way Jesus leads his followers? Why doesn't anyone notice?

*   *   *

5. Quoted by Charles Taylor, *Sources of the Self: The Making of Modern Identity* (Cambridge, Mass.: Harvard University Press, 1989), p. 224.

Jesus' metaphor, kingdom of God, defines the world in which we live. We live in a world where Christ is King. If Christ is King, everything, quite literally, every *thing* and every *one*, has to be re-imagined, re-configured, re-oriented to a way of life that consists in an obedient following of Jesus. This is not easy. It is not accomplished by participating in a prayer meeting or two, or signing up for a seven-step course in discipleship at school or church, or attending an annual prayer breakfast. A total renovation of our imagination, our way of looking at things — what Jesus commanded in his no-nonsense imperative, "Repent!" — is required.

The ways and means promoted and practiced in the world are a systematic attempt to substitute human sovereignty for God's rule. The world as such has no interest in following the crucified King. Not that there isn't plenty of lip-service offered along the way across a spectrum ranging from presidents to pastors. But when it comes down to an actual way of life, most of the language turns out to be court protocol — nothing to do with the *way* we actually order our affairs.

Those of us who understand ourselves as followers of Jesus seem to be particularly at risk of discarding Jesus' ways and adopting the world's ways when we are given a job to do or mission to accomplish, when we are supposed to get something done "in Jesus' name." Getting things done is something that the world is very good at doing. We hardly notice that these ways and means have been worked out by men and women whose ambitions and values and strategies for getting things done in this world routinely fail the "in Jesus' name" test. Once we start paying attention to Jesus' ways, it doesn't take us long to realize that following Jesus is radically different from following anyone else.

The one positive thing that can be said for the ways and means approved and rewarded in this world is that they work, sometimes magnificently, in achieving grandly conceived ends. Wars are fought and won, wealth is accumulated, elections are won, victories posted. But the means by which those ends are achieved leaves a lot to be desired. In the process a lot of people are killed, a lot of people impoverished, a lot of marriages destroyed, a lot of children abandoned, a lot of congregations defrauded.

My concern is with the responsibility of Christians, *every* Christian, to develop awareness and facility in the ways of Jesus as we go about our daily lives following Jesus in home and workplace, neighborhood and congregation, so that our following is consonant with his leading. I want to develop discernments that say an unapologetic "no" to ways that violate the gospel of Jesus Christ.

What I hope to call attention to is the undiscriminating way in which so many of us embrace and adopt the very ways and means that Jesus rejected, taking up with the world in ways suggested by the promises of the devil: assurances of power and influence, domination and success. Every such practice diverts energy from the community of Jesus, blurs the distinctiveness of the way of Jesus, and (whether intentional or not, usually not) insinuates a defiant element of resistance to the prayers of millions of Christians who pray daily, "Thy kingdom come."

The Laity Myth

I welcome any within earshot to enter the conversation, but I have a particular interest in getting the ear of the so-called laity — the nonprofessionals, the amateurs, the "mere" Christians, the members of the Christian community who say, "I'm just a layperson." These are the men and women who have occupied most of my attention in my fifty years as a pastor.

"I'm just a layperson" is usually spoken in the same self-deprecating inflection as "I'm just a homemaker," or "I've never been to seminary," or "Who am I that I should go to Pharaoh?" (Moses in Exod. 3:11), or "I'm only a boy" (Jeremiah in 1:7). It is an age-old habit, endemic to the human condition: if we don't have a socially sanctioned role, or a professionally certified position, or a recognized position in a family or community hierarchy, we feel inadequate and apologetic. As ourselves, just as ourselves, we have no "standing." Just as ourselves, we are *just* laypersons.

I have spent much of my life attempting to expose that "laity myth" for the lie that it is. Along with many colleagues, some of whom I know, most of whom I don't know personally, I have been trying to scrub the words "laity" and "layperson" of any and every hint of condescension and to recover biblical dignity, restore gospel vigor, to every random follower of Jesus.

I want Christian men and women to carry the designation layperson boldly into workplace and marketplace, home and church, without deference, without apology. I want them to know that in the vocabulary of Scripture they are the *people* of God (*laos* in the Greek of the New Testament is "people"); they are the laity, the laypersons, capable just as they are, as able as Mary and Elizabeth, as Peter and John — all laypersons — to hear, obey, love, and help one another along with the best of them as they follow Jesus.

Within the Christian community there are few words that are more disabling than "layperson" and "laity." The words convey the impression — an impression that quickly solidifies into a lie — that there is a two-level hierarchy among the men and women who follow Jesus. There are those who are trained, sometimes referred to as "the called," the professionals who are paid to preach, teach, and provide guidance in the Christian way, occupying the upper level. The lower level is made up of everyone else, those whom God assigned jobs as storekeepers, lawyers, journalists, parents, and computer programmers.

It is a barefaced lie, insinuated into the Christian community by the devil (who has an established reputation for using perfectly good words for telling lies). It is a lie because it misleads a huge company of Christians into assuming that their workplace severely limits their usefulness in the cause of Christ, that it necessarily confines them to part-time work for Jesus as they help out on the margins of kingdom work. It is particularly damaging in matters of ways and means, for we are used to deferring decisions in these matters to qualified experts or professionals.

It is not difficult to account for this pervasive "laity" putdown among us. After all, we spend our most impressionable years smaller, weaker, less knowledgeable, more inexperienced than most of the people with whom we grow up. Is it any wonder that we carry these feelings of inadequacy into our adult lives? We commonly compensate by getting academic degrees, professional certification, awards and trophies, as evidence of accomplishment. Or we join a club, follow a guru, buy a late-model car, dress in the latest fashion, wear a cap that identifies us with an athletic team. We acquire significance by taking on a role that defines our place in society or performing a function that is rewarded with applause or money.

What others think of us and how much they pay us go a long way in disguising feelings of inadequacy from our friends, our neighbors, and our fellow workers. There is at least one area of life in which we are not "just a layperson." If I am a mechanic, I know more about the car you drive than you do. While I am working on your car I am not a "layperson." If I am a physician, I know more about your body than you do. When I have a stethoscope around my neck and a scalpel in my hand I am not a layperson. If I am an English professor, I know more about the language you speak than you do. As long as I am lecturing in a classroom I am not a layperson. And on and on and on.

But in the company of Christians, that hierarchy of expertise simply doesn't work. There are no experts in the company of Jesus. We are all beginners, necessarily followers, because we don't know where we are going. On reflection it is difficult to understand how the term "laity" and the assumptions drawn from it continue to marginalize so many Christians from all-out participation in following Jesus. After all, didn't Jesus call only laypersons to follow him? Not a priest or professor among the twelve men and numerous women followers. And Paul, the tentmaker.

Our common identity as Christians is given most explicitly in baptism. If there is any need to distinguish the term "Christian" from its secularized usage as someone who is not a communist, not an atheist, not a Buddhist, my preference is to use "company of the baptized," or "baptismal identity," or "baptized Christian." Baptism marks us as the work of the Father, Son, and Holy Spirit. It is not an identity that we achieve on our own or a mark of superiority to others. And so throughout this conversation, I will from time to time use variations on the term "baptism," as reminders of our common identity.[6]

---

6. For an elaboration of baptism as a term of definition see my *Christ Plays in Ten Thousand Places,* pp. 300-331.

The plain fact is that most people who set out and continue to follow Jesus are laypersons. So why do so many of us habitually and pliantly take a subordinate position under certified experts in matters of faith? As a pastor myself, I've never gotten over my surprise — and dismay — at being treated with doggish deference by so many people. Where do all these Christians, who by definition are "new creatures in Christ" and therefore surely eager to taste and see for themselves (a universal characteristic in newborns) that the Lord is good, pick up this deprecating self-understanding? They certainly don't get it from the Bible or from the gospel. And certainly not from Jesus. They get it from the culture, both secular and ecclesial.

They get it from leaders who love the prerogatives and power of expertise, who bully people by means of their glamorous bravado into abdicating the original splendor of a new life in Christ and then declining into the wretched condition of the consumer. The consumer is passivity objectified: passive in the pew, passive before the TV screen, vulnerable to every sort of exploitation and seduction, whether religious or secular. And worst of all, passive in the matters of ways and means in following Jesus, letting others who we think must know better tell us how to do it.

*   *   *

But none of us has to live that way. We can — we must! — take responsibility for the way we live and work in our homes and neighborhoods, workplaces and public squares. We can refuse to permit the culture to dictate the way we go about our lives. We do not have to passively let professionals decide the ways we will follow Jesus.

When the Hebrews, recently enslaved but now free, were gathered at Sinai to begin their formation as a free people, God spoke the words that defined them over against their four centuries of slavery in the highly hierarchical kingdom of Egypt. One of the defining phrases was "kingdom of priests" (Exod. 19:6 RSV). "Priest" was a privileged and highly influential position in the culture from which they had just been rescued, a far cry from anything they could ever have imagined for themselves. And now they were all priests! It would take them a long time to assimilate what that meant. Many of them never did get it. Many of us still don't get it.

Twelve hundred years or so later, the phrase was picked up by Peter as he wrote to his congregation of beleaguered first-century Christians in the process of helping them understand and live out their baptismal identity in Jesus: "a royal priesthood" (1 Peter 2:9). John of Patmos, who gets the last scriptural word in these matters, also used the term "priest," this basic term of self-understanding out of the Hebrew tradition, to identify the Christians in his congregations: "priests serving his [Jesus'] God and Father" (Rev. 1:6) and "priests serving [Jesus'] God" (Rev. 5:10).

One of the severely crippling misunderstandings of the Reformation assertion of "the priesthood of all believers" is to assume (or worse, insist) that each of us can function as our own priest — "I don't need a priest, thank you, I can do quite well on my own, me and Jesus." But that is certainly not what Martin Luther intended when he included the priesthood of all believers as a fundamental tenet for reforming the church. He meant that we are all priests, not for ourselves, but for one another: "I need you for my priest, and while we are at it, I'm available to you as your priest."

The priesthood of all believers is not an arrogant individualism that, at least in matters dealing with God, doesn't need anyone. It is a confession of mutuality, a willingness to guide one another in following in the way of Jesus, to assist and encourage, to speak and act in Jesus' name, and to be guided by another to speak and act in Jesus' name. In the community of the baptized, there is no one, absolutely no one, who is not involved in this priestly leading and being led, for even "a little child shall lead them" (Isa. 11:6).

The intent throughout this conversation is to explore the ways in which Christians follow Jesus. The ways become clear in the act, and only in the act, of following Jesus on the terms enacted by Jesus. None of the ways can be abstracted from Jesus, depersonalized into a principle or strategy. I also want to post warnings against the many well-advertised ways and means that send us off on tangled detours or hopeless dead ends. And, not least, I want to recruit my friends in Christ for the work defined by Maritain as the "the Purification of Means."

Ways and means that are removed or abstracted from Jesus and the Scriptures that give witness to him amount sooner or later to a betrayal of Jesus. In this kingdom-of-God world, the person that we follow is the primary shaping influence on the person that we become. Christians follow Jesus.

*   *   *

Part One, "The Way of Jesus," will develop the metaphor of the way: the way that Jesus brought to full expression in his life, death, and resurrection. The way of Jesus did not originate with Jesus, although he certainly provided its final and definitive articulation. Jesus did not give explicit lectures and seminars on how to live in the kingdom of God. He simply said "Follow me." Jesus was anticipated by eighteen hundred years of men and women who walked in the "way of the righteous" (Ps. 1:6). We know some of their stories well and so can place not only the way that Jesus walked in Palestine in the first century, but the way many others walked in a wide-ranging historical and theological landscape that is large enough for us to see Jesus whole, in relation to his predecessors who were anticipating and preparing the way for his coming.

In addition to Jesus, I select six representative figures who preceded Jesus in the "way of the Lord." Each contributes an element that gives texture and depth to the way completed by and in Jesus: Abraham and the way of faith, Moses and the way of language, David and the way of imperfection, Elijah and the way of marginality, Isaiah of Jerusalem and the way of The Holy, and Isaiah of the Exile and the way of beauty.

Part Two, "Other Ways," considers Jesus in the context of three prominent leaders in the first century who did not follow the Jesus way. When Jesus appeared on the scene and said "Follow me," he did it in the company of well-established and highly successful leaders who represented rival ways of getting on in the world, ways that could easily have obliterated the way of Jesus at the three pivotal points of his life: Herod at Jesus' birth, Caiaphas at his death, and Josephus in the years following his resurrection. Jesus ignored them. Each of these leaders, in addition to making his considerable mark in the world, provoked strenuous lay opposition movements fueled by religious intensity and concern for God, thus providing yet other contrasts to the way of Jesus. The way of Herod, master of political ways and means, was countered by the Pharisees; the way of Caiaphas, master of religious ways and means, was countered by the Essenes; the way of Josephus, master of celebrity ways and means, was countered by the Zealots. Jesus ignored all of them. The masters of the day in the ways of politics, religion, and celebrity, along with lay protest movements that each provoked, continue to be well represented in our times; they provide contrasts that bring out what is distinctive in the way of Jesus and the discernments required of those among us who take up Jesus' command, "Follow me."

*   *   *

Over a period of eighteen hundred years or so, the Hebrews, our ancestor people of God, lived in proximity to a succession of great world civilizations — absolutely stunning civilizations, extravagantly splendid in architecture and art, masters of all the latest technologies, with military accomplishments that boggle the imagination still, sophisticated organizational and bureaucratic systems capable of directing huge work forces and an international economy, and religious establishments that articulated religious systems capable of integrating entire populations in a common belief and practice. None of these cultures were fly-by-night or flash-in-the-pan. Their influence endured for hundreds, some of them for thousands, of years.

The Hebrews were fortunate to happen to be in just the right place and at just the right time to benefit from them, see with their own eyes these cultures in operation. The people of God were *there*, experiencing firsthand the finest the world had to offer. The roll call of the empires quickens the pulse still: Sumeria, Egypt, Assyria, Babylonia, Persia,

Greece, Rome. Their leaders stand tall in the Leadership Hall of Fame: Hammurabi, Ramses, Tiglath-Pileser III, Nebuchadnezzar, Cyrus, Alexander the Great, Caesar Augustus.

But there is also this: through all these hundreds of years, with all that brilliantly executed empire-building going on around them — elaborate religious processions, magnificent building operations, exhibitions of art, military prowess — the Hebrew people kept to their own ways and maintained a unique counterculture, and in particular a counterculture in matters of ways and means. It is one of the wonders of the world that they were not absorbed by the power and beauty and wealth and learning brandished and celebrated by the kings and queens, the generals and priests, the gods and goddesses of those empires. The Hebrews seemed impervious to the whole show. They maintained what was always, given the sociopolitical forces around them, a precarious identity. But maintain it they did. How did that happen?

At one point the Hebrew people came close to obliteration. In approximately 1000 B.C. they decided that they wanted to be like "the other nations," the successful nations, the world-class nations. They wanted a king. Samuel, their spiritual leader at the time, reluctantly caved in to their demands. Saul, the first king, had an impressive inaugural, but it soon fizzled. David, appointed to replace him, achieved considerable local fame but was a nonentity in the military, political, and international scene of the day. His son Solomon made something of a splash with his elaborate temple-building and sexual exploits, but after years of posturing and despite a reputation for wisdom, at his death the kingdom split and the whole king business more or less fell apart. The falling apart was protracted — five hundred years of chaos and confusion — but when all was said and done, there were no more kings and no more kingdom.

But all through those centuries, from Abraham to Jesus, the people of God were developing ways of living in "the kingdom of God" that became fully expressed in Jesus, the very ways that turned out to be definitive for the salvation of the world.

For Christians who live in countries that inherit a Christian tradition, however thinned out, it is sometimes difficult to discern how different we are from the world. We speak the same language, eat the same food, drive the same cars, vote in the same elections. But we follow a very different leader, one who in virtually every detail guides us in a way of living that is counter to that of the world, a leader who not only leads but tells us, without qualifications, "Follow me."

*   *   *

The Jesus Way: A Conversation on the Ways That Jesus Is the Way continues the conversation in spiritual theology that I began with *Christ Plays in Ten Thousand Places* and continued in *Eat This Book: A Conversation in the Art of Spiritual Reading* (particularly the reading of the Bible). I intend the term "conversation" to be taken quite literally — a back-and-forthness between writer and reader. Matters of spiritual theology in general, and the spirituality of the ways of our Lord taken up in this conversation, are not categorically precise and cannot be pinned down with formulaic definitions or prescriptions. There are ambiguities that can be worked out only in prayer and practice while on the way.

The way of Jesus cannot be imposed or mapped — it requires an active participation in following Jesus as he leads us through sometimes strange and unfamiliar territory, in circumstances that become clear only in the hesitations and questionings, in the pauses and reflections where we engage in prayerful conversation with one another and with him. After all, we are not just learning how to think right about God. For that we would enroll in a classroom so that we could concentrate, protected from distractions. And we are not just practicing ways to behave right before God. For that we would go to a training camp set up for behavioral modification that would provide the necessary protection from interruptions.

We cannot remove ourselves from the way in order to have more favorable conditions for learning the way. We are already "on the way," acquiring insights and developing habits of obedience, following Jesus in our homes and neighborhoods and workplaces, gradually and incrementally maturing in the way so that who we are and what we do is realized coherently and comprehensively.

I

THE WAY OF JESUS

Follow me. . . . I am the way. . . .

JESUS, IN MARK 8:34 AND JOHN 14:6

. . . biblical leadership always means a process of being-led.

MARTIN BUBER, *Israel and the World*

CHAPTER 1

Jesus: "I Am the Way . . ."

Jesus is the Way. In the sixth of his seven great "I Am" self-definitions in St. John's Gospel he said so: "I am the way, the truth, and the life." It is among his most memorable and frequently quoted statements. It is also among the most frequently dismissed in the present-day culture of North America. The fog of inattention that surrounds the statement is to be expected from those who do not follow this "way," but it is astonishing and distressing among the men and women who give guidance and direction in the ways and means of living in the community of Jesus and as leaven in the world.

"Follow me" is the third imperative spoken by Jesus in Mark's telling of the gospel story (Mark 1:17). It is preceded by "Repent" and "Believe" (1:15). The three imperatives are the first commands that Jesus speaks after his radical, inaugural announcement, "The kingdom of God is at hand" (1:15 RSV). As the story proceeds, it turns out that by using the term "kingdom," Jesus is defining reality comprehensively as God's reality (you can't get more comprehensive than "kingdom"). Kingdom is what Jesus reveals, patiently but insistently, word by word, act by act. Real life, the real world, is a vast theater of salvation, directed by our wise and totally involved God. The three imperatives are invitations to live precisely *this* reality, *this* kingdom, following Jesus.

The first imperative, "Repent," requires a decision to leave one way of life and set out on another. It commands a change of mind or heart that results in a change of direction. The second imperative, "Believe," requires a personal, trusting, relational involvement in this comprehensive reordering of reality. And the third imperative, "Follow," gets us moving obediently in a way of life that is visible and audible in Jesus, a way of speaking and thinking, imagining and praying, that is congruent with the present, immediate ("at hand") kingdom realities.

To follow Jesus implies that we enter into a way of life that is given character and shape and direction by the one who calls us. To follow Jesus means picking up rhythms and ways of doing things that are often unsaid but always derivative from Jesus, formed by the influence of Jesus. To follow Jesus means that we can't separate what Jesus is saying from what Jesus is doing and the way that he is doing it. To follow Jesus is as much, or maybe even more, about feet as it is about ears and eyes.

*   *   *

When Jesus said "I am the way . . ." he used a word to define himself that is rich in resonance. Two thousand years later, one of our canonical American poets, Robert Frost, used the same metaphor in a poem that became the defining creed among a few but, as it turned out, not many of his fellow citizens: "I took the [road] less traveled by. . . ." The sentence is a Jesus classic: brief, punchy language that opens up wide vistas on reality.

Way: a simple noun designating a road that leads to a destination, but then opening up as a metaphor that ramifies into many and various "ways" — not only the way we go, as in the route we take, but the way we go on the way whether by foot or bike or automobile. The way we talk, the way we use our influence, the way we treat another, the way we raise our children, the way we read, the way we worship, the way we vote, the way we garden, the way we ski, the way we feel, the way we eat. . . . And on and on, endlessly, the various and accumulated "ways and means" that characterize our way of life.

*　　*　　*

"Way" is a stock metaphor in both our Scriptures and the traditions that have developed from them. At the entrance to our prayer book, the Psalms, the opening meditation uses this metaphor to set two ways of life before us. Will you live a solid life of prayer, listening to and answering God, rooted in the soil of God's revelation, your life growing like God's Torah, a tree with fruit-laden branches? Or will you live an insubstantial life of chatter and gossip, using words without God-context, oblivious of God, your life reduced to a pile of incoherent syllables, leaves blown every which way by the wind? Choose your way.

The Psalms in their extensive exploration of a life lived attentively and responsibly before God are conspicuous in their use of the metaphor, employing it ninety-seven times (twenty-one of these uses in the elaborately intricate Psalm 119). But the Psalms are in no way unique in their use of the metaphor. "Way" is employed extensively in both the Hebrew and Greek testaments, providing an intricate web of associations that keeps us alert to the pervasive and unrelenting necessity of being involved in a discerningly participatory way in all truth (doctrine) and all action (obedience), the truth and the action all of one piece, quite as much as a traveler and the road are of one piece. Jesus repeats and develops the Psalm 1 imagery of the two ways in his Sermon on the Mount when he contrasts the popular and easy road to death with the demanding road to life (Matt. 7:13-14).

It is significant that the primary term for identifying the followers of Jesus in the early church was "the Way." Luke in writing the story of the first Christian community uses it six times (Acts 9:2; 19:8, 23; 22:4; 24:14, 22), most famously, perhaps, recording Paul in his sermonic defense before Felix: "this I admit to you, that according to the Way, which they call a sect, I worship the God of our ancestors . . ." (24:14). "Christian," used in Antioch to refer to these people, is used only once (Acts 11:26).

Metaphor

"Way" is a metaphor. Which is to say that it both is and is not what it names. Way is a road, a street, a path. It is formed by clearing out boulders and stumps, paving the ground with asphalt or concrete. Stop signs are provided and "No Passing" warnings posted, along with directions and mileage to the next city. But when Jesus tells us that he is the Way, he is obviously not saying anything like that. He is not something for us to walk on. He is covered with skin, not asphalt. He cannot be summarized by a numbered line on a map. To call Jesus a way is obviously nonsense.

But even though we know that it is nonsense we say the word anyway, with serious intent. None of us for a moment supposes that Jesus is something that we walk on after having cleared out the underbrush and deadfalls in the forest. Calling Jesus the Way (or any of its synonyms — street, sidewalk, avenue, highway, trail, and so on) doesn't cause even a moment's confusion in our minds.[1]

For at the same time that we know it is nonsense we know it is *not* nonsense. Without hesitation we receive this word, "way," as an invitation to imagine the interconnectedness of the visible and invisible. We realize that there is more to Jesus, the Way, than we can see or hear, touch or taste. Our imaginations go to work, we try this, then that, we acquire an aptitude for dealing with all the interconnected visibles and invisibles inherent in reality.

We live in an intricate web of relationships that comprises the visible and the invisible, and so we need words that at one and the same time designate what is immediate to us via our senses and also immediate to us by faith. Ours is the world of dirt and stone, roads and houses, lilies and leopards, Saturn and San Diego, cradles and coffins, *and* simultaneously the world of sin and forgiveness, patience and per-

---

1. It did, however, seem to have confused Thomas, perhaps the most literal-minded of the apostolic twelve. When he heard Jesus say it, he thought that Jesus was the way as in "the road to Capernaum" or "the road to Bethany." But Jesus quickly got him to understand the term as metaphor. See John 14:5.

sistence, holiness and evil, faith, hope, and love, of which the greatest is love. These are not two worlds that coexist: the two worlds are the same world. The two aspects are indivisible. Metaphor is language that in a single word conveys the indivisibility of visible and invisible, of seen and unseen, of heaven and earth.

The simple fact is that life is mostly invisible, inaudible, untouchable. Life may be ultimately inaccessible to our five senses, but without the evidence supplied by our five senses it would for the most part elude us. It turns out that the quickest and most available access to the invisible by means of language is through metaphor, a word that names the visible (or audible, or touchable). A metaphor is a word that carries us across the abyss separating the invisible from the visible. The contradiction involved in what the word denotes and what it connotes sets up a tension in our minds, and we are stimulated to an act of imagination in which we become participants in what is being spoken. Metaphor is our lexical witness to transcendence — to the more, the beyond, the within — to all that cannot be accounted for by our microscopes and telescopes, by our algebra and geometry, by pulse rate and blood pressure, by weights and measures . . . a witness to all the operations of the Trinity.

The writers of Scripture are all masters of metaphor, language as a witness to the interconnectedness of all things visible and invisible. A metaphor takes a word that is commonly used to refer to a thing or action that we experience by means of our five senses and then uses it to refer to something that is beyond the reach of our immediate senses. Rock, for instance, refers to a hard mass of minerals that can be held and weighed, seen and painted. It designates what I stub my toe on, or throw through a window. There is no ambiguity in the word. It stays the same no matter what. And then one day Jesus looks at Simon and says, "You are a rock." What is that supposed to mean? By means of the miracle of metaphor, the word, taking the man with it, is launched into another realm of meaning altogether. Simon has been Rock (Peter, *petros*) ever since. We are still trying to come to grips with all the connections and implications set in motion by that metaphor.

At the simplest level, words identify things or actions. A word is a label. But when used as a metaphor, a word explodes, comes alive — it starts *moving*. I imagine myself entering a museum where every exhibit is identified by a word or words. The exhibits of animals and birds and artifacts are fascinating — there is so much to know! I observe and read and learn. Then suddenly, without warning, pterodactyls are flying; lions are running and growling and hunting for their supper; the women in the exhibits are trying on Egyptian gold necklaces and competing for attention, while the men grab Greek javelins and go into combat. The place is no longer a museum in which I can study or admire inert things; it is a world teeming with life and movement and action in which I am a participant — dodging the animals, admiring the women, avoiding the javelins — whether I want to or not.

Metaphor does that, makes me a participant in creating the meaning and entering into the action of the word. I can no longer understand the word by looking it up in the dictionary, for it is no longer just itself. It is alive and moving, inviting me to participate in the meaning. When the writers of Scripture use metaphor, we get involved with God, whether we want to or not, sometimes whether we know it or not.

When metaphor is banished and language is bullied into serving as mere information and definition, as happens so often in our computerized culture and cultural religion, the life goes out of the language. It also goes out of us. When this reduction happens in relation to God and all that pertains to God, we end up sitting around having study and discussion groups in religious museums. If we are lucky, one of the descendants of David or Hosea, Jonah or Habakkuk, shows up and with the simple expedient of a metaphor, said or sung, drags us outside into the open air where all the stuff we are studying is alive and moving and colliding with us. This certainly happens when Jesus shows up and says, "I am the way. . . ."

Which, of course, is why metaphors are so prominent in our Scriptures. And why "way" is used by these writers who are intent on getting us involved in the action of Father, Son, and Holy Spirit. "Way" gathers into itself everything that has to do with "ways and means." "Way" has a literal denotation of road, path, highway, street, and so on. But it simultaneously expands with connotations ranging broadly and comprehensively into the way we talk (boldly or hesitantly, kindly or sarcastically, lovingly or angrily, smoothly or roughly, reverently or blasphemously), the way we walk (leisurely or hastily, confidently or confusedly, strongly or weakly), the way we appear (groomed or slovenly), the way we behave (uprightly or criminally, straightforwardly or deviously, openly or slyly, generously or stingily, courteously or rudely).

Discernment

The relation between ends (where we are going) and means (how we get there) is a basic distinction in science, technology, philosophy, morality, and spirituality. Fitting the right means to the desired ends is required in virtually everything we do, from things as simple as getting across the street and frying an egg to the complexities involved in a mission to the moon or writing a novel. But here's the thing: the means have to be both adequate to and congruent with the end. Means have to fit ends. Otherwise everything falls apart.

It is far easier to decide on a desired end, a goal, than it is to acquire adequate means. "What do you want to do [or be] when you grow up?" evokes a kaleidoscope of answers for the first twenty or so years of our lives. Setting the goal requires little effort, no commitment, and no skill. But finding the means for reaching the goal, achieving that identity, is a matter of diligent concentration, responsible perseverance, and keen discernment.

Discernment of means adequate for living to the glory of God and congruent with our identity as baptized Christians has always been demanding, which is why the biblical writers use the metaphor of *way* so frequently. But with the unprecedented proliferation of technology, discernment makes demands on us in a way not anticipated by our biblical writers. For us, technology has taken over the business of means. Technology has a monopoly, at least in the minds of most, on answering questions regarding means. But technology for the most part restricts the term to matters visible: the means for making cars, getting to London, amassing a fortune, winning a game, killing the enemy. It is a very impressive monopoly. In our awed admiration we hardly notice that there is little skill or wisdom or concern given to the way we actually live. A technologized world knows how to make things, knows how to get places, but is not conspicuous for living well.

My concern is that the prominence of the *way* in our Scriptures and traditions, showing us how to glorify God and realize our baptismal identity, has been transferred in contemporary life into ways of getting money, getting jobs, and getting power. The authority of Scripture and Jesus in discerning and employing means has been taken over by technology, the god Technology. And this proliferation of technology obscures the vital organic connections between means and ends in everything that permeates our ordinary living. When technology calls the shots in matters of means, "standard of living" has nothing to do with how well we live, only with how much money we spend annually.

Temptation

The way in which Jesus is the Way is not a matter of style or expedience. Nor is it a generality, a vague pointing in an upward direction. Prayerfully and scripturally attentive, Jesus deliberately chose the way he would live. If we choose to follow him, we must be just as prayerful, scripturally attentive, and deliberate. The other ways are no ways.

Before they launch us into the story of the way of Jesus, our first three Gospel writers (in Matt. 4:1-11, Mark 1:12-13, and Luke 4:1-13) provide us with an arresting bold-print clarification on the way in which Jesus is the way — and the ways in which he is not.

After a few introductory matters, each writer places John the Baptist prominently before us. John is the last and greatest of the Hebrew prophets, prophets who from the time of Abraham have been preparing the "way of the Lord." John baptizes Jesus. The Spirit, like a dove, descends and alights on Jesus — a validation from heaven. The baptism is then endorsed by the voice from heaven, "This is my beloved Son, with whom I am well pleased." Jesus' lifework as Messiah — revealing God to us, leading us to God — is launched.

A glorious beginning. A great start. The baptism, the descent of the dove-Spirit, the voice from heaven. Yes. Momentum is up. Jesus is on his way. And we who are ready to follow Jesus are also on his way.

And then our canonical friends stop us in our tracks: "Hold on. Not so fast. Don't be in such a hurry. Pay attention to this." We are eager to get going but now we sit back — reluctantly, impatient with the interruption. We listen to the story of Jesus tempted by the devil.

"Immediately" (Mark's word) the Spirit drove Jesus out into the wilderness where he was tempted by the devil. Necessity is underlined. This has to take place before the story can continue. The word *peirazō* can also be translated "test" as it is in Genesis 22:1, when God brought Abraham to the time of testing on Mount Moriah. Apparently there are wrong ways to be on "the way of the Lord." The wilderness provides the place and time to clarify what is involved. We necessarily (this is not an option) have to pay close attention to the *way* we are on the way of the Lord, how we do this. Jesus had to do it; we have to do it.

The temptation clarified at the very outset the ways in which Jesus would do his work as Messiah. *Who* he was needed no letters of reference: the Holy Spirit descending like a dove and alighting on him was verification enough. His qualifications needed no further endorsement: "This is my beloved Son . . ." is definitive in that department. But *how* would he go about this messianic work, this comprehensive reconciliation of all things, "whether on earth or in heaven" (Col. 1:20), this salvation? *This* needs to be looked at closely, carefully considered, examined, rigorously tested. The stakes are high, eternally high.

*   *   *

Paul's time spent in the wilderness after his conversion to the way of Jesus ("I went away at once into Arabia," Gal. 1:17) suggests that not only did Jesus need to go through a time of testing and temptation but all of us who follow Jesus need to do so. Who we are and what we are to do is clear enough. But how will we do it? What ways will we use?

We grow up in a world in which the devil's ways of "doing good" are lavishly praised and practiced. Before we took up with Jesus, these ways seemed to work well enough, so well that we were only transiently aware that there even was a devil. But now in the clear desert air, discernments take place. We discern illusion behind the mask of goodness. We discern lies woven into the fine rhetoric of the pursuit of happiness. We discern incongruities between pretense and performance. We discern a disorienting extravagance in a promise that, like a bright light, dazzles us, temporarily blinding us to the details involved in our dailiness.

Wilderness time. Desert time. Time to see the way of Jesus tested against the devil's way. Time to feel the terrible pull of temptation away from the way of Jesus and realize that it is a temptation, as all temptation is, to embrace illusion, to believe a lie. Time to become aware of the immense but hidden abyss between the way of Jesus and the ways of the devil.

Time in the wilderness guards the way of Jesus from presumption and misapprehension, from naiveté and self-absorption. We give close attention to what is going on in the testing and tempting of Jesus and note that the devil does not suggest that Jesus in any way renounce his call, turn back to something simpler, avoid responsibility, deny the validity of his baptism, or doubt the voice from heaven. The devil is content to leave the matter of ends — the goal, the purpose, the grand work of salvation — uncontested. His tempting is devoted exclusively to *ways*, to the means that are best suited to accomplish the end to which Jesus is the way.

*   *   *

The first temptation: turn stones into bread. Jesus is hungry. The devil wants to use Jesus to do good. Jesus can begin by providing himself with a good meal. He can turn the stuff of creation into a commodity and do something useful with it — an obvious and good thing to do. It will launch him on a career of doing good: meet people's needs; satisfy their hungers whether physical, emotional, or mental; fulfill them; give them self-esteem.

The devil wants us to do the same: follow Jesus but then *use* Jesus to fulfill needs, first our own and then the needs of all the hungry people around us. It is the temptation to deal with myself and others first and foremost as consumers. It is the temptation to define life in consumer terms and then devise plans and programs to accomplish them "in Jesus' name."

Not that there are not needs aplenty in this world that need tending to. And not that there is not urgent gospel work to be done giving ourselves to lifework in alleviating hunger and poverty, working for justice, healing the sick, teaching what needs to be known, caring for the land, raising crops and cooking meals, telling stories and singing songs, protecting the weak. But the temptation is to *reduce* people, ourselves and others, to self-defined needs or culture-defined needs, which always, in the long run, end up being sin-defined needs — and use Jesus to do it.

The American economy is defined primarily in terms of meeting needs. We are better at it than probably any society in history, but meeting needs has not made us any better as people. Some of our critics say that we are the most selfish, self-centered, self-deceived people who have ever lived, and they might be right. And for all our ability to meet needs, we have an astonishing capacity for not noticing the needs of those we don't like or who will overly inconvenience us.

Jesus was active in meeting needs all his life and he means for us to be similarly active, but the way he lived was not reduced to, although it always included, meeting needs.

The second temptation: jump off the roof of the temple. The devil wants to use Jesus to dazzle the crowds of people on the street below with a miracle, to put a little excitement into their dull lives. "Jump, Jesus — these people will never forget it; it will change their lives. For years to come they will be telling their children and grandchildren of that angel-rescue, a convincing witness that God is supernaturally at their beck and call." The temptation is to embark on a circus career in miracles. And what could be better than a career in God-miracles, religious miracles, entertaining crowds, supplying ecstasy on demand?

The devil wants us to do the same, use Jesus as a hedge against boredom. Use Jesus as some people use drugs and alcohol, sex and fast cars, danger and thrills, television and guns. Use Jesus for his miracle potential. Use Jesus as a reprieve from the humdrum. Package Jesus as a commodity for weekend diversions.

Certainly there is no shortage of emotionally drab people in the world, living dead-end lives, drifting from one fix to another. No shortage of men and women devoid of an inner life, missing out on so much, and therefore vulnerable to addictions of all sorts — sex, drugs and alcohol, food, the adrenaline rush that comes in criminal acts and gambling. There is much to be done here. For there is no question but that Jesus wants us to live abundantly. He said he did (John 10:10). There is so much joy and beauty and ecstasy in the way of Jesus. Jesus' way is never tight-fisted or scrimped or penny-pinching. The temptation is to *reduce* Jesus to escapism and thrills: an impersonal rescue, an irresponsible diversion, a manipulative reprieve from the ordinary.

The American entertainment industry is second to none in providing cheap diversions and borrowed ecstasies. A temporary detachment from daily responsibilities, a vacation from demanding intimacies, is most useful — it can return us to our dailiness, our jobs and friends and families, energized and renewed. Our lives can be refreshed and energized by entertainment. But in excess it defeats what it sets out to do for us: we are herded into the bleachers as spectators to the aliveness of life, reduced to the passivity of a couch potato, satiated into sloth. Careful observers repeatedly warn us that we are entertaining ourselves to death.[2]

Jesus was certainly capable of taking that jump off the temple roof. Why didn't he do it? Jesus refuses to entertain us with miracles, just as he refused to entertain Herod Antipas (Luke 23:8-9). Jesus is not interested in diverting us from life, but in revealing the "more" that is in life beyond what we can cobble together on our own, dimensions of beauty and challenge, depths of gladness, our mouths "filled with laughter" (Ps. 126:2). What is more impressive than the miracles that Jesus performed is that he performed so few of them. Jesus never used

2. See Neil Postman, *Amusing Ourselves to Death* (New York: Vintage Books, 1985).

miracles as shortcuts or labor-saving devices. "No Christian will suppose that Jesus in his carpentry shop ever laid aside the hammer and used the Holy Ghost to drive an awkward nail."[3] His very occasional miracles were a way to show us the "more" that is inherent in life, a revelation of the depth available to us in a life of love and obedience. The way of Jesus is not a sequence of exceptions to the ordinary, but a way of living deeply and fully with the people here and now, in the place we find ourselves.

The third temptation: rule the world. The devil wants to use Jesus to run the world, take charge of the world — "all the kingdoms of the world and their splendor." What an offer! Who is more qualified? Here is the opportunity to establish a rule of peace and justice and prosperity. Create a government free of corruption. But of course it would have to be on the devil's terms, a rule conditioned by the unholy *if* — "if you will fall down and worship me." The devil's way would necessarily be an imposed, impersonal way. The devil's way would be absolutely perfect in its functions, but with no personal relations.

The devil wants us to use Jesus in the same way. Use Jesus to run our families, our neighborhoods, our schools, our governments as efficiently and properly as we can, but with no love or forgiveness. Every man and woman reduced to a function. That is the only way that you can have a just and peaceful and prosperous government. If you let people have a say in these matters, suddenly you will find yourself operating in a maelstrom of prejudice, egotism, ambition, superstition, ignorance, greed, avarice — you name it. Our newspapers and newscasts do name it every day. Meanwhile the devil is at our elbows, tempting us to impose "the right" by eliminating freedom. Gandhi used to talk disparagingly of "dreaming of systems so perfect that no one will need to be good."[4]

Not that there is not a lot of good to be done in the world of poli-

---

3. Austin Farrer, *The Triple Victory* (London: Faith Press, 1965), p. 44.

4. Quoted by E. E. Schumacher, *Small Is Beautiful* (New York: Harper and Row, 1973), p. 24.

tics and government, the cause of peace and the work of justice, marriage and family, business and trade. Despite numerous attempts to develop utopian communities down through the centuries, the human race has never been very good at taking care of these matters, providing a way for men and women to make a living, work with each other for common goals, look out for the needs of the weak and damaged. War has always been the classic way of choice to impose our idea of what is good on the people we don't like or disapprove of. It still is. In the century just completed "all the kingdoms of the world," led by the most advanced kingdoms economically and educationally, outdid themselves in not getting along. George Steiner summarizes it as "a time out of hell."[5] The facts and statistics are indisputable: the smarter we get, the more prosperous we are, the more murderous we become.

American democracy, assumed by many, maybe most, to be one of the brighter spots in the history of the world's governments regarding human rights and prosperity, is by no means unblemished — certainly not without "spot or wrinkle." The vision of our early political leaders that we would be a "city on a hill," showing the way for the world, has long since faded. The rhetoric that we are a Christian nation is not supported by the performance of our political leaders, our business community, or our institutions of learning. Meanwhile, every Christian has an important voice and presence in the way our country is run and our culture is formed — but we are dupes of the devil if we suppose that we can speak in a language and act in a style other than or counter to the ways that Jesus spoke and acted.

Jesus has a great deal to say about how we run the world — "kingdom" and "world" figure largely in what he was and is about. But he values our souls too much to "de-soul" us in order to make us good. He will not impose his way on any of us — no, not one of us. He invites and he forgives. He seeks the lost and heals the hurt. He rebukes the proud and turns the other cheek. The final word that our Scriptures give us on Jesus is triumphant as the "ruler of the kings of the earth"

5. George Steiner, *Grammars of Creation* (New Haven: Yale University Press, 2001), p. 4.

(Rev. 1:5) — the identical exalted position offered by the devil, but ruling, as it turns out, first from the Golgotha cross and now "seated at the right hand of the Father," carrying out the grand and comprehensive work of salvation in which all "will bow in worship before this Jesus Christ, and call out in praise that he is the Master of all, to the glorious honor of God the Father" (Phil. 2:10-11 *The Message*).

Jesus was tempted to rule from a throne-bureaucracy of abstract rules and disembodied principles imposed on men and women apart from relational trust and worshiping love. He refused. The rule of Jesus is never impersonal, never nameless.

*   *   *

Each of the devil's temptations has to do with the *way* that Jesus is the way, the way he will go about his work. Will he reduce and depersonalize the way by imposing his will on the rocks, using them to provide for human needs, first taking care of himself and then feeding a lot of people? Will he put on a circus spectacular, demonstrating the miraculous, ever-present providence of God to the people on the street but never dealing with them as persons? Will he rule the world by means of a faceless bureaucracy, efficiently enacting justice and prosperity without getting his hands dirty?

Jesus said no to each one in turn. Jesus gave a definitive, Scripture-backed no to each temptation. And why? Because in each case it would have been an impersonal way, a way abstracted from relationships, a way disengaged from love, a way imposed from the outside. It would have been a way ripped out of the comprehensive story of salvation, and therefore ripped out of participation in people's lives. Whatever the way of Jesus means, bullying force is not part of it. It is certainly not what takes place when a fuse of dynamite (named after the Greek word for power, *dunamis*) is lit. The way of Jesus is always exercised in personal ways, creating and saving and blessing. It is never an impersonal interference from the outside.

In the three great refusals, Jesus refuses to do good things in the wrong way. Each temptation is wrapped around something good: feed a lot of people, evangelize by miracle, rule the world justly. The devil's temptation strategy is to depersonalize the ways of Jesus but leave the way itself intact. His strategy is the same with us. But a way that is depersonalized, carried out without love or intimacy or participation, is not, no matter how well we do it, no matter how much good is accomplished, the Jesus way. We cannot do the Lord's work in the devil's ways. The devil has great ideas — brilliant ideas! The devil is the consummate idealogue, but he is incapable of incarnation. He uses people to embody his projects in functional rather than personal relationships. The devil is the ultimate in disincarnation. Every time that we embrace ways other than the ways of Jesus, try to manipulate people or events in ways that short-circuit personal relationships and intimacies, we are doing the devil's work. Vigilance is required. It has always been required. It is required still in this America where doing good work in impersonal ways is epidemic.

Ways

So. Jesus the Way, the ways of Jesus. He shows the way. He also *is* the way. He doesn't point out the way and then step aside and let us get there on our own as best we can. Jesus points out the way, but then he takes the initiative, inviting us to go with him, taking us with him across land and sea, through all kinds of weather, avoiding dead ends and seductive byways, watching out for danger and alerting us to enemies.

One of the things that comes into focus as we consider Jesus the Way is that we cannot account for the distinctiveness of Jesus' way by assembling pertinent adjectives and adverbs for who he is and how he acts. The way is not an abstraction, a slogan, a principle. It is a metaphor: a road, a path, a street, a highway, a trail, and simultaneously a person, a body that we can see and a spirit that we cannot see, speaking words that we can understand, sitting down to dinner with friends, teaching in a synagogue in Capernaum and along the shores of Galilee Lake, sailing in a boat and riding on a donkey, throwing a picnic featuring bread and fish for five thousand men and women with their children, spending the night praying for us in the mountains, dying on that Golgotha cross, rising from the dead and breathing his resurrection life into us.

The primary documents that tell us about this way are narratives of the way Jesus lived and the way he proclaimed the good news message. There are — and their absence is conspicuous — no summaries of his attributes, no test results of his intelligence or aptitudes, no lists of his accomplishments. Every detail is embedded in his metaphor-studded story. We are intended to enter by imagination and faith and prayer into the story, this narrative, and get a feel for what is involved, the relationships that make up the web of this way.

*   *   *

There is also this: Jesus is our way to God, but at the same time Jesus is God's way to us. Heraclitus, the pre-Socratic Greek philosopher, is known among us today only in fragments. We don't have a book, nor even so much as an essay. We have just fragments of his speech, many of them enigmatic. In the context of this conversation on the way of Jesus, here is one that I like very much: "The way up and the way down is the same way."[6]

The way we come to God is the same way that God comes to us. God comes to us in Jesus; we come to God in Jesus. It is the same way, the Jesus way. God comes to us in Jesus speaking the words of salvation, healing our infirmities, promising the Holy Spirit, teaching us how to live in the kingdom of God. It is in and through this same Jesus that we pray to and believe, hear and obey, love and praise God. Jesus is the way God comes to us. Jesus is the way we come to God. "The way up and the way down is the same way."

Jesus is the way of salvation. We follow his way. Jesus is the way of eternal life. We follow his way. The way Jesus does it is the way we do it. Jesus is the way we come to God. Period. End of discussion.

6. Charles H. Kahn, *The Art and Thought of Heraclitus* (Cambridge: Cambridge University Press, 1979), p. 74.

And Jesus is the way God comes to us. On earth, Jesus is the way of faith and obedience and prayer — to God. From heaven, Jesus is the way of God's revelation, God's salvation, God's blessing — to us.

Everything we need to know of God comes by way of Jesus: "The Word became flesh and dwelt among us, full of grace and truth; we have beheld his glory" (John 1:14 RSV). St. John's Gospel, carefully and in a most leisurely way — "unresting, unhasting, and silent as light"[7] — tells us the story, all the operations of the Holy Trinity revealed to us in Jesus, the Christ.

Several decades ago Charles Sheldon wrote a book that was widely read, *What Would Jesus Do?* Good question. But if another question is not given equal billing alongside it, it yields answers that are only a half-truth. We must also ask, *What is God doing?* Jesus tells us what to do; at the same time he tells us what God is doing. Jesus is God in action. Jesus is God speaking. Jesus is God touching lepers. Jesus is God forgiving a condemned and dying criminal and an adulterous woman hounded by men holding rocks and poised to kill her. Jesus is God blessing children. Jesus is God giving sight to Bartimaeus, life to Lazarus. Jesus is God calling down judgment on religious posturing. Jesus is God weeping over Jerusalem.

Jesus. Jesus. Jesus. Jesus is the way we come to God. Jesus is the way God comes to us. And not first one and then the other but both at the same time. Not God's way to us on Sundays and our way to God on weekdays. It is a two-lane road. Much mischief has been perpetrated in the Christian community by not keeping both lanes open. The road up and the road down are the same road.

Psalm 84 speaks of men and women "in whose hearts are the highways to Zion." We know something about highways and we know what happens when an accident blocks the lane we are in. We sit there stuck, while the cars on the other side of the road are free to drive home, or to work, or to the mountains to ski, or to the ocean to surf and swim. It is not enough to have a single lane. We require a highway

7. From the hymn by Walter Chalmers Smith, "Immortal, Invisible, God only Wise," *The Hymbook* (Philadelphia: Presbyterian Publishing Co., 1955), p. 82.

with the traffic going both ways — Jesus. Our way to God. God's way to us.

*   *   *

There is more. The people who told this story, primarily Matthew, Mark, Luke, and John, were also conversant with earlier narratives that anticipate this one. They tell the story of the way of Jesus in the narrative context of centuries of story-telling in such a way that the stories of the preceding two thousand years are filled out and completed in the story of Jesus.

If we want to get the full impact of the story of Jesus and the way of Jesus, there is no substitute for taking a long, slow, leisurely pilgrimage through the pages of Genesis to Malachi, getting that river of narrative flowing through our bloodstream, observing the enormous attention given to place and person, so that this story is rooted in the immediate and the local, in named people in the neighborhood, among the animals and angels alive in those forests and deserts. In the remaining chapters in this section I want to bring into the conversation six of these people who embraced, prefigured, and prepared the way of Jesus: Abraham, Moses, David, Elijah, Isaiah of Jerusalem, and Isaiah of the Exile.

We cannot understand the way of Jesus by means of summary accounts of those two thousand years of history and belief and worship that preceded Jesus. If a summary could provide adequate preparation, the Holy Spirit would surely have supplied it and saved us the trouble of making ourselves at home in that narrative country, learning the language of faith, finding our way around the kingdom of God.

*   *   *

I want to counter the common reduction of "way" to a road, a route, a line on a map — a line that we can use to find our way to eternal life; such reduction means the elimination of way as a metaphor, the reduction of way to a lifeless technology. The Way that is Jesus is not only the roads that Jesus walked in Galilee and to Jerusalem but also the way Jesus walked on those roads, the way he acted, felt, talked, gestured, prayed, healed, taught, and died. And the way of his resurrection. The Way that is Jesus cannot be reduced to information or instruction. The Way is a person whom we believe and follow as God-with-us.

Years ago I was traveling along a spectacular mountain road with an old college friend who was visiting from Texas. This road is one of the scenic wonders of North America. My friend had a map open on her knees. I kept pointing out features in the landscape around us: a five-hundred-foot waterfall, a glacial formation, a grove of massive Western Red Cedars, a distant horizon of mountains on which a storm was forming. She rarely looked up; she was studying the map. When I, with some impatience, tried to get her attention, she told me that she wanted to "know where we are." And "knowing where we are," for her, was defined by a line on a map. She preferred the abstraction of a road map to the actual colors and forms, the scent and texture of Mount Reynolds, the roar of Logan Creek, an alpine meadow on the way to Piegan Pass, luxurious in bear grass.

A variation on my friend's preference for abstractions over an actual world of wonders occurred years earlier. My wife and I, with our children, had spent many glorious hours hiking in these same mountains that my friend reduced to a map. When our two sons became adolescents they also became impatient with the pace of their parents on any ascent up a mountain. We would be on a trail no more than ten minutes when they were out of sight. For them the trail, the *way*, was reduced to one thing and one thing only: the way to the top of the mountain. They set out with all deliberate speed to conquer (their verb of choice) the mountain, get to the peak, write their names in the metal box containing the names of successful climbers. They always took a couple of pictures to document their feat. And then, reeking with boredom, they waited for their slowpoke parents who were carrying the lunch. "What took you so long? Did you lose your way? We've been waiting for *hours!*"

What *did* take us so long? Well, there was a lot to see, to savor, to absorb, to enjoy: a mountain goat posing regally on a cliff, a blue-fringed gentian to look at again as for the first time, the wind-sculpted trunk of an ancient white-bark pine, a water ouzel playing in a waterfall, the nectarine that we relished as we sat and took in the next range of mountains that had just come into view (why do nectarines taste so much better at altitudes above eight thousand feet?). *Way* for us was far more than a way to get to the top. It was a way of being present to everything on the way — spruce fragrance, brook music, glacier-cut rock formations, bear-grass elegance, and (saving the best for last) leisurely conversation of reminiscence and appreciation in the easy company of one another. Our sons' reduction of *way* to way-to-the-top was a considerable improvement over my friend's reduction of it to a line on a map, but it was a reduction all the same. I remember reading something along this same line by Robert Pirsig: "To live only for some future goals is shallow. It's the sides of the mountain which sustain life, not the top. Here's where things grow. But of course, without the top you can't have the sides. It's the top that *defines* the sides."[8]

I am interested in releasing all the metaphorical nuances in the way of Jesus. Too many of my faith-companions for too long have been reducing the way of Jesus simply to the route to heaven, which it certainly is. But there is so much more.

Dorothy Day, one of our iconic American pilgrims, a sturdy and discerning traveler on this way, loved to quote St. Catherine: "All the way to heaven is heaven, because He had said, 'I am the way.'"[9]

8. Robert Pirsig, *Zen and the Art of Motorcycle Maintenance* (New York: William Morrow, 1974), p. 198.

9. Dorothy Day, *The Long Loneliness: An Autobiography* (San Francisco: Harper and Row, 1952), p. 247.

CHAPTER 2

Abraham: Climbing Mount Moriah

The defining event in the way of Abraham takes place on Mount Moriah: the Binding of Isaac, the *Akedah* (the term the rabbis use for this story, after the Hebrew word for "binding"), Abraham binding Isaac and offering him as a sacrifice on the altar that he has just built expressly for this purpose. This story has absorbed the imagination of the people of God and plunged generation after generation of us into facing and dealing with the fundamental mystery that is God: There is so much here that we cannot comprehend, so much that violates our pious sensibilities, so much that refuses to conform to our expectations. How can God command a murder? And not just murder in general but the murder of a beloved son? How can God go back on the miracle-promise fulfilled in the birth of Isaac? How can God, who our parents and pastors have taught us loves us from eternity, command this cold-blooded cruelty? How can God, who Jesus tells us has such a tender heart that he is moved even by the death of sparrows, command a father to kill his son, without so much as a hint of explanation?

We can't handle this. When we try to imagine ourselves as either Isaac submitting to the binding or Abraham lifting the knife to slit his throat, we cannot do it. It is too terrible to admit into our consciousness, especially a consciousness that includes a good and sovereign God. We look for explanations and answers, we ransack libraries and cultures in search of something or other to mitigate the unbearable harshness. We hire theologians and pastors to abstract the story into a principle or dogma or lesson that will insulate us from the offending details. But there is no getting around it: The *Akedah*, the Binding of Isaac on Mount Moriah, the knife poised at Isaac's throat, is not only the defining event in the way of Abraham, but the "midpoint of *Genesis* . . . the paradigmatic narrative of the entire book."[1] There it stands: a huge, impassible boulder blocking the way.

Alexander Whyte, the formidable Edinburgh pastor, doesn't try to moralize or theologize or psychologize: "I do not understand this dark dispensation of God — all the seed of Abraham are often compelled to say — all is dark, is midnight to me."[2]

A striking element in the Abraham story is the spare, austere language, the economy of words used in drawing us in as participants, involved in what we will never comprehend. An intolerable tension between the highest and noblest human feelings and expectations (love, fatherhood, a God-ordained leadership place among the people of God — everything that gives human life meaning and wholeness) is created by a command to abandon it all, give it up in obedience to an unexplained and arbitrary command of God. Everything that God has given and gives, surrounded with promises and blessings, now taken away without explanation, without reason. There is nothing in the telling of this story that invites us into the inner workings, nothing that makes us want to be a participant, nothing that brings us, as we say, "alongside" God and his salvation.

Why did our ancestors place this story so imperiously on the very threshold of the Way? Didn't they know that many of us coming on this story so early on, offended and outraged, would just shut the book and go shopping for something or someone more benign to guide us in our spiritual quest, like, say, the Buddha?

---

1. Everett Fox, *The Five Books of Moses* (New York: Schocken Books, 1995), p. 92.
2. Alexander Whyte, *Bible Characters* (London: Oliphants, 1952), vol. 1, p. 77.

Faith

Abraham is remembered among the people of Israel and the people who later became the followers of Jesus as father of the people of God. The story is unmistakably a story of a human being. In all essential details he is like us. It is the story of a man who obeyed God's call to leave his country and follow the leading of his God to a place that he knew nothing about. It is a story in which, with Paul as our teacher, we become acclimated to the word "faith" — trusting obediently in what we cannot control, living in obedient relationship to the One we cannot see, venturing obediently into a land that we know nothing about.

Faith has to do with marrying Invisible and Visible. When we engage in an act of faith we give up control, we give up sensory (sight, hearing, etc.) confirmation of reality; we give up insisting on head-knowledge as our primary means of orientation in life. The positive way to say this is that when we engage in an act of faith we choose to deal with a living God whom we trust to know what he is doing, we choose a way of life in which bodily senses and physical matter are understood as inseparable and organic to vast interiorities (soul) and immense beyonds (heaven), and we choose to no longer operate strictly on the basis of hard-earned knowledge, glorious as it is, but over a lifetime to embrace the mystery that "must dazzle gradually/Or every man go blind."[3]

It is most certainly not a disposition, an "inner life." It is an obedient life, a deliberate engagement of the will, a fusion of body and spirit, visible and invisible fused, taking us somewhere.

This involves considerable risk. The supposed security of objective certainty recoils from such risk. But for those who take it, it also results in inhabiting a vast, previously unperceived, reality. It also involves considerable retraining in virtually everything involved in being a man, a woman. The introduction of the word "faith" into our language produces a radical and total reorientation from a flat-earth existence,

3. Emily Dickinson, *The Complete Poems*, ed. Thomas H. Johnson (Boston: Little, Brown, and Company, 1925), p. 507.

plotted along the monotonous lines of a suburban subdivision, to a multidimensioned "on earth as it is in heaven," in which God's presence is the dominant and defining reality with whom we have to do.

The way of Abraham continues today along these same lines. Somewhere along the way we realize that we are not in charge of our own lives. The life of faith does not consist in imposing our will (or God's will!) either on other persons or on the material world around us. Instead of making the world around us or the people around us or our own selves into the image of what we think is good, we enter the lifelong process of no longer arranging the world and the people on our terms. We embrace what is given to us — people, spouse, children, forests, weather, city — just as they are given to us, and sit and stare, look and listen until we begin to see and hear the God-dimensions in each gift, and engage with what God has given, with what he is doing. Every time we set out, leaving our self-defined or culture-defined state, leaving behind our partial and immature projects, a wider vista opens up before us, a landscape larger with promise.

*   *   *

The Binding of Isaac is introduced as a test: "After these things God tested Abraham" (Gen. 22:1). After what things? Well, after enough details have accumulated to show us that Abraham was a person of faith, a person who listened to God and obeyed with his life. Abraham is our prototypical person of faith, not faith as a doctrine to be taught and learned but a certain way of being in the truth that extends beyond reason's ability to fully grasp. The faith word "believe" ("faith" is the noun and "believe" the verb of the same root word in Hebrew, *aman*) is used only once in the story of Abraham's life. ("And he *believed* the LORD; and the LORD reckoned it to him as righteousness," Gen. 15:6.) But when Paul in his great, grounding letter to the Romans called up Abraham as a key witness in his case for the gospel, he zeroed in on just this, his faith:[4]

---

4. The noun "faith" (*pistis*) and the verb "believe" (*pisteuō*) are also from the same root word in Greek.

"Abraham *believed* God. . . . [S]uch *faith* is reckoned as righteousness" (Rom. 4:3, 5); "*Faith* was reckoned to Abraham as righteousness" (4:9); "the ancestor of all who *believe*" (4:11); "the example of *faith* that our ancestor Abraham had . . ." (4:12); "those who share the *faith* of Abraham" (4:16); "hoping against hope, he *believed*" (4:18); "he did not weaken in *faith*" (4:19); "he grew strong in his *faith*" (4:20).

Paul's choice of Abraham as the prototypical person of faith is echoed in the grand recital of the epic of faith from Abel to Jesus that is a high point in the Letter to the Hebrews (11:1–12:2). In this passage, the term "faith" is used twenty-six times in connection with nineteen named persons, but it is Abraham who is cited most often, four times. (Moses with three citations comes in a close second.)

What did these writers see in Abraham that they named faith? Was it not this lifetime of internalizing the commanding and promising but invisible God and then stepping out on the road in obedience? Was it not this readiness to leave wherever he was and leave whatever he had in order to embrace the vision, the covenant, the command? Was it not a life of responsive openness to God and a matching indifference to whatever conditions he found himself in? Was it not a lifetime disposition to receive God rather than to satisfy himself?

Faith is a trusting, obedient life on the road, the *way*. Faith is a resolute "Yes" to the promises and commands of the living God, God as *present*. And faith is a firm "No" to an idol subject to manipulation and control, a god that we can see and touch and test.

Among Scripture-taught people of God, "our father Abraham" (Luke 1:73 RSV; John 8:53; Acts 7:2; Rom. 4:16; and so on) is the dictionary in which we look up the meaning and get a feel for what is involved in the life of faith. What we get, it turns out, is not a definition but a story, a story in which traveling, journeying, walking, running, coming and going on roads and paths under the commands and promises of God, life on the *way*, permeates the narrative.

The first verb in the story of Abraham, the person of faith, is "*Go . . .*" (Gen. 12:1). Abraham's faith comes to expression as he sets out on a journey: "So Abram *went . . .*" (Gen. 12:4). Six more verbs in quick succession keep Abraham before us as a God-commanded man walking on the road from Haran to Canaan: *departed* (12:4) . . . *set forth to go* (12:5) . . . *had come* (12:5) . . . *passed through* (12:6) . . . *moved on* (12:8) . . . *journeyed on* (12:9).

The walking and traveling verbs let up slightly in the narration as other elements enter the story, but that Abraham is on a *way*, a way commanded by God, is never far from our awareness. There are sixteen verbs for walking or journeying between the introductory 12:1-9 and the climactic 22:1-9.

But then as Abraham sets out for Mount Moriah in chapter 22, the *way* Abraham walks once again comes into focus with six verbs — *go to the land of Moriah* (22:2) . . . *set out and went* (22:3) . . *the boy and I will go* (22:5) . . . *the two of them walked on together* (22:6) . . . *the two of them walked on together* (22:8) . . . *arose and went together* (22:19) — similar to the eight-verb emphasis on the *way* of Abraham that marked the opening paragraph (12:1-9).

*   *   *

The fatal thing is to reduce faith to an explanation. It is not an explanation, it is a passion. To tell the story of Abraham is to enter a narrative that throws self-help, self-certification, self-discipline — all our paltry self-hyphenations — into a junkyard of rusted-out definitions.

The story of Abraham very early on sets a certain tone, a context, an atmosphere so that we understand that this way on which we walk is not primarily about duty (although there are duties to perform). Nor is it primarily about making the most of our prospects (although our prospects are included in the journey). The story of Abraham is a story of the way of faith. Doing our best and making the most of our chances are peripheral matters, not the point of the story.

No, the Abraham story narrates a way of living in which God is personal and immediate, in which God is embraced and followed, in which God speaks and is obeyed, in which we recover and practice a language that we knew quite well in infancy and early childhood but, in Newman's haunting phrase, "lost awhile"[5] — a language learned in the company of grandparents and playmates, birds and unicorns, the rose of Sharon and the lilies of the valley, among prophets and poets, singers and weavers. It is a language of story and metaphor, immediacy and relationship, vision and dream, wisdom and the kerygma that is Holy Scripture, all said and sung in holy worship as we are washed in holy baptism and eat and drink the holy Eucharist: the Word made flesh, the words that Jesus lived and spoke, the words and sighs that the Spirit prays in us. This is a way of living in which we gradually, over a lifetime, learn to live with God personally and believingly "the days that were formed for me, when none of them as yet existed" (Ps. 139:16), whether consciously or unconsciously, as written plainly in Scripture and sacrament, and attested between the lines and on the margins of each page.

Faith designates a way of life that takes place in an intimate web of visible and invisible, silence and speech, light and darkness, chaos and cosmos, knowledge and mystery, God and us. It is far too complex to explicitly define or explain. And since all the dimensions and elements are re-configured uniquely in each human soul, there is no immediate model that can be copied or followed. It cannot be predicted or programmed; it can only be realized by participation, by setting out and continuing on a journey, a way, the way of Abraham, the way of faith.

Abraham is set before us as our father in the faith. Given the importance ascribed to Abraham in all matters of faith, it is astonishing how austere the defining story is, how few details are given. Out of a lifetime of 175 years, we are given seventeen stories. In providing this introductory initiation into the way of faith, our Lord the Spirit is careful not to give us too much lest we try copying Abraham's life instead of living our own.

For faith cannot be learned by copying, not by imitating, not by mastering some "faith-skills." We are all originals when we live by faith.

---

5. "And with the morn those angel faces smile,/which I have loved long since and lost awhile." John Henry Newman, "Lead, Kindly Light," *The Hymnbook* (Philadelphia: Presbyterian Publishing Co., 1955), no. 331.

Sacrifice

But "faith" is not commonly used in this hard-traveling way. More often it is clichéd into a feeling or fantasy or disposition — a kind of wish upwards, an inclination indistinguishable from a whim and easily dissipated by a gust of wind or the distraction of a pretty face.

And so the way of faith requires repeated testing so that we can discern whether we are dealing with the living God or some fantasy or illusion we have cooked up in a mulligan stew of lust and anger, envy and sloth, pride and greed. The testing of faith involves continuous honing, re-orienting, re-adjustment, timely rescues from self-deceit, gracious deliverances from the devil's illusions. The test is conducted by means of sacrifice, sacrifice that in Abraham's life of faith has its fullest exposition in the Binding of Isaac on Mount Moriah.

Sacrifice exposes spiritual fantasy as a masquerade of faith. Sacrifice scraps any illusion, no matter how pious, that is spun by the devil. Sacrifice plucks out the avaricious eye. Sacrifice lops off the grasping hand. Sacrifice is a readiness to interrupt whatever we are doing and build an altar, bind whatever we happen to be carrying with us at the moment, place it on the altar, and see what God wills to do with it.

Abraham was a veteran in the sacrifice business. After leaving Ur and Haran his first named activity consisted in building altars at which sacrifices were made. Shechem, Bethel, and Hebron are named. Each altar became a place of prayer: "Is this the way God commanded and promised, or is this a version of the command and promise that I have customized to my convenience?" At each altar he learned a little more, acquired a deeper discernment, a sharper insight into God's command and promise in contrast to his innate willfulness and indulgence but also in contrast to the anti-faith world of Ur with its imposing ziggurat.[6] Altars built at many a crossroads, a life of repeated sacrifices, each

---

6. A ziggurat in Ur from the time of Abraham was discovered by archaeologist C. L. Wooley. It is a pyramid-like structure, not as imposing as the Egyptian pyramids, but, at three stories in height, still impressive. See *The Anchor Bible Dictionary* (New York: Doubleday, 1992), vol. 6, p. 766.

sacrifice an act of discernment, separating the chaff of illusion from the wheat of promise.

The spare reticence of the narration invites a participating imagination — all that leaving, over and over. Habits of relinquishment became deeply ingrained in Abraham. They become deeply ingrained in us as we read. Leaving Ur and Haran, leaving Shechem and Bethel, leaving Egypt and Gerar, leaving Beersheba. Leaving, leaving, leaving. But every leaving was also a lightening of self, a further cleansing of the toxins of acquisition. A life of *getting* was slowly but surely replaced by a life of *receiving* — receiving the promises, receiving the covenants, receiving the three strangers, receiving Isaac, receiving circumcision, receiving a ram in the thicket — being transformed into a life that abandons self-sovereignty and embraces God-sovereignty. Abraham did that for a hundred years: "*sacrifice*/Is slow as a funeral procession/In rush-hour traffic, the sort of word/Other words pass, honking. . . ."[7]

In the process of leaving behind, Abraham became more, gradually but certainly realizing that relinquishment is prerequisite to fulfillment, that letting go of a cramped self-will opened up to an expansive God-willed life. Faith.

When we travel the way of Abraham this happens: the word "sacrifice" is gradually transformed from a sour whine of resentment to a robust embrace of affirmation. Every time Abraham left one place, the road lengthened and the landscape widened. Mount Moriah would provide him his largest experience of God. On Mount Moriah Abraham was empty enough of Abraham to take in salvation whole. Faith.

*   *   *

A sacrificial life is the means, and the only means, by which a life of faith matures. By increments a sacrificial life — an altar here, an altar there — comes to permeate every detail of life: parenthood, marriage, friendship, work, gardening, reading a book, climbing a mountain, re-

---

7. Jeanne Murray Walker, "Sacrifice," in *A Deed to the Light* (Chicago: University of Illinois Press, 2004), p. 17.

ceiving strangers, circumcising, and getting circumcised. Abraham did not become our exemplar in faith by having it explained to him but by engaging in a lifetime of travel, life on the road, daily leaving something of himself behind (self-sovereignty) and entering something new (God-sovereignty).

Sacrifice is to faith what eating is to nutrition; it is the action that we engage in that is transformed within ourselves invisibly and unobserved into a life lived in responsive obedience to the living God who gives himself to and for us, sacrifices himself for us. Faith, of which Abraham is our father, can never be understood by means of explanation or definition, only in the practice of sacrifice. Only in the act of obedience do we realize that sacrifice is not diminishment, not a stoical "This is the cross I bear" nonsense. It does not result in less joy, less satisfaction, less fulfillment, but in more — but rarely in the ways we expect. Who could have expected what would take place on Mount Moriah?

*   *   *

I have no intention of being glib regarding the details of what is involved in sacrifice — it takes years to get a feel for all that is involved. Mount Moriah and the Binding is a standing rebuke against the glib. And we need all the help we can get in this business; sacrifice requires preparation and allies. Even after all his years on the road, all those altars, all those sacrifices, Abraham still required assistance in getting to Mount Moriah for the sacrifice: the three days' walk to the mountain, the two servants, saddling the donkey, chopping the wood for the burnt offering, the fire pot, the knife — and, of course, Isaac. The capacity and readiness for sacrifice is an accumulation of small but significant details.

Altar-call rhetoric is conspicuously absent. The conversation involved in the Binding is brief, without embellishment, without any display of emotion. It begins with God saying *"Abraham,"* to which Abraham's answer is simply *"Here am I."* Three days later on the mountain this brief exchange is repeated almost word for word, but with Isaac taking the initiative this time, *"My father,"* and Abraham responding to his son in the same words he had used earlier in response to God, *"Here am I, my son."* Abraham is present to God in the same way he is present to his son, present to his son in the same way he is present to God. The same terse exchange occurs a third time at the altar on which Isaac has been bound for sacrifice. God in the form of the angel says, *"Abraham, Abraham"* (emphasis by repetition), and Abraham answers as is his wont, his third *"Here am I"* — present and ready, obedient still.

Testing

The test that takes place on Mount Moriah can be understood only in the full context of Abraham's journey, the *way* of Abraham: all those years and hundreds of miles of travel west from Ur to Haran to Canaan and eventually as far south as Beersheba, the numerous altars built and worshiped at throughout Canaan, the faithless detour to Egypt, the generosity to nephew Lot, the tithe paid to Melchizedek, the covenant vision and sacrifice, the conception and birth of Ishmael, a second covenant vision and its commanded rite of circumcision, hospitality to the strangers at the Oaks of Mamre, intercession for and judgment on Sodom and Gomorrah, negotiations with Abimelech, the Hagar and Ishmael drama — everything leads up to the *Akedah* on Mount Moriah. But always traveling, always on a journey. Then the purchase from Ephron the Hittite of a cemetery plot for Sarah at Machpelah and subsequent arrangements for Isaac's marriage to Rebekah bring the *way* of Abraham to a quiet terminus. The Moriah test is embedded in a life of obedience and disobedience, a life of faith and unbelief, a life of horizontal travel and vertical prayer. Visible and invisible are inextricably woven together in a fabric that we call faith, believing obediently the Voice, the Presence.

Abraham's life of faith that God brings to the test at Mount Moriah is not an abstraction. It is a way of life lived on real ground with actual people. It is not a test that takes place in the controlled conditions of a laboratory or a prayer meeting. The Mount Moriah text is embedded in a context. The text covers three days; the context is elaborated across a span of a hundred years, years in which the *way* of Abraham — the way he lived his life — had been repeatedly put to the test on the way — the actual roads — Abraham journeyed. It is a test of his faith, what is discerned in Romans and Hebrews as the characteristic feature of his life.

*   *   *

The Moriah test in matters regarding God and the soul is this: Are we using God or are we letting God use us? The temptation is to think that God is there to serve us. The temptation is to come to God as a consumer shopping for the gospel as a commodity. The temptation is to reduce God to a cozy domesticity. The test question is blunt: "Have I been kidding myself all along?" In all matters of faith, in this life lived in passionate inwardness and responsive obedience in the presence of God, we need repeated reality checks.

Has Abraham been dealing with God all these years, the God who spoke, the God who promised and fulfilled promises, the God who gave visions and issued commands? Or has he been making it all up? Mount Moriah tests the possibility that he has, all along, been attempting to get God on his own terms. But God's will is to give himself to Abraham on God's terms and only on God's terms, terms that may far exceed our pitifully limited comprehension.

If there is one thing that is certain in these matters, it is that "the heart is deceitful above all things, and desperately wicked" (Jer. 17:9 KJV). So why would any of us suppose ourselves to be exempt? Our faith, all faith, everyone's faith, needs testing. And we cannot be trusted to test ourselves. We are too full of self-interest and self-deceit. We are too devious in devising ways of cooking the books to document the evidence that serves our illusions. When we look at the track record of priests and temples, pastors and churches, missionaries and missions, it is obvious that religion in all its forms, including most emphatically Christianity, is a perpetual breeding ground for violence, abuse, superstition, war, discrimination, tyranny, and pride. Religion and spirituality is a bottomless pit breeding illusion, deceit, and oppression. So — testing.

It is both common and easy to develop a concept of faith in which God is pledged to give us whatever we want whenever we ask; that faith means being a consumer of gospel goods and services; that faith means that we are baptismally certified to administer the test on God, to calculate and evaluate God's performance in our lives; that faith qualifies us to explain God and call him to account when he doesn't make sense. And many are the leaders and friends who encourage us along this line.

There is far more to this life than we can comprehend, huge stretches of the unknown both before (west of Haran) and above and within us (God). How do we deal with all this, this God-created, God-permeated reality? Do we reduce the world to land and people that we can take charge of, and then employ our minds and imaginations to figure out how we can get God to help us do it? Or do we live by faith?

We need testing. God tests us. The test results will show whether we are choosing the way of awe and worship and obedience (which is to say, God), or whether, without being aware of it, we are reducing God to our understanding of him so that we can use him. Have we slipped into the habit of insisting that God do what we ask or want or need him to do, treating him as an idol designed for our satisfaction? Does God serve us or do we serve God? Do we require a God that we can fully understand and control or are we willing to be obedient to what we do not understand and could never control? Is God a mystery of goodness whom we embrace and trust, or is God a formula for getting the most out of life on our terms? The test results will show whether we have been blithely assuming that God is pledged to give us whatever we want whenever we ask. Have we thought all along that God is there to serve us? The test will tell us. Do we want God in our own image or do we want the God who is beyond us and over us, who we trust will do for us what only God can do in the way that only God can do it — no strings attached . . . no reservations . . . no caveats . . . the whole hog? The test will tell us.

And we will be glad enough to have the test results so that we can get on with the resurrection-shaped life God has for us. This does not always happen without some pain, for we can get very attached to our little projects of self-deification, but it doesn't take us long to be glad to have gotten rid of them.

*   *   *

Nothing in our Scriptures is as demanding on our faith as the *Akedah*, this Binding of Isaac, narrated in such bare but excruciating detail as to leave no doubt that the stakes are eternally high. We ask, "Why this quite unimaginable severity at Moriah?" Isn't there another way? Couldn't certificates of baptism include a warning, "Use only as directed," and let it go at that? Søren Kierkegaard in his passionate search for an authentic life of faith probed the Moriah test relentlessly and left no room for an easy detour, a comfortable alternative.[8] He warns against every attempt to trivialize faith into a vacation getaway in the mountains, or a place of influence in the city, or an entertainment park in the suburbs. The way of faith does not serve our fantasies, our illusions, or our ambitions. Faith is not the way to God on our terms, it is the way of God to us on his terms.

A three-day walk to Mount Moriah exposes the banality of all such bogus faith. At Mount Moriah we accept and worship a God beyond our understanding. At Mount Moriah we embrace a mystery that is light-filled, but no less a mystery for all that.

Abraham and the *Akedah*: the Christian way cannot be programmed, cannot be guaranteed: faith means that we put our trust in God — and we *don't know* how he will work out our salvation, only that it is our salvation that he is working out. Which frees us for anything. We must be the ones tied down, so that we can be the ones set free. The *Akedah* is an open door to living faithfully, without calculation. There necessarily will be renunciations all along the way: "Renunciation . . . is a piercing virtue."[9]

8. See Søren Kierkegaard, *Fear and Trembling*, trans. Walter Lowrie (Garden City, N.Y.: Doubleday, 1954 [first published in 1843]).

9. Emily Dickinson, "Renunciation — is a piercing Virtue," in *The Complete Poems*, p. 365.

Jack Leax's poem accurately expresses what happens on Mount Moriah.

> The Spirit must scream
> Plummet down
> Like a bird of prey
>   And sit   fierce
> Talons clenched
> In your bleeding lips
>
> And your words become
> His Word
> And his Word become
> Your words
> That your speech
> Dead in the agony of self
> Might be resurrected
> In self-extinction.[10]

*   *   *

Erich Auerbach, in pehaps the most perceptive analysis of Mount Moriah ever, wrote that since everyone knows that this is a story about a hidden God, we should not be surprised to be surprised at what happens.[11] Still, even after many years of reading this story I am surprised

---

10. Jack Leax, "On Writing Poetry," in *Grace Is Where I Live* (La Porte, Ind.: Word-farm, 1993, 2004), p. 74. In commenting on his own poem, Leax refers to the influence of T. S. Eliot's words: "What happens is a continual surrender of himself as he is at the moment to something which is more valuable. The progress of an artist is a continual self-sacrifice, a continual extinction of personality." In Abraham's way "artist" is synonymous with "Christian."

11. "So much in the story is dark and incomplete, and since the reader knows that God is a hidden God, his effort to interpret it constantly finds something new to feed upon." Erich Auerbach, *Mimesis*, trans. Willard Trask (Princeton, N.J.: Princeton University Press, 1968), p. 15.

to find myself surprised. I am surprised that Abraham, Isaac bound and knife raised, is not surprised to hear the voice tell him that there is a ram in the thicket. And Isaac is not surprised to end up not sacrificed. Not a word in the narrative indicates anything like surprise. Not a word of surprise, not a single emotion of surprise in the story as written.

Why am I surprised and Abraham and Isaac are not?

Here is what I think: The *Akedah* was a three-day journey for Abraham, but it cannot be understood apart from a hundred years of road-tested faith that comprises the Abraham story. The way of Abraham is the first chapter of the people of God to whom Abraham is father, the one in whom all the people of the earth will be blessed. Abraham furnishes the context that permeates everything that follows. The *Akedah* is not isolated, not a text without a context; it is a summing up and clarification of a long life of reorientation from the ziggurat in Ur to the altar on Moriah, from self-aggrandizement to God-gifting.

God has tested Abraham's faith at every turn. To live by faith — better, to live a faith life — means to be tested. Abraham's faith did not always survive the test: his faith failed the test in Egypt, failed the test in Gerar, failed the test with Hagar. Untested faith does not yet qualify as faith. Untested faith, having the appearance of faith, the feeling of faith, the language of faith, may be only wishful thinking, or an adolescent illusion, erotic dreaming, satanic delusion, a cultural cliché, a cover for self-sovereignty — whatever. Kierkegaard named all such as "caricatures of faith."[12] There are many occasions in which the word "faith" is used for something or other that is not faith.

The test is the catalyst in which our response to God, the raw material of faith, is formed into a *life* of faith. Or not. If the test dissolves whatever we were calling faith into romanticized sludge or pietistic ooze, we are blessedly rid of what will dissipate our life in self-deception.

Abraham left Ur and Haran freely obedient to a command of God, a single-syllable imperative, unsupported, unexplained, unadorned: "Go." He went in what we might call good faith, that is, without calculation, without suppressed motives, without superstitious

12. Kierkegaard, *Fear and Trembling*, p. 48.

fear. He wasn't enticed; he wasn't bullied. He was commanded, "Go." He went. His faith was perfectly adequate to get him going, but it also required repeated testings along the way. By the time of the *Akedah*, Abraham's faith had been tested, and tested, and tested. Sometimes (in Egypt with the Pharaoh, at Gerar with Abimelech, in dealing with Hagar and Ishmael) the testings had exposed his so-called faith as no faith at all. But incrementally, across those miles and through those years, his faith deepened and matured.

The *Akedah* strikes us as outrageous, the God of promises and covenant acting totally out of character. But maybe not to Abraham. Sacrifice was the motif by which he had lived for years, the letting go, the leaving behind, the traveling light. Faith, repeatedly tested by sacrifice, was a way of life for Abraham. Each sacrifice left him with less of self and more of God. Each sacrifice abandoned something of self on an altar from which he traveled onward with more vision, more promise, more Presence. In the command to leave Ur, Abraham had abandoned his past. He has been learning how to do that now for thirty-five years or so, losing nothing in the process. Now he is asked to abandon his future. By now he has a lived history in which God has provided for him in unanticipated, unexpected ways. Maybe by now he is used to living trustingly in the seemingly absurd, that which he could not anticipate, that which is beyond his imagining. Maybe he is accustomed by now to the operations of providence. If we arrive at Mount Moriah without having prayerfully and imaginatively participated in the decades of Abraham's testings, God seems to us to behave outrageously out of character. But not to Abraham. He is by now a veteran in the way of faith that is at the same time the way of the faithful God. He is not nearly as surprised as we are. Mount Moriah is the centerpiece of a life of faith that is completed in Jesus, who absorbed the *Akedah* entire in his Gethsemane prayer, "Not my will but thine. . . ." It certainly occupied a prominent place in St. Paul's mind when he assured all of us who walk in the way of Jesus that "No testing has overtaken you that is not common to everyone. God is faithful, and he will not let you be tested beyond your strength, but with the testing he will also provide the way out so that you may be able to endure it" (1 Cor. 10:13).

CHAPTER 3

Moses: On the Plains of Moab

More words in our Holy Scriptures are ascribed to Moses than to any other single speaker or writer. The words of Moses, written in the first five books of the Bible, are the foundational words of the revelation of God to us. In the Hebrew tradition, both ancient and modern, everything following the Books of Moses is either commentary or elaboration on Moses.

Who could have anticipated this? In the opening event that catapulted Moses from a shepherd-life in Midian to leading God's people from Egyptian slavery, Moses responded to the voice from the burning bush by begging off on the grounds that he wasn't good with words. He described himself as a tongue-tied stutterer ("I am slow of speech and slow of tongue," Exod. 4:10). What good is a leader if he is no good with words? Forty years later the closing scene on Moses has this one-time "slow of speech" shepherd holding forth from his Plains of Moab pulpit, pouring out a torrent of words (thirty-one pages in English translation, seventy of Hebrew text), generous and eloquent in a sermon that brought all those years — the life of salvation that he and the people had lived together from Egypt to Sinai to Canaan — up-to-date and compressed into an urgent *Today*.

There is considerable irony in these juxtaposed scenes: from a shepherd who couldn't talk to a preacher who couldn't stop talking —

giving his name to the five books that provide our introductory immersion in the language that God uses to reveal himself "for us and for our salvation," a way of language that received its final articulation in Jesus, the Word made flesh.

Moses and the Five Books

But over the past roughly three hundred years, the name of Moses, so long identified with the Five Books, the Torah, was gradually effaced from the spine of the books, much as names disappear from centuries-old, weather-scoured cemetery markers. In this case the weather did not consist of wind and rain, snow and sleet, but of historical criticism, a new way of reading the Bible.

Historical criticism, this new way of reading the Bible, treated the text exclusively as a historical document, dismissing all literary or faith considerations. When critics employed the tools of historical research only, the traditional identification of Moses with Torah didn't pass historical muster. The great pioneer of historical criticism, Benedict Spinoza (1632-1677), got the historical-critical ball rolling. By the time that Julius Wellhausen published his classic, *Prolegomena to the History of Ancient Israel* (1879), Moses had been replaced as author of the Five Books by historically reconstructed source documents designated by the letters J, E, D, and P. In the practice of this method, tons of historical information were gathered that have proved of enormous use. No one regrets the gains in historical understanding. But there has also been severe loss.

In academic circles at least, the long practice of reading the Bible as a book of faith has taken second fiddle to reading it strictly as history. The story — the narrative of a lived faith in God — has been obscured if not lost altogether. The scholars who read the Bible this way (and they have dominated the academic study of Scripture for a long time now) ignore the literary context of the Bible and take it apart looking for development and historical change. They challenge the historicity of foundational events and traditional ideas of authorship — that Moses wrote the Pentateuch and that the Evangelists wrote the

Gospels — and then reconstruct the history, but leave the Bible itself a midden of fragments from various times and places. They take the text apart, but in Harvard University professor Jon Levenson's blunt indictment, they "lack a method for putting it back together again."[1] They have no interest in the literary and theological coherence of the text.

The motivation in the practice of historical criticism is academically well-intentioned. But the replacement of Moses' authorial presence in the Five Books by mostly impersonal sources has had the unfortunate even if unintended effect of obscuring and sometimes destroying the integrity of the material itself. The historical critics suppose that by getting "behind" the Moses books, they can serve us forth a better or truer "truth." But most writers are highly offended when people get more interested in the contents of their wastebaskets and filing cabinets than in the books they write. "Read the book!" The meaning is in the book, not in the information in or about the book.

When I was twelve years old, the year 1944, my father bought a disreputable '36 Plymouth, drove it home, and parked it in the alley behind our house. There it died. It never ran again. I don't think my father ever went out back and looked at it again. But I put it to good use. I was a couple of years away from getting my driver's license and so sat in that old wreck most days for an hour or so after school and practiced using the gear shift, shifting from first to second to third and back down again, using the brake and clutch pedals, my hands on the steering wheel, imagining myself in the act of driving over mountain roads and through blizzards.

After a few months I had mastered the moves. But having used up my imagination in driving the inert machine, I thought I might as well try to find out what made it tick when it did tick. I think I had a vague idea that maybe I could make it run again. I took it apart, piece by

---

1. Jon D. Levenson, *The Hebrew Bible, the Old Testament, and Historical Criticism* (Louisville: Westminster/John Knox, 1993), p. 2. Levenson argues that the "price of recovering the *historical* context of sacred books has been the erosion of the largest *literary* contexts that undergird the traditions that claim to be based on them" (p. 4). He does not dispute the value of historical criticism but challenges (I think convincingly) its imperialistic pretensions.

piece, self-educating myself in the ways of carburetors, cooling systems, transmissions, and brake drums. After a few months I was familiar with all the parts now laid out on the grass, but I never did figure out what made it run. And of course by the time I had completed my investigative work, there was no chance of it ever running again.

This is essentially Levenson's criticism of the historical critics.

*   *   *

Is it possible to appreciate the work of the historical critics that in large part (not completely) removes Moses as the author of the Five Books and at the same time affirm the traditional Mosaic presence that has provided a cohesive and personal authorial voice, the story line, that has kept all the parts together for both Jews and Christians for so long? Is it possible to take the Torah apart historically and then put it back together again as a book of faith with theological and literary integrity? I think it is.[2] It is not only possible, but worth any effort it might take.

The world that we now read of in our Bibles was an essentially oral world, although there is plenty of evidence that much of the speaking also got written. Language in itself, in its origins and in most of its practice, is oral. We *speak* words long before we write and read them. And even after we start writing and reading them, our spoken words far outnumber the words we write and the words we read. And that goes even for the men and women — journalists, novelists, poets, diarists — for whom writing is a vocation. The world we live in today continues to be primarily oral. Orality does not mean primitive. Words spoken are both previous to and even inherently superior to words written even in the most literate of cultures.

Among our Hebrew ancestors, generations of orally transmitted traditions developed and matured their unique people-of-God mem-

2. Brevard Childs employs "canonical criticism" as a methodology to this end. See his *Introduction to the Old Testament As Scripture* (Philadelphia: Fortress, 1979), pp. 132-35. See also James A. Sanders, *Torah and Canon* (Philadelphia: Fortress, 1972).

ory. Here and there, now and then, the words got written down and preserved, copied and collected, honored and read. Moses is remembered as one of those who wrote down the words (Exod. 24:4; 34:27; Deut. 31:9, 24). The words became books. In all that was said or sung or written, the memory and words of Moses provided the story line that kept it all together. Over time the telling and the writing became the Five Books of Moses.

Moses' presence — his leadership, his integrity, his ordained authority as the leader of the people of God out of the slavery of Egyptian bondage into the service of God, his Sinai mediation of God's revelation, his provision and instruction for centering the life of the people in worship, his pastoral care of his flock all those years in the wilderness — shaped all the seemingly disparate stories, instructions, directions into a coherent whole. Moses looms still as the architect of the huge, sprawling house of language — assembled and constructed by the many voices, the many pens and much parchment — that is Torah, the Five Books, the founding document for the faith of Israel and the Christian gospel: *Torah* — the revelation of God written for the people of God, Jew and Christian alike. Not "author" in a strictly literal sense, but *authority* in an encompassing literary and Spirit-inspired sense.

Jesus, who confined his language to the spoken word, and those who wrote his story for us, commonly referred to the Torah ("the Law") simply as "Moses." In the early church, Moses is the most prominent ancestral name, whether as leader of the people of God or as mediator of the revelation of God in Torah.[3] Torah and Moses were virtual synonyms in both Judaism and church.

Walter Ong reflects on the interplay of the living voice and the written word embedded in the Moses tradition and carried over into the Gospels:

> To assure maximum presence through history, the Word came in
> the ripeness of time, when a sense of the oral was still dominant

---

3. Moses turns up eighty-one times in the New Testament, compared to runners-up David and Isaiah, with fifty-six and twenty-three respectively.

and when at the same time the alphabet could give divine revelation among men a new kind of endurance and stability. The believer finds it providential that divine revelation let down its roots into human culture and consciousness after the alphabet was devised but before print had overgrown major oral structures and before our electronic culture further obscured the basic nature of the word.[4]

*   *   *

It is tempting to caricature the historical-critical reconstruction of the Five Books with scenes of bookish editors busy with scissors and paste around makeshift tables under tamarisk trees in the Sinai desert, later in the shade of willows by the waters of Babylon, putting together somewhat clumsily and at times arbitrarily documents that ended up being ascribed ignorantly to Moses. Umberto Cassuto, a leading Hebrew scholar in these matters, has a much better image, much more congruent with the living process involved: "The stream of this tradition may be compared to a great and wide-spreading river that traverses vast distances; although in the course of its journey the river loses part of its water . . . and it is also increasingly augmented by waters of the tributaries that pour into it, yet it carries with it . . . some of the waters that it held at the beginning when it first started to flow from its original source."[5]

*   *   *

Language scholars use two terms, diachronic and synchronic, that help us to distinguish the living, authoritative voice of Moses from the actual Spirit-directed writing that became the Five Books. The distinc-

4. Walter J. Ong, S.J., *The Presence of the Word* (New Haven: Yale University Press, 1967), p. 191.
5. Umberto Cassuto, *The Documentary Hypothesis and the Composition of the Pentateuch*, trans. I. Abrahams (Jerusalem: Magnes, 1961), pp. 102-3.

tion at the same time helps us to keep peace between reading for information and reading for revelation.

When we approach language diachronically we are in charge, looking for information that we can use, fixing its place and use in history. We read a catalogue this way, and an almanac, and the telephone directory. When we approach language synchronically we submit to the authority of the language, remembering everything we've been told, anticipating where the words might lead us, letting the language use us — the way we read a poem or a novel. When we read diachronically, the word is inert, silent on the page; when we read synchronically, the word is a living something, like sound, something going on.

Reading language *diachronically* means reading it according to a linear continuum through history. There may or may not be any meaningful connection from one page to the next. This sentence was written first, this one second, this one third by various persons who may or may not have known one another. You can stop at any word or sentence and attempt to fix its meaning in terms of the place and time it was written and from whatever you can conjecture of the purpose for which it was written. Reading a language *synchronically* means reading it as if all the words are operating at once in sequence and in relation with one another. No one sentence or phrase has its intended meaning apart from all the other words on the page or the book in precisely the way they are put down. Diachronic and synchronic readings don't have to be at odds. At their best they work in partnership.

For two thousand years the Bible has been read by Christians (for Jews even longer) synchronically, as personal revelation, a vast organically webbed narrative composed of the accumulated voices of generations listening and answering God and one another, not as bits of impersonal information. Maimonides (1138-1204), perhaps the greatest of all medieval Hebrew Scripture scholars, insisted on the internal coherence of the Books of Moses (but not on Mosaic authorship) in his principle of literary simultaneity. He wrote, "there is no difference between verses like, 'And the sons of Ham were Cush and Egypt' (Gen. 10:6), or 'And his wife's name was Mehetabel' (Gen. 36:39), or 'Timna was a concubine' (Gen. 36:12) and verses like 'I am the Lord your God' (Ex. 20:2) and 'Hear, O Israel' (Dt. 6:4). For all of them come from the mouth of God." Jon Levenson, using Maimonides to reinforce the synchronic reading of the Five Books of Moses, comments: "although in historical-critical discourse the notion of Mosaic authorship of the Pentateuch is indefensible, the underlying and antecedent ideas of the unity and divinity of the Torah *must remain* relevant considerations. . . ."[6]

Every Idle Word . . .

Words are holy — all words. But words are also vulnerable to corruption, debased into blasphemies, trivialized into gossip. The honor given Moses as the authorial presence in our foundational Five Books invites us into an immersion and training in language as inherently sacred, the means by which God brings us and all things into being, provides us with the means of realizing *meaning,* the meaning of our lives, the meaning of God's salvation for us.

The opening page of our Scriptures presents us with God speaking words: *saying* the entire creation and us into being. "And God said . . . and God said . . . and God said . . ." — eight times the phrase is used. After the eighth "and God said," everything is in place: light and sky; land and sea; vegetation and trees; sun, moon, and stars; fish and birds; animals wild and domestic; reptiles and insects; man and woman. Language is previous to and foundational for all that is.

Everywhere and always as Christians follow Jesus we use words that were first used by God in bringing us and the world around us into being. Our language is derivative (as everything about us is!) from the language of God. Our common speech is in continuity with the language of God. Words are essential and words are holy wherever and whenever we use them. Words are inherently holy regardless of their employment, whether we are making up a shopping list, making conversation with an acquaintance on a street corner, praying in the name of Jesus, asking for directions to the bus station, reading the prophet

6. Levenson, *The Hebrew Bible,* p. 65 (italics added).

Isaiah, or writing a letter to our congresswoman. We do well to reverence them, to be careful in our use of them, to be alarmed at their desecration, to take responsibility for using them accurately and prayerfully. Christian followers of Jesus have an urgent mandate to care for language — spoken, heard, or written — as a means by which God reveals himself to us, by which we express the truth and allegiance of our lives, and by which we give witness to the Word made flesh. Jesus was severe in his warning against "every idle word" (Matt. 12:36 AV) and insistent that "anyone with ears listen" (Matt. 13:9). Each of the seven urgent messages by John of Patmos to his congregations concludes with the identical phrase, "let anyone who has an ear listen" (Rev. 2–3). When the poet of Psalm 12 surveyed the degradation around him, it was the abuse of language that most appalled him: "They utter lies to each other; with flattering lips and a double heart they speak . . . as vileness is exalted among humankind" (Ps. 12:2, 8).

But by and large reverence for language is not conspicuous among us, in or out of the Christian community. Contemporary language has been dessicated by the fashions of the academic world (reductive rationalism) and the frenzy of economic and industrial greed (reductive pragmatism). The consequence is that much of the talk in our time has become, well, just talk — not much theological content to it, not much personal relationship involved, no spirit, no *Holy* Spirit.

But speech is the "life-blood of society," as Eugen Rosenstock-Huessy has so passionately demonstrated.[7] If there is going to be a healthy community, there has to be a healthy language. We need protection against the "winds and doctrines" of spiritual consumerism. We need a feel for vocabulary and syntax that is able to detect and delete disembodied ideas, language that fails to engage personal participation. We need a thorough grounding in the robustness of biblical story and grammar that insists on vital articulated *speech* (not just the employment of words) for health of body and mind and soul. Moses

---

7. Eugen Rosenstock-Huessy, *Speech and Reality* (Norwich, Vt.: Argo Books, 1970), p. 10.

gives us a feel for the biblical pulse and rhythm, biblical reverence as well as biblical meaning.

We need discernment and then courage to distance ourselves from the presumptuous historical criticism that places itself *above* the Scriptures. And then we need to deliberately and believingly place ourselves *under* them, submitting to the revelation as provided for us by these marvelous writers with their riveting prose, their scintillating poetry, their dancing metaphors and syntax.

Words don't just sit there, like bumps on a log. They have *agency*. Scott Cairns, reflecting on his work as a poet working with words in the context of the believing community reading the Scriptures, says that we "are attending not only to a past (an event to which the words refer), but are attending to a present and a presence (which the words articulate into proximity for their apprehension) . . . leaning into that articulated presence, participating in its energies, and thereby participating in the creation of meaning, with which we help to shape the future." We understand the Scriptures, he says, not simply as "narratives of past events nor simply as exhortations to believe (though I believe they are both of these); they are also scenes into which the believer (whether patristic author or contemporary pilgrim) enters in order to make something new of them, in order to develop into something new — a new creature, say — receiving the Scriptures' empowering assistance."[8]

A Congregational Language

Moses is, by all accounts, a magnificent leader: bold, relentless, untiring. But in the biblical tradition that formed around him, mostly he is a man of words. The way of Moses is paved with language: the word from the burning bush that called and credentialed him to lead the people out of a slave life in Egypt into a life of free obedience under God, the word delivered from Sinai that became the constitution and

8. "A Conversation with Scott Cairns," *Image* (Seattle: Center for Religious Humanism), no. 44 (Winter 2004-2005).

bill of rights of the twelve tribes, the words he used for forty years and across many a wilderness mile of trial and temptation that brought the people to the entrance of Canaan, poised for the conquest of the land that God had promised them in his covenant with Abraham, the words that formed the family stories of the salvation people — all those forty years of words that came together on the Plains of Moab as he preached his artful valedictory sermon, re-voicing (which is what sermons do) words that had been said and sung under the sovereignty of God's word. The words that are ascribed to Moses and the way he used them, more than those of any other person, Jesus alone excepted, have given us a vocabulary and syntax for the way God reveals himself to us and how we in our turn respond to him.

The way of language in which Moses is our first teacher is most accurately described, I think, as a congregational language, a language textured by the give and take of congregational life under the formative influence of God's word, the kind of language that develops in a worshiping congregation that invokes God and then listens and prays. It is the language of a community of faith, a mixed community of struggling sinners and faltering saints, preachers and teachers, people on pilgrimage telling their family stories, passing on the counsels and promises of God.

Richard Pevear, reflecting on the complexity and wide-range of Russian voices that went into Dostoevsky's *The Brothers Karamazov,* observed that "The community of speech is simultaneous: the words of the dead are heard by the living, the words of the past are heard in the present."[9] The Books of Moses are just such a community of speech, congregational in that they are not dominated by a single voice, a domineering pulpit language, but rather are a language used by souls-in-congregation (not private); a personal language of relationship, covenantal and promissory (not impersonal or abstract); a storied language (not moralistic or didactic); a practical matter-of-fact language (not vague or general) that can get you across the street without adjec-

9. Introduction to *The Brothers Karamazov,* by Fyodor Dostoevsky, trans. Richard Pevear and Larissa Volokhonsky (San Francisco: North Point, 1990), p. xviii.

tives or adverbs. It is a language composed of voices that arrive from various times and places, but throughout there is a consistent presence and reliable story line that provides a discernible coherence to a very unsystematic gathering of material. In this case the story line and coherence has a name: Moses.

The vocabulary and syntax of this souls-in-congregation language, this Moses language, sets the standard and permeates the language of revelation that we now recognize as biblical, language that reveals God's presence and purpose among us. Three elements stand out in the language of revelation used by this community of souls-in-congregation: names, stories, and signposts. These elements are in constant need of refurbishing and recovery lest they degenerate into "idle words," the ones Jesus warned us about, and then get swept into the dustbin.

Names

Names abound in Moses. Names are honored: personal names, God names. We don't get very far along on this way of language before we realize the enormous significance of names. The story of God-with-us is chock-full of names. It is not possible to walk along this "highway . . . called the Holy Way" (Isa. 35:8) without hearing names, names from the right, names from the left, names echoing those ahead of us, names resonating from those behind us. What numbers are to a mathematician and what colors are to a landscape artist, names are to Christian language.

The genealogy, a bare, unadorned listing of names, a much under-appreciated literary feature in the language of Moses, has profound implications for the way we understand the interpersonal context in which God works among us, working out our creation and salvation. In Genesis ten genealogies ("these are the generations . . .") provide the organizing structure of the book.[10] Lists of names con-

10. Genesis 2:4 (heaven and earth), 5:1 (Adam), 6:9 (Noah), 10:1 (Noah's sons), 11:10 (Shem), 11:27 (Terah), 25:12 (Ishmael), 25:19 (Isaac), 36:1 (Esau), 37:2 (Joseph).

tinue to turn up in various forms and for a variety of purposes throughout the Hebrew Bible. One scholar, a specialist in this genre, counts "about 25 genealogies."[11] And when Matthew and Luke sit down to write their account of Jesus, they both use the idiom of genealogy that was introduced in Moses. Some complain about the long lists of names that they encounter in their reading of Scripture, and impatiently treat them as deadfalls in the forest impeding their passage. But if I found my name in the list, would I be offended or bored?

Rosenstock-Huessy insists that the greatest forms of human speech are names.[12] Names root language in the personal, in the particular man, woman, and child. Abstractions, generalities, and great cosmic ideas can come later. But if they get too far removed from personal names, they degenerate. The words and grammar diminish in vitality and become anemic.

Story

A name is a seed. When it germinates it becomes a story. Moses is not just a name-dropper; Moses is a storyteller. The storytelling way of language that we find in the Five Books goes on to gather momentum conspicuously in David and then definitively in Jesus.

In our Holy Scriptures story is the primary verbal means for bringing God's word to us. For this we can be grateful, for story is our most accessible form of speech. Young and old love stories. Literate and illiterate alike tell and listen to stories. Neither stupidity nor sophistication put us outside the magnetic field of story. The only serious rival to story in terms of accessibility and attraction is song, and there are plenty of those in the Bible, too.

Stories continue to hold a prominent role in the language that re-

11. Robert R. Wilson, in *Anchor Bible Dictionary,* ed. David Noel Freedman (New York: Doubleday, 1992), vol. 2, p. 930.

12. Eugen Rosenstock-Huessy, *The Origin of Speech* (Norwich, Vt.: Argo Books, 1981), p. 5.

veals God and God's ways to us. Storytellers in Christian communities carry a major responsibility for keeping us alert to story and the ways story works. Our best storytellers still learn their craft from Moses and Jesus.

But there is another reason for the appropriateness of story as a major means of bringing us God's word. Story doesn't just tell us something and leave it there. It invites our participation. A good storyteller gathers us into the story. We feel the emotions, get caught up in the drama, identify with the characters, see into nooks and crannies of life that we had overlooked, realize that there is more to this business of being human than we had yet explored. If the storyteller is good, doors and windows open. Moses is good both in the artistic and moral sense.

Another thing about stories: honest stories respect our freedom. They don't manipulate us, don't force us, don't distract us from life. They show us a spacious world in which God creates and saves and blesses. First through our imaginations and then through our faith — imagination and faith are close kin here — they offer us a place in the story, invite us into this large story that takes place under the broad skies of God's purposes in contrast to the gossipy anecdotes that we cook up in the stuffy closet of the self.

Not all stories, of course, are honest. There are sentimentalizing stories that seduce us into escaping from life; there are propagandizing stories that attempt to enlist us in a cause or bully us into a stereotyped response. And so when an honest storyteller comes along, respecting our dignity and freedom, we are grateful. Moses is honest, inviting us into the story as participant in something truer than our culture-stunted ambitions.

We read these stories and recognize ourselves as participants in a larger family, whether willing or unwilling, in the life of God: stories of Adam and Eve, Noah and his sons, Abraham and Sarah, Isaac and Rebekah, Jacob and Rachel, Joseph and Asenath, Moses and Zipporah, Aaron and Miriam, Balaam and his donkey, Joshua and Caleb, and on and on, centuries of stories until the "fullness of time" and the story of Jesus.

Unfortunately, we live in a language world in which story has been pushed from its biblical frontline prominence to a bench on the sidelines, condescended to as "illustration" or "testimony" or "inspiration." Our contemporary unbiblical preference, both within and without the church, is for information over story. We typically gather impersonal (pretentiously called "scientific" or "theological") information, so that we can take things into our own hands and take charge of how we will live our lives. We want to make up our own stories. But we don't live our lives by information; we live life in relationships, family-of-faith relationships in the context of a community of men and women, each one an intricate bundle of experience and motive and desire, and in the presence of a personal God who has designs on us for justice and salvation. Consulting the experts in order to gather information leaves out nearly everything that is uniquely *us* — our personal histories and relationships, our sins and guilt, our moral character and believing obedience to God.

Telling a story, on the other hand, is the primary verbal way of accounting for life the way we live it in actual day-by-day reality. There are no (or few) abstractions in a story — story is immediate, concrete, plotted, relational, personal. And so when we lose touch with our lives, our *souls* — our moral, bodily, spiritual, God-personal lives — story is the best verbal way of getting us back in touch again. That is why God's word is so prodigal in its storytelling. Back to Moses!

Signposting

There is yet another element of language used in the Books of Moses that is necessary for souls-in-congregation. I will call it signposting: laws are posted, directions given, instructions provided. The most prominent of these are the *Ten Words* (The Ten Commandments, the basic rules for living, Exod. 20:2-17) and the *Shema* ("Hear O Israel . . . ," the basic creed for believing, Deut. 6:4-9). These are succinct and punchy: there is no ambiguity, no "ifs, ands, or buts." They are not debatable. Not discussion-starters. These are fundamental in all aspects of behaving and believing. Understandably, they hold our attention to what is central.

But there are also signposts designated the "Book of the Covenant" (Exod. 20:22–23:33; 24:7) and the "Statutes and Ordinances" (Deut. 12:1). These are neither succinct nor punchy. They are endlessly detailed, full of "ifs, ands, and buts." They are an elaborate witness to the painstaking attention that is given among the people of God to the details involved in day-to-day living in community.[13]

Community is intricate and complex. Living in community as a people of God is inherently messy. A congregation consists of many people of various moods, ideas, needs, experiences, gifts and injuries, desires and disappointments, blessings and losses, intelligence and stupidity, living in proximity and in respect for one another, and believingly in worship of God. It is not easy and it is not simple. Not every situation can be anticipated. Novel combinations of circumstances take us by surprise. No community worth its salt has ever existed very long without attending painstakingly to particular conditions.

The care given to the overarching directions for the way we live (the commandments) and what we believe (the creed) extends into the nittygritty of particular cases, into areas of ambiguity where things are not cut and dried. What if you kill a person but didn't mean to (Exod. 21:13)? What if you get in a fight with your slave and knock his or her tooth out (Exod. 21:27)? What if you borrow a donkey and it gets injured or dies (Exod. 22:14)? What's the penalty for a man who seduces a virgin (Exod. 22:16-17)? How old must a newborn goat be before it can be offered as a sacrifice (Lev. 22:26)? What's the recipe for how much flour you use in baking bread for the tabernacle (Lev. 24:5)? What is your responsibility regarding your relatives who have fallen on hard times (Lev. 25:35)? If a man is jealous of his wife, though he has no evidence of her unfaithfulness, what is he to do (Num. 5:11-22)? In a judicial case if you can't decide whether it is manslaughter or murder, what do you do (Deut. 17:8-13)?

And on and on and on . . .

When I was a teenager I had friend who lived on a cattle ranch.

---

13. Other similar gatherings of laws covering the wide-ranging details of everyday living together are in Exodus 34:11-28, Leviticus 17–26 (the "Holiness Code"), and Numbers 5–6, 19.

Sometimes I was invited out for a visit. On one of those visits I learned a phrase that I had never heard before, *idiot savant,* French for "learned or wise idiot." One of the chores to which my friend was routinely assigned by his parents was what they called "riding fence." It was mindless work: he simply rode his horse along the barbed wire fence that enclosed the cattle, who were always, it seems, looking for breaks or weaknesses. When he found one he repaired it. There were miles of fence. Some days he would ride for hours without finding what he was looking for.

He told me that cattle are the dumbest members of the entire livestock family, animals, as Pooh Bear might put it, "of little brain." But in one thing they are absolutely brilliant: they have a genius for finding a hole or weak place in a fence. And the moment they find it they are through it, leading their sister cows and brother bulls after them into dangerous terrain where they have no skills for protecting themselves or avoiding calamity. You then have to spend the next two or three days rounding them up and returning them to where they belong and can be kept alive. My friend called cattle the *idiot savants* of the livestock world. And so it was necessary to "ride fence" to protect the cattle who didn't know enough to take care of themselves but were absolute geniuses at finding a hole and escaping from the confines of the community where there were adequate provisions for keeping them healthy.

One day while reading Moses and finding myself in the middle of a long passage of "Statutes and Ordinances" in Deuteronomy it occurred to me that this was something very much like my friend riding fence on his parents' cattle ranch — and me in my congregation. Christians in congregations are certainly not mentally defective, but there is considerable evidence that we might be spiritually defective, with one exception: We have an absolute genius for finding whatever might serve as a loophole in the commandments and creed.

*   *   *

Language used in relation to God and the soul is particularly liable to abstraction and depersonalization. Men and women entrusted with leading others in the way of following Jesus, parents and pastors and teachers and our many, many companions on the way — all of us in this kingdom of priests — are easily tempted to use a language that is large and impressive in order to provide authority and urgency. But we must not. We must pay attention to the way words are used, lest we detract from or blaspheme the way of Jesus. The way language is used — context and syntax, grammatical mood and poetic rhythm — provides the meaning. *God* out of context, without syntax, can be either blessing or blasphemy. Impersonal, story-less talk and writing is a blight on the world of discourse. Moses keeps us story-trained, and our lives story-responsive, congregation-rooted, congregation-relational.

"Gospel Me to the Garden"

In the Christian New Testament, the four Gospels of the Evangelists hold a place comparable to the Five Books of Moses in the Old. Matthew, Mark, Luke, and John were modest writers (not a typical trait among writers) and none claim authorship, but they clearly learned the craft of writing from Moses. The early generations of those who read the Gospels wrote the Evangelists' names soon enough (as earlier generations had supplied the name of Moses to the Five Books). The Jesus community not only named the writers but kept the four together as a company: Matthew, Mark, Luke, and John. They have kept congenial company ever since as heirs to Moses in the way of language. An old nursery rhyme addresses them in prayer:

> Matthew, Mark, Luke, and John
> Bless the bed I lie upon.
> And if I should die before I wake,
> I pray the Lord my soul to take.

This gospel quartet appears again in the more sophisticated context of Robert Lowell's poem "At the Indian Killer's Grave":

John, Matthew, Luke and Mark,
Gospel me to the Garden. . . .[14]

Lowell's use of "gospel" as a transitive verb catches the conviction of readers of Scripture that these four Gospels, like the Five Books of Moses that preceded them, take us someplace, someplace that we want to go to. They are not entertainment or speculation, inspirational slogans, insider lore, apologetic arguments, historical reconstructions, consumer psychologies, meaningful encounters, bullying threats, or energizing challenges. They are a *way,* the language way of Moses and Jesus: "*Gospel* me to the garden."

14. Robert Lowell, *Lord Weary's Castle and the Mills of the Kavanaughs* (New York: Harcourt, Brace and World, 1951), p. 63.

CHAPTER 4

David: "I Did Not Hide My Iniquity"

Perfectionism is a disorder that occurs frequently in the Christian community. It is way of perceiving Christians in two categories: carnal Christians and spiritual Christians. There are variations in the terminology for dividing up the church and putting each of us in our place: mere believers and serious disciples; water-baptized Christians and Spirit-baptized Christians; lukewarm and on-fire; the rigorist and the relaxed. Perfectionism has a way of claiming the term "spiritual" for itself — some Christians are spiritual and by implication the others are not. In this context the term "spiritual" is marked by a particular intensity of interiority or something of the kind that introduces a sharp dichotomy into the Christian community between the common and the elite. You are either gray and ordinary, or conspicuously resplendent in an aura of light. There is no diversity and particularity of color, no spectrum, among the men and women among whom our Lord the Spirit is shaping the life of Christ in his church. Inevitably the rigorist comes to look on the relaxed with considerable condescension.

From time to time, the rigorist party sharpens the dichotomy and, going beyond perfectionist tendencies, actually talks about achieving perfection in the Christian way: If we take this life with unrelenting seriousness we can actually live a perfect life in Christ. When that happens rigorist condescension turns into polite (but not always polite) contempt of the relaxed.

The church as a whole has discouraged, sometimes with great vigor, this sort of dividing up the community of Jesus into graded classes, but the way of perfection has a way of surfacing century after century under a variety of banners: Messalians, Donatists, Quietists, Pietists, and Holiness movements that, inventive with numerous variations, try to convince the Christian community that the way of Jesus is a way of perfection. Since we are commanded to follow Jesus and Jesus is perfect, the way of Jesus is a way of perfection. It is not only desirable but required that we live or at least aspire to live perfect lives if we are serious about the Christian faith.

Perfectionism: a most ruinous deviation from the way, a detour from the way of Jesus. It is unlikely that it will plunge us headlong into damnation, but it certainly makes us most undesirable company with others on the pilgrim way. Perfectionism is a perversion of the Christian way. It is responsible for disabling countless sincere and devout Christians for common usefulness in the company of their neighbors on pilgrimage to Jerusalem. The perfectionist has neither time nor taste for quotidian holiness.

The attempt to impose perfection on either oneself or another, whether parent on child, pastor on congregation, CEO on a company, teacher on student, husband on wife, wife on husband, is decidedly not the way of Jesus.

*   *   *

And how do we know? In large part because of David, the ancestor of Jesus, who was unembarrassed to be called Son of David. David provides a large chunk of the evidence that disabuses us of the idea that perfection is part of the job description of the men and women who follow Jesus. More narrative space is given in our Scriptures to the story of David than to any other single person, and there are *no* perfectionist elements in it. The way of David is, from start to finish, a way of imperfection.

*   *   *

The way of David is rich in so much of what is involved in dealing with what we all deal with — men and women, enemies and friends, sex and children. The story is woven in a vast tapestry of love and war, deeply textured in all the emotions that express the highs and lows of daily existence. David is nothing if not *interesting*. There is a charismatic verve to his life that compelled the attention of everyone. The stories about him quickly developed in Israel into something approaching a national myth. The people of Israel remembered and talked about everything and everyone that had to do with this man.[1]

*   *   *

The David story is framed by giant-killing. Before he is old enough to vote he steps onto the stage of history by killing Goliath, the formidable Philistine giant from Gath. In the last Philistine battle recorded, David is too old and tired to kill anymore, but his nephew Jonathan does it for him, kills the grotesque Philistine giant (also from Gath) with six fingers on each hand and six toes on each foot (2 Sam. 21:20-21). David's larger-than-life story, bookended by a slain Philistine giant at either end, was assured a place in the giant-killer hall of fame.

Everyone, it seems, loved David. He captured the imagination of the entire country. His popularity was expressed in spontaneous parades in villages whenever David returned from another battle triumph, as women poured out of whatever village he entered, singing and dancing, festive with tambourines and lutes. The hit song of those early David years was

Saul kills by the thousand,
David by the ten thousand. (1 Sam. 18:6-7 *The Message*)

1. For more on David see my *Leap over a Wall: Earthy Spirituality for Everyday Christians* (San Francisco: HarperSanFrancisco, 1997).

*   *   *

All of us have an insatiable curiosity on every detail of what it means to be involved in being a man, a woman — the human condition: "Who am I? What does it mean to be me? And what exactly am I doing here?" We are looking for verification of what it means to be alive, truly alive, in this world. That is why we read, reread, and continue to read stories: stories by Dostoevsky and Tolstoy, stories by Balzac and Dickens, stories by Faulkner and Stegner, stories by Updike and Undset. Doris Lessing, a master storyteller herself, says that she reads and rereads stories "as I think they should be read, for illumination, in order to enlarge one's perception of life."[2] High on the list of stories available to us that we can read and reread to enlarge our "perception of life" is the David story, the *way* of David, this extensive and detailed probing of the human condition.

Robert Alter in his superb translation of the David story writes that "the anonymous Hebrew writer, drawing on what he knew or thought he knew of the portentous historical events, has created this most searching story of men and women in the rapid and dangerous current of history that still speaks to us, floundering in history and the dilemmas of political life, three thousand years later."[3]

The human interest that pulls us into this story deepens and expands as we extend our reading of the David story into the David prayers, preserved for us in the Book of Psalms. The prayers are the inside story of the human life that is given to us from the outside in the biographical account of what David did, the men and women he lived with, the way he lived in the society of his time, and the way he functioned as a leader. The story shows us David dealing with Samuel and Saul, Jonathan and Joab, Michal and Bathsheba, Amnon and Absalom, Mephibosheth and Ahithophel. The prayers show us David dealing with God: sin and repentance, despair and hope, doubt and praise, guilt and grace.

2. Doris Lessing, *A Small Personal Voice* (New York: A. A. Knopf, 1974), p. 5.
3. Robert Alter, *The David Story* (New York: W. W. Norton, 1999), p. xxiv.

David was a person of prayer. As it turns out, we end up knowing far more about David's dealings with God than we do about his dealings with Goliath and Saul, Jonathan and Abigail, Bathsheba and Tamar. And we need to know this, for God is the large, totally encompassing reality in which "we live and move and have our being." John Calvin described the Psalms as "an anatomy of all the parts of the soul."[4] We will never understand the first thing about who we are and what we are doing if we know ourselves only from the outside. Not that the inside can be understood apart from the outside (nor the outside apart from the inside). We need access to both: the story and the prayers. And we have both. There are some ancient manuscripts in which copyists left a gap after each incident in David's life into which the reader could insert an appropriate psalm, praying his or her human action into God's presence and action.[5]

There is not the slightest effort given in the biblical story to make David admirable in any moral or spiritual sense. And yet there is the assumption in all of this that flawed and faithless and failed as he is, he is representative — not a warning against bad behavior but a witness, inadvertent as it was, to the normalcy, yes, the inevitability of imperfection.

The scriptural witness to David's way of imperfection consists of two large elements: the narrative of his life told in the Books of Samuel (1 Samuel 16 through 1 Kings 2), and the prayers of David that are gathered in the Psalms.

The Narrative

My favorite in the grand cycle of David stories takes place at the cave at En-gedi. En-gedi is a small oasis alongside the Dead Sea, the large lake

---

4. John Calvin, *Commentary on the Book of Psalms*, trans. James Anderson (Grand Rapids: Eerdmans, 1949), p. xxxvii.

5. Peter Ackroyd, *Doors of Perception: A Guide to Reading the Psalms* (London: SCM, 1978), pp. 35-36, 74-76.

of salt water at the southeastern corner of Israel. Today there is a little park for picnickers and swimmers — a cluster of palm trees, a stand where you can buy soft drinks, a bathhouse for changing clothes and for rinsing off the salt after a swim. There are usually a dozen or so swimmers — or floaters (it's hard to swim in that dense salt water). I spent several hours at En-gedi a few years ago. It was a spring day. I wanted to get a feel for the country where David had survived during the years he was a fugitive from King Saul. I climbed up the cliffs, ducked into the caves, trying to imagine the kind of life that David eked out in that harsh environment.

About three hundred yards to the west of the Salt Sea, a precipitous rise of cliffs pushes up two thousand feet to where they are topped by tableland. The plateau and cliffs are deeply grooved by erosion, making a tangle of canyons and caves. This is the wilderness of En-gedi, a vast expanse of badlands, a country as harsh and inhospitable as any you're likely to find on this earth. Hyenas, lizards, and vultures are your hosts.

On the run from King Saul, David and a few of his men hide in one of the caves overlooking the Dead Sea. The day is hot and the cave is cool. They are deep in the cave, resting. Then there is a shadow across the mouth of the cave. They are astonished to see that it is King Saul. They didn't know that he was that close in his pursuit. Saul enters the cave but doesn't see them: fresh from the hard glare of desert sun, his eyes haven't adjusted to the darkness and don't pick out the shadowy figures in the recesses of the cave. Besides, he isn't looking for them at that moment; he has entered the cave to respond to a call of nature. He turns his back on them.

When David and his men see what is going on, they know that Saul, oblivious to their presence, is as good as dead. The men are ready to pounce, but David silently forbids them to kill him. Instead, he moves along the wall of the cave to where the king's garment has been tossed, cuts off a piece of it, and then slips back with his men. In a short while King Saul pulls on his garment, straps on his sword, and leaves. David lets him walk a healthy distance away and then goes to the mouth of the cave and calls out to him. By now the king is across the canyon. David calls, "My lord the king!" (1 Sam. 24:8). Saul looks back, astonished. David bows down, reverently honoring the king. And then he speaks, "Why do you listen to those who tell you I am your enemy? See what I have in my hand? It is the skirt of your robe. Just now, instead of cutting your robe, I could as easily have cut you, *killed* you. But I will not do that. I will never do that because you are Yahweh's anointed" (my paraphrase).

As Saul was outlined from the opening of the cave against the cobalt blue of the Dead Sea, with the red cliffs of Moab beyond, David saw something his companions didn't see: David saw not an enemy but the magnificent, albeit flawed, king anointed by God. And he did obeisance.

All the ingredients for a scene of coarse vulgarity are here: the king on his "throne," viewed from the backside, taking a dump. But David, earthy as he was, was not vulgar. He turned the scene into an act of generous homage, a sacred moment, an improbable and incredible witness (considering the circumstances). Reverence for life.

But the reason David's refusal to kill King Saul catches and holds my attention is that it strikes me as completely uncharacteristic of David. David got his start by killing the Philistine giant Goliath. From that moment on, killing Philistines was a leitmotif in David's life. He made a specialty of killing Philistines: He killed a hundred as a bride-price to Saul for Michal's hand in marriage (1 Sam. 18:27). He acquired a fast-rising reputation as a Philistine-killer that eclipsed all of King Saul's warriors combined (1 Sam. 18:30): the "heavy defeat" of Philistines who were marauding Keilah (1 Sam. 23:1-5), the rout of Philistines at Baal-perazim (2 Sam. 5:17-21) and again in the valley of Rephaim (2 Sam. 5:22-25), the capture of Metheg-ammah from Philistines (2 Sam. 8:1). But not just Philistines — Geshurites, Girzites, Amalekites, Jerah-meelites, Kenites, Moabites, Aramaeans, Edomites, and Ammonites also contributed substantially to David's body count.

In the welter of all that killing, the thing that interests me most is the man he didn't kill. He didn't kill King Saul. And King Saul was the one man he had the most reason and motivation to kill. King Saul was obsessed with killing David. A maniacal jealousy consumed Saul.

Twice in his own house he tried to kill David at the very time when David was trying to soothe the emotionally distraught king with his music (1 Sam. 18:10-11). Failing in all those attempts, Saul sent him out against Philistines as a commander of just a thousand soldiers intending that he be killed in the line of duty. But David came back triumphant (1 Sam. 18:12-16).

Killing David became an obsession with the king. He could think of nothing else: "Saul spoke with his son Jonathan and with all his servants about killing David" (1 Sam 19:1). One time while David was again playing music for the king he narrowly escaped death from the royal javelin (1 Sam. 19:9-10). One night when Saul surrounded David's house with assassins, David's wife Michal let him out through the window and he got away (1 Sam. 19:11-17). Later Jonathan helped David escape the king's evil passion (1 Sam. 20). When Saul learned that the priests at Nob had given aid and comfort in protecting David from his murderous plot, he ordered their massacre: eighty-five priests along with "men and women, children and infants, oxen, donkeys, and sheep" — leaving the "city of priests" awash in blood (1 Sam. 22:6-23).

From then on, David was on the run. By the time we come upon him hiding in the cave at En-gedi he had a band of men with him, surviving by their wits in the Wilderness of Ziph. Saul was determined to get him — he "sought him every day" (1 Sam. 23:14). When the Ziphites betrayed his whereabouts to Saul, David escaped to the Wilderness of Maon (1 Sam. 23:25-29). And from there to En-gedi.

David the giant-killer. David the Philistine-killer. But he didn't kill Saul. King Saul, who did everything he could think of to kill David, who nurtured a murderous passion to murder the young man who had saved his kingdom from the Philistines, who hunted David through the wilderness wadis and canyons like a wild pig, was not killed by David.

But this glorious exception at the Cave of En-gedi throws into stark relief the norm by which he lived, thoroughly assimilated into the bloody barbarism of Iron Age Canaanite culture. But aren't leaders supposed to *lead*? Lead beyond the culture-determined standards? The only thing that distinguishes David from the surrounding Canaanite kings is that he killed more and better than they did. Is that what we expect from a leader anointed by God? Shouldn't there be at least some hint that there is another way, a way articulated so winningly by Isaiah of Jerusalem, who lived in a culture just as barbarous as David's, a way to God's Mountain where

> He'll show us the way he works
>> so we can live the way we're made . . .
> [where] they'll turn their swords into shovels,
>> their spears into hoes.
> No more will nation fight nation;
>> they won't play war anymore. (Isa. 2:3-4 *The Message*)

And it is not as if it was only the surrounding culture that David failed to transcend. He was no more admirable in the matter of personal and family virtues. His infamous adulterous affair with Bathsheba, with its cover-up murder of Uriah, gets the headlines, but it's just as difficult to find much to write home about on other fronts: he had eight wives, twenty-one children, and a harem of concubines — so much for monogamy and focus on the family. In the stories that are told of two of his sons, Absalom and Amnon, he comes across as a thoroughly indifferent and mostly failed father. He tolerated the brutality and perfidy of his right-hand man, Joab, letting him do what he himself would have been embarrassed to do openly. There is one poignant moment that in its tragic pathos rivals David's later heart-wrenching grief over the death of his son Absalom — the grief of Paltiel over the loss of his wife; but this time David was the cause of the tragic grief, not the recipient of it. The matter of Paltiel exposes David as calloused and calculating.

The details are heartrending. After Saul's death, his field commander Abner offered to come over to David's side as an ally. But David insisted on a condition: that his former wife, Saul's daughter Michal, be returned to him. But by now she was no longer his wife. After David had escaped from Saul's assassins, Saul had married off Michal to a man named Paltiel. Now David wanted her back. The motivation was purely political, an act of brutal disregard for either Michal's wishes or Paltiel's feelings. David wanted his former wife, Saul's daughter, returned to back up his claim to be Saul's legitimate successor. So Michal was forcibly removed from husband and home and taken to David. Paltiel followed her, "weeping as he walked behind her all the way to Bahurim. Then Abner said to him, 'Go back home!' So he went back" (2 Sam. 3:16). We have no words from Paltiel, only his eloquent tears paving the way to and from Bahurim, a village just south of Jerusalem. It is a heartbreaking scene, Paltiel and Michal, husband and wife, ripped apart by a peremptory self-serving political stratagem. There is no evidence that David felt any emotion about what he had done. He was oblivious to both Michal and Paltiel. David was not going to permit personal feelings to interfere with what we might today call realpolitik. David's role as leader obliterated David's soul. If David at En-gedi showed David at his best, in the matter of Paltiel he is at his worst — a man who sacrifices his humanity at the altar of power.

There is more to be said on the nobility of David than En-gedi. There is his intimate friendship with Jonathan (1 Sam. 18–20); David's response to Abigail (1 Sam. 25); a second refusal to kill Saul at the hill Hachilah (1 Sam. 26); David's generosity at the brook Besor (1 Sam. 30); David's lament over the deaths of Saul and Jonathan (2 Sam. 1); David worshiping before the Ark of the Covenant (2 Sam. 6); David repentant before the prophet Nathan (2 Sam. 7); David's compassion for Mephibosheth (2 Sam. 9); David's humility before the curses of Shimei (2 Sam. 16); David's kindness to the old man Barzillai (2 Sam. 19); and David's tribute to the bravery of the warriors who risked their lives to bring him water from the Bethlehem well (2 Sam. 23). And, reading between the lines, much, much more.

But there can be no confusion about what is conveyed in this narration. The life of David is a labyrinth of ambiguities, not unlike our own. What we admire in David does not cancel out what we abhor, and what we abhor does not cancel out what we admire. David is not a model for imitation; David is not a candidate for a pedestal. The David story is an immersion in humanity, no different from the humanity conditioned by our culture and flawed by our sins. The story of David is not a story of what God wants us to be but a story of God working with the raw material of our lives as he finds us. David's story is told with so much detail so that we will have spread out before us exactly what goes on in a thoroughly lived human life in which God is shaping a life of salvation. David is a man of God, but not by any means a perfect man of God.

The Prayers

Alongside the stories of David, we have the prayers of David, gathered in the book of Psalms, 150 prayers that are the primary text on prayer for Jews and Christians. The David stories give us his life from the outside; the David prayers give us his life from the inside. The person in Scripture who has the most extensively told story is the same person who is shown to be most at prayer. Not all the prayers in the Psalms are David's prayers. Several are connected with other names (Solomon, Asaph, Ethan, Korah, Heman, Moses). Thirty-four are anonymous (the tradition calls them "orphan psalms"). Nor is it likely that David himself composed all of the seventy-three prayers attributed to him. "A Prayer of David" can also be translated, "a Prayer in the David tradition" or "a Prayer for David." The Hebrew *l'dawid* is not precise. Some were written by him, others written in honor of him, most written in awareness of him. He was the most prominent of those who wrote prayers in Israel. He was remembered by all as the "sweet psalmist of Israel" (2 Sam. 23:1 RSV). In the tradition of the people of God, David's name gives cohesion and authority to the whole collection of Israel's prayers that were gathered and arranged in the book of Psalms.[6]

*   *   *

---

6. This is not unlike the way that the name of Moses gives authorial coherence to the grounding narrative of the Five Books as discussed in Chapter 3.

We are interested in understanding as well as we can the nature of this man who holds such a prominent place in our Scriptures and in the continuing traditions of the church as a "man after his [God's] own heart" (1 Sam. 13:14; see also Acts 13:22), the man who for forty years and more held a key position in Israel. The stories tell us clearly that it was a way of imperfection. What about the prayers? The prayers are the same, prayed on the way of imperfection.

The Psalms express everything we are capable of experiencing: exuberant praise and reverent meditation, but also questioning doubt, victimization, lament, pain, penitence, and repentance. Most of them, two-thirds in fact, are prayed by men and women in trouble of one kind or another. Of these the Christian community early on designated seven of them (6, 32, 38, 51, 102, 130, 143) as "penitential," prayers prayed out of a sense of sin and guilt, failure and trouble, prayers prayed out of a sense of need and inadequacy. These are prayers prayed on the way of imperfection, prayers prayed by those who don't "have it all together," prayers prayed out of shame and sorrow for sin. They provide our praying imaginations with Holy Spirit antibiotics to protect us from perfectionist expectations, perfectionist pretensions, perfectionist illusions. They provide us a way of praying in detail what we inevitably experience on the way of imperfection.

Psalm 6: I drench my couch with my weeping.

The trouble that we are born into "as sparks fly upward" (Job 5:7) provides the content to this first penitential prayer. We are not told what the trouble is: God's anger provoked by sin (v. 1)? Sickness? (Healing is mentioned in vv. 2-3.) Persecution? (Foes, workers of evil, and enemies are referred to in vv. 7-8, 10.) Probably all of these, but more. The sin in the world breaks out in troubles all over the place. Every once in a while one of the troubles triggers an avalanche of dismay and sorrow that simply overcomes us. There are times when an accumulated sense of the sheer mass of trouble in the world just knocks the wind out of us, knocks the *prayer* out of us — all the sin, all the sickness, all the meanness: damaged lives, broken hearts, child abuse, raped women, rampant hunger, torture, the grinding poverty of the poor, the un-checked greed of the rich, desecrating violations of our land and water and air, brutal arrogance in high places. Details pile up. There is a lot wrong with the world. We have moments when the apocalyptic bru-tality and blasphemy loose in the world tramples our life to the ground (Ps. 7:5). Those moments are compounded when we realize that some of the wrong is in us — we are not just observers of it, we are part of it. Sin is not a Them thing; it is also Us. When the two moments come to-gether — the Them wrongs and the Us wrongs — the hurt and hate, the guilt and sin catalyze an enormous sorrow. We find ourselves in the middle of Psalm 6 weeping our prayer:

> I am weary with my moaning;
>> every night I flood my bed with tears;
>> I drench my couch with my weeping.
> My eyes waste away because of grief,
>> they grow weak because of all my foes. (Ps. 6:6-7)

The language is extravagant — crying every night and waking up with pillow and mattress tear-soaked. But is it exaggerated? Maybe not. Not at least if this prayer comes out of a heart that is in touch with the catastrophic dimensions of sin and all the tears of despair and (some-times) repentance that flow night and day, year after year pooling into a great salt sea of sorrow: the tears of the tortured, the tears of the be-trayed, the tears of the dying, the tears of the lonely, the tears of Rachel weeping for her children, the tears of Paltiel weeping for Michal, the tears of David weeping over Absalom, the tears of Peter weeping outside the court of Caiaphas, the tears of the women on the Via Dolo-rosa, the tears of Jesus — weeping over Lazarus, weeping over Jerusa-lem, weeping in Gethsemane. Tears, tears, tears. We find ourselves swimming in a sea of tears.[7]

---

7. The verb translated "flood" is literally "I swim...." We can translate, "I swim in a river of tears." See Isaiah 25:11 and Ezekiel 47:5. Charles Briggs, *The Book of Psalms* (Ed-inburgh: T&T Clark, 1952), vol. 1, p. 50.

The way of imperfection takes us through slums and suburbs, across battlefields and into refugee camps, to hospitals and homeless shelters. We find common ground with the addicts and the abused, the victims and victimizers, the down and out and the up and out. On the way of imperfection we find ourselves following Jesus to the well in Samaria, the sycamore tree in Jericho, the pool of Siloam, the cross on Golgotha where "Christ is in agony to the end of the world."[8]

There is much laughter and singing and dancing on this way, palm branches and hosannas. But there are also tears and laments, rivers of them, every tear a prayer and not one unnoticed — "my tears in your bottle!" (Ps. 56:8).

Psalm 32: When I declared not my sin, my body wasted away.

The great, great grandaddy of all sins is the denial of sin, the refusal to admit sin. Such refusal is odd because, as G. K. Chesterton once observed, sin is the only empirically verifiable item in the entire Christian/Jewish belief system. No one has seen God at any time, but we see sin with our own eyes all the time. And yet denial is commonplace.

When we follow Jesus, we are not more than a mile or two down this road of imperfection when we realize that we are going to have to deal with sin — all this sin on the road and rubbing shoulders with all these sinners. We had expected to be in better company than this.

Praying with David, who knew a good deal about sin, we soon learn that the remedy for sin is not the extermination of sin, not long training in not-sinning, not a rigorous program conditioning us in a pavlovian revulsion to sin. The only effective remedy for sin is the forgiveness of sin — and only God can forgive sin. If we refuse to deal with God, we are left dealing with sin by means of punishment or moral education or concocting some strategy of denial. None seem to make much of a dent in the sin business. No. The way, the only way, is to get in on God's forgiveness. And we do that by confession. No ex-

---

8. Blaise Pascal, *Pensées* (New York: Random House, 1941), #552, p. 176.

cuses, no rationalizations, no denial, no New Year's resolutions, only "I will confess. . . ." Psalm 32 is straightforward:

> I acknowledged my sin to thee,
>   and I did not hide my iniquity;
> I said, "I will confess my transgressions to the LORD";
>   then thou didst forgive the guilt of my sin. (Ps. 32:5 RSV)

Most of us, maybe all of us, when caught doing what is wrong, resolve or promise not to do it again. Those resolves and promises serve us well for our first few years. But not for long. After awhile they begin sounding tinny in the ears of our parents and teachers and friends. And then they begin sounding tinny to us.

But confession doesn't sound tinny. Confession is a way out of the puny, self-deceiving, mulish contrivances we attempt in order to manage sin on our own. Confession is entrance into the vast world of forgiveness, encompassed with God's deliverance and steadfast love.

Psalm 38:   There is no health in my bones because of my sin.

Sin makes us miserable. As inevitable as it is and as unavoidable as it turns out to be, it is not congenial to our image-of-God created selves. Sin introduces a foreign substance into our souls. This is not the way we were intended to live.

This prayer is conspicuous in its portrayal of the physical dimensions of sin — the sheer quantity of bodily parts and postures that are listed: no soundness in my *flesh*, no health in my *bones*, *wounds* that fester, utterly *bowed down and prostrate*, *loins* filled with burning, utterly *spent and crushed*, tumult of *heart*, *heart* throbs, *strength* that fails, light of my *eyes*: eight bodily parts, four bodily postures. Sin and the effects of sin are not simply matters of the spirit or misdirections of the will or disobedient acts. The whole person is involved. There is no inner and outer in matters of sin.

Also, there is frequent reference to others who are involved in sin. *Friends, companions, kinsmen, those who seek my life, who seek my hurt, who meditate treachery, my foes, those who hate me, who render me evil for good, my adversaries:* ten references to others whose sin affects me. There is no us and them in matters of sin. Which means, of course, that I cannot deal with sin by dealing exclusively with my inner life. Neither can I hope to deal with sin by converting or eliminating those who are against me.

So what is left? God is left. God is the one with whom we must deal. The prayer refuses to listen or respond to what others say, whether in accusation or by way of advice. We cut to the chase, we address and attend to God: "for thee, O LORD, do I wait; it is thou, O LORD my God, who wilt answer" (v. 15 RSV).

The psalmist certainly takes responsibility for the personal consequences of his or her sin (*my* sin, *my* iniquities, *my* foolishness). But the social dimensions are also very much involved: no illusions that if I just get "right with God" everything is going to be fine, no fantasies that if I can just convert or conquer and so get rid of my detractors I will be home free. God is the one with whom I must deal. My inside world is not, nor will it ever be, perfect. The outside world is not, nor will it ever be, perfect. In all matters of sin, my business, first and foremost, is God: "Make haste to help me, O Lord, my salvation" (v. 22).

Psalm 51: Purge me with hyssop, and I shall be clean; wash me, and I shall be whiter than snow.

The penitential prayer of confession that is Psalm 51 is identified with David's adulterous sin with Bathsheba. It is a genuine cry of contrition that stands out among the people of God as *the* prayer for forgiveness, the prayer most memorized and most prayed by men and women conscious and convicted of sin.

The primary metaphor for sin in this prayer is dirt that makes us dirty, requiring a vigorous scrubbing: *wash* me thoroughly, *cleanse* me, *purge* me, *blot out* all my transgressions/iniquities, create in me a *clean* heart.

The frequency with which we use "dirty" as an adjective of disapprobation commands notice: dirty clothes, dirty face (and hands, feet, ears, mouth, hair), dirty plates, dirty tricks, dirty work, dirty mind, dirty sex, dirty air, dirty words, dirty books, and so on. But dirt, as such, has no negative connotations when it is in its proper place, in, say, a garden or flower pot or beet field. There is nothing negative in the Genesis statement that the human being is formed by God from dirt. Just the opposite. The dirt from which we are made and to which we will return is identical with the dirt beneath our feet, a witness to our organic relation with the entire creation, giving dignity to the nonhuman world. It is only when the dirt is in the wrong place that it becomes a defiling adjective: dirty.

And that tells us something about sin. Every single thing in the entire God-given creation — inorganic or organic; mineral, vegetable, animal, or human — is good, but yet can also can be used in the wrong way and end up defiling us. And since we are immersed in the materials of a good creation and cannot live any other way, we are continuously vulnerable to defilement.

Further, it is the very goodness of creation (dirt) that renders sin so attractive and seemingly innocent. Sin, in a sense, has no substance in itself. It can exist only as a perversion or distortion of the good, the true, the beautiful, which it is its genius to defile. We therefore cannot eliminate the source of sin without destroying the very goodness and truth and beauty that we inhabit. The possibilities of sin are always at hand, both within and without.

We can no more live a sinless life than we can plant potatoes without getting our hands dirty. But neither do we have to go around all day with dirty hands. There are washbasins well-supplied with soap in our homes and workplaces — and baptismal fonts and baptistries in our sanctuaries. The way, the only way, to deal with sin is through washing, a primary metaphor for forgiveness. And connecting with God's forgiveness, like washing, requires frequency.

To object that this trivializes the gravity of sin and opens the door to profligacy is anticipated by St. Paul's rebuke of the hypothetical person who says, "Well, let's just keep on sinning so God can keep on forgiving" (in Romans 3:8 and 6:1). The fact is that there is no other way to deal with sin except through God's forgiveness, God's endless and most merciful forgiveness.

Psalm 102: He will regard the prayer of the destitute, and will not despise their supplication.

We are made for one another. We are not ourselves by ourselves. And among these "one anothers" is the Other — God: Father, Son, and Holy Spirit. The emphatically (three times!) relational three-personed God created men and women in his relational image: "It is not good that the man should be alone; I will make him a helper as his partner" (Gen. 2:18). When this relational reality is severed or denied or distorted, we are dealing with sin. It is immaterial whether the refusal or failure in relationality is between a person and God, or between one person and another who are both in the image of God: it is sin all the same.

One familiar consequence of sin — one of several consequences — is isolation. Psalm 102 gives witness to this experience of isolation. Early in the prayer the images of solitary confinement pile up: shunned by God, shut up in a hot furnace, grass cut from its roots and withered, a vulture or owl in an uninhabited wasteland, a solitary bird on a bare rooftop, taunted by enemies, eking out life on a diet of ashes and tears, the averted eye, the deaf ear. Isolated, alone, ignored, abandoned. Godless and friendless.

There is no lack of detail provided here. But what is interesting and most significant is that the groveling, if that is not too harshly put, stops abruptly: *But.* "But thou, O LORD, art enthroned for ever . . ." (v. 12). The prayer, by some inner logic (no transition is evident) shifts to God: the action and presence of God takes over. At the same time the pronouns change; "I" and "me" give way to nouns and pronouns of community: Zion, thy servants, the nations, all the kings, the destitute, their supplications, generations to come, people yet unborn, peoples, kingdom, the children of thy servants, their posterity. There is a last, brief gasp of desperation in verses 23-24, but it is soon dwarfed and quieted against the endless prairie horizon of God's royal presence (vv. 25-28).

The vision of the road to heaven as a way of perpetual palm branches and hosannas is not a vision, it is a mirage. Jesus wept lonely tears in a festival parade on that very road. Betrayed by Judas, deserted in Gethsemane, forsaken by his Father on the cross, reviled by taunts.

The way is pot-holed by sin and sinners. There are moments of isolation and disconnection from God and family, God and friends, God and community. And if Jesus was not insulated from feeling and dealing with the isolating and lonely effects of our sin, we are well-advised not to attempt to build or find a road more to our liking and convenience.

**Psalm 130: I wait for the LORD, my soul waits,
and in his word I hope.**

For people on the way, waiting is a grievous imposition. Being on the way means that we are headed for a destination. For an eager, determined traveler, waiting can be experienced only as an interruption, a delay. Running, strolling, driving a car, walking the dog, riding a horse, whatever, on the way is what we *do* on the way. Why else would we be on the way?

But there are times when we are incapacitated from making our way along the way. A broken leg, an accident that leaves us crumpled in the ditch, a promising shortcut that leaves us mired helplessly in a bog. That's when we wait. We have no choice. It makes no difference how many cheerful passersby shout encouragement to us, cheerleading us to heaven, calling out advice, quoting Scripture ("gird up your loins" . . . "take up your cross and follow" . . . "run with perseverance . . ."). We can't do it. We are at the end of our rope. We are in over our heads. We pray. We pray because there is nothing we can do for ourselves, and there is nothing anyone else can do for us. We pray "out of the depths."

"Out of the depths" launches the prayer. "Depths" is a term from the lexicon of geography — valley, ravine, deep waters, pit, trench — that is frequently used as a metaphor: unfathomable, depth of corruption, distress, apostasy. Sin is certainly implicated throughout these depths. Sin is not a superficial blemish on either soul or body, it penetrates to the depths. Sin does not respond to cosmetic treatments, it requires work at the foundation of our lives.

But here's the thing. The sin does not disqualify us from being on the way. Sin does not expel us from our place on the way. We may be stuck, incapacitated, lost, depressed, angry, puzzled, confused, but we are still on the way: "If thou, O LORD, shouldst mark iniquities, Lord, who could stand? But there is forgiveness with thee, that thou mayest be feared" (vv. 3-4 RSV). Another way to put that is "If you, GOD, kept records on wrongdoings, who would stand a chance? As it turns out, forgiveness is your habit, and that's why you're worshiped" (*The Message*). We are on the David way, are treated in the Jesus way; there is, therefore, as St. Paul put it, "now no condemnation" (Rom. 8:1).

The long and short of it is that there is a lot more going on on the way than getting to a destination. And there is a lot more going on on the way than what we are doing. There is what God is doing. Which is why we "wait for the Lord." We stop, whether by choice or through circumstance, so that we can be alert and attentive and receptive to what God is doing in and for us, in and for others, on the way. We wait for our souls to catch up with our bodies. Waiting for the Lord is a large part of what we do on the way because the largest part of what takes place on the way is what God is doing, what God is saying. Much of the time, disabled or enervated by sin, we can't do what must be done, so we wait for God to do it in us. Much of the time, we don't know what to do, so we wait until we understand what God commands us to do. The waiting is not just an indolent "waiting around." We wait "for the morning," which is to say that we wait in hope. We wait while we are being "ransomed, healed, restored, forgiven." We wait for God to do what we cannot do for ourselves "in the depths." When he has done it, we are once more on the way.

Psalm 143: Enter not into judgment with thy servant;
for no man living is righteous before thee.

There is a lot wrong with the world. There is a lot wrong with me. Prayer is not a whitewash of the wrong whether in the world or in me. It is rather a leisurely and devout attentiveness, as often as every day, to the conditions in which I find myself as I walk this way of imperfection.

The fundamental finding of the prayer that is Psalm 143 is that the conditions are not primarily what can be compiled into a thick catalogue of all the wrongs, sins, imperfections, faults, crimes, and enmities that journalists report daily and that moralists condemn roundly. The conditions mostly have to do with God, the faithful and righteous God of steadfast love.

The world's catalogue of sin is immense, with pages added every hour. It turns out that there is not much to be said for men and women in this world on the righteousness front: Psalmist and Paul team up to make sure we get it: "There is no one who does good, no, not one. . . . [A]ll have sinned . . ." (Ps. 14:3 and Rom. 3:23). The libraries of the world are stuffed with the documentation. Go ahead: read up on it.

But reading is not the preferred way for dealing with what is wrong with the world. We already have plenty of documentation. Information is readily available. In this world in which sin is so in-your-face, it is common enough for men and women to get obsessed with wrongs, sins, crimes, enmities. They become collectors of sin-gossip. They rage against the decadence of the culture. Or they are forever scrupulously examining their own souls for blemishes.

But that is not the David way. The David way is to immerse ourselves in the God conditions that prevail on the way. We do that not by taking a book from a library shelf and reading up on God. No, we pray. Prayer is not a research paper into the varieties and extent of sin. Instead, "I stretch out my hands to thee. . . ."

> I meditate on all that thou hast done;
> I muse on what thy hands have wrought. (v. 5 RSV)

The moment we do that, remembering and meditating and musing, sin ceases to be hot news or salacious gossip or the raw stuff of outrage. *God* fills our minds and imaginations — we remember, we notice, we hear . . . God.

As we pray, the proportions of what we see taking place on the way change radically. The many wrongs and sins that plague our human condition are collapsed into just three references to enemies (vv. 3, 9, 12). Now it is the presence and action of God that dominates: four times God is addressed directly; twenty pronouns for God keep the name of God at front and center. There are twelve imperative verbs addressed to God for help along this sin-littered roadway compared to a mere three that ask for God to deal with enemies.

So even though sin provides the background for this seventh prayer, it is God who provides the subject matter and produces the action. Which is fitting for this final penitential prayer. Naiveté regarding sin is dangerous as we follow Jesus, but an obsession with sin is decidedly unhealthy. It is God's business to take care of the sin; our business is with God as he does his work in and with us.

*   *   *

Conspicuous by its absence in this immersion in the seven penitential prayers that deal with sin and sinners is even the hint of a resolve to "not do it again." Not a single moral/spiritual resolution shows up in these prayers. Dealing definitively with sin is God's business, and God's way of dealing with the sin business is forgiveness.

This does not mean that moral intentionality and effort is useless or inappropriate on the way, only that sin as a thing-in-itself is beyond our power to get rid of whether within ourselves or in the people or institutions for which we have responsibility. In dealing with sin we don't do it on our own, we deal with God as he deals with sin. Dealing with the intricacies, the subtleties, and the pervasiveness of sin requires God in his mercy. And the overall way that he does it is to forgive.

*   *   *

The way of David is the way of imperfection. The story David lived and the psalms he prayed provide us with an imagination that is capable of understanding the operations of God to do his perfect work in us, not our capacities to perfect ourselves. The stories tell us that nothing about us, whether good or bad, is without significance; the prayers tell us that everything within us, whether good or bad, has to do with God. The stories and prayers together free us from a role and performance mentality, free us from the perfectionist expectations of others and perfectionist ambitions we set for ourselves. If we believingly take in what is given to us in the stories and prayers of David, we are inoculated against the soul-debilitating germs of perfectionism.

This way of imperfection manages to get challenged in every generation, and a way of perfection offered as a replacement. But perfection is not an option. It is a seduction. It is the devil's offer to avoid dealing with sin by various sleight-of-hand verbal and behavioral strategies. Perfectionist talk and perfectionist illusions are generated by that fast-talking master of illusion, the "angel of light" St. Paul warns us about (2 Cor. 11:14).

The David text in stories and prayers is a powerful bulwark against all perfectionist tendencies. As we read this text, learning to find our place in the kingdom, our way in following Jesus, our way in leading others to follow Jesus, we find ourselves in the company of this splendid (the man who didn't kill King Saul) but also seriously flawed (the man who violated Paltiel) man as our praying companion. We need to know, without equivocation or rationalization, that the way of Jesus absorbs the way of David into it. The Holy Spirit is not out recruiting an elite, all-star holiness team for the Jesus way. Jesus is able "to sympathize with our weaknesses" (Heb. 4:15). "He is able to deal gently with the ignorant and wayward" (Heb. 5:2). And we need to know that for two thousand years now his way of imperfection has been affirmed and elaborated on by our most mature and tested leaders, Catholic, Orthodox, and Protestant.[9]

9. See Simon Tugwell, O.P., *Ways of Imperfection* (Springfield, Ill.: Templegate, 1985).

CHAPTER 5

Elijah: "Hide Yourself by the Brook Cherith"

Elijah. His name is his prophetic witness: "My God is Yahweh" — *Eli* (my God) *is Yah* (short for Yahweh). Yahweh is the uniquely personal name revealed by God to Moses at the burning bush. Now, roughly four hundred years after Moses, the name Yahweh is used to form the name of the prophet Elijah, who will be the prophet of Yahwism at a critical time that threatened to obliterate the Name.

*　　*　　*

Six days after Peter's confession of Jesus as the Christ at Caesarea Philippi and Jesus' soberingly austere conversation regarding his approaching crucifixion (take up *your* cross and follow me . . .), Jesus climbed a mountain with three of his disciples, Peter, James, and John (Matt. 17). There, in a private showing, Jesus' appearance changed, becoming dazzling bright in the company of Moses and Elijah. The three were deep in conversation. It was a moment filled with light: Jesus' face was all sunlight, Jesus' garments blazed with light, a light-filled cloud descended on Jesus and Moses and Elijah, and then God's voice spoke from the cloud, "This is my beloved Son; listen to him." The moment was over as suddenly as it had begun: "when they lifted their eyes, they saw no one but Jesus only."

Moses and Elijah, who appear together in conversation with Jesus at his transfiguration, lived their lives formed and defined by the Name, Yahweh. They bring into the conversation with Jesus on the mountain everything that Jesus brings together coherently and in completeness in his "Word made flesh," the Way. The Gospel writers mean for us to understand that everything that God revealed in the words and actions that preceded Jesus is now fulfilled in Jesus. *Moses:* the name we associate with the foundational word of God that brought creation, salvation, and community into being and that continues to furnish us with the language we have used to listen and pray ever since. And *Elijah:* the name we associate with the recovery of that language when it is forgotten, distorted, or obscured; the preached and proclaimed — prophetic! — word of God that gets our attention and gets us back on the way when we have willfully left it or mindlessly strayed from it.

The name of Moses is associated with an enormous output of words, ranging over the first five books of the Bible. The name of Elijah, in contrast, is featured in a mere six chapters comprising just nine stories (1 Kings 17–19 and 21; 2 Kings 1–2). But Elijah's influence over our understanding of prophets and prophecy is far out of proportion to the six chapters, the nine stories. Alexander Whyte, the Scots preacher who like a craggy druid in his prophetic Edinburgh pulpit bore a strong family resemblance to Elijah, expressed the consensus of the church: "The prophet Elijah towers up like a mountain in Gilead above all the other prophets. There is a solitary grandeur about Elijah that is all his own.... He was a Mount-Sinai of a man, with a heart like a thunderstorm."[1]

*   *   *

Over a period of several hundred years, the Hebrew people gave birth to an extraordinary number of prophets, men and women distinguished by the power and skill with which they presented the reality of God — his commands and promises and living presence — to communities and nations who were living on god-fantasies and god-lies.

1. Alexander Whyte, *Bible Characters* (London: Oliphants, 1952), vol. 1, p. 362-63.

Lots of people more or less believe in God. But most of us do our best to customize God to suit our convenience by adapting and modifying, making him "relevant to our situation." Prophets insist that God is the living center or nothing. Our task is to become relevant to his situation. They insist that we deal with God as God reveals himself, not as we imagine him to be. I say "insist," present tense, because what they said and wrote, canonized in the Jewish and Christian Scriptures and re-voiced century after century in the preaching and teaching of synagogue and church, continues to wake us up to the most important things going on in and around us — *Yahweh*, the living and present and self-revealing God.

There are many other prophets who take their place among the people of God, some named, some unnamed, some who write what they preach, some (like Elijah) who don't. But Elijah's eminence is incontestable.

*   *   *

I was attracted to Elijah at a young age. I think it may have been because he came from the hills and mountains, was at home in a wilderness similar to the Montana Rockies I grew up in. I imagined him formed in Gilead, comfortable with solitude and silence, occasionally coming out into public to expose the idolatries and compromises of the country and give witness to the word and presence of God. I liked his boldness on Mount Carmel taking on the priests of Baal, but I also identified with his cowardice before that witch woman, Jezebel. I admired the attention and care he extended to the obscure and unnamed widow of Zarephath and his fiery indignation over the frame-up and murder of the underdog neighbor Naboth. And Mount Horeb (Sinai) — I'm still trying to take in all that took place there in that cave. And even though I felt some guilt in doing it, I couldn't help taking secret delight in the delicious irony surrounding the fate of King Ahaziah. Then that final whirlwind rapture in the chariot and horses of fire — fire that consumed the Mount Carmel altar, fire that consumed Ahaziah's supplicant soldiers, and now the fire that takes Elijah to heaven.

Elijah and fire.

I grew up imagining the ways that Elijah's passion was conceived and nurtured in the mountains of Gilead, beside the brook Cherith, under the broom tree south of Beersheba, and in the cave on Mount Horeb. He was immersed in the culture and politics of his day but not shaped by them. He lived on the margins, and when he showed up in public, his energy and imagination were undiluted by opinion polls and proffered compromises.

My attraction to Elijah was confirmed in early adulthood when I found myself immersed in a sea of needs and pressures that threatened to obscure or even erase my baptismal identity as Christian. As I entered the adult world, virtually everyone I met presented me with an agenda; the items on the list were usually well-intentioned and socially approved but more often than not they involved employing an idol that could be used in substitute for the God and Father of our Lord Jesus Christ in a culture dominated by consumer-idolatries. How could I maintain my Christian identity? I thought one way was by keeping prayerful company with Elijah.

Ahab

Elijah's first recorded sermon (1 Kings 17:1) is to a congregation of one, Israel's King Ahab. Abrupt and brief, it consists of seventeen words in Hebrew (twenty-five in English). At first hearing it sounds like nothing much more than a weather forecast: There is going to be a drought for an undetermined length of time — "these years." We are not told whether Ahab said anything in response.

But we are told that God immediately told Elijah to cross the river and hide: "Get away from here; cross the Jordan and hide out by the brook Cherith." That would be in Gilead, the wilderness country that Elijah was from.

Why does God command Elijah to go into hiding? And particularly when Ahab shows no apparent sign of hostility toward him?

I think it is because it was going to take a while for Elijah's "weather forecast" to sink in. But once it does, once Ahab realizes what Elijah is actually telling him, Elijah's life will be at risk.

Ahab and his wife Jezebel had made the worship of the Phoenician/Canaanite god Baal the official religion of Israel. Baal had always maintained a cultic presence in Israel, but when Jezebel, the princess of Tyre (a center of Baal worship), married Ahab the cult virtually took over. Jezebel brought to Israel a passion for the cult of Baal and assembled 450 Baal prophets and 400 prophets of Asherah (Baal's consort) in her service. Ahab built a temple for Baal, the rain god, featuring a Baal altar, and installed an image of the popular sex and fertility goddess Asherah with her cult of sacred prostitution.

Ahab may have been a little slow in interpreting Elijah's message but Jezebel probably was not. She would have seen the weather forecast of drought for what it, in fact, was: a message to Israel that Baal was impotent, his reputation as the rain god a barefaced lie. The corollary to his impotence would be Asherah's sterility, her womb dry as a cracked cistern. The drought would advertise the barrenness of the Baal/Asherah cult of fertility.

$$* \quad * \quad *$$

Ahab was king of a fairly young nation, a mere fifty years of history behind it when he took the throne. The kingdom that David had united out of the twelve tribes split after the death of Solomon. Israel was formed as a separate nation. The schism took place when years of pent-up resentment over Solomon's arrogant and oppressive measures of forced labor exploded and ripped the country apart. The ten northern tribes rebelled. They installed Jeroboam son of Nebat as their king. Solomon's son Rehoboam got the leftovers, the two southern tribes of Judah and Benjamin.

It didn't take long to see that the kingdom was not only split into north and south politically but also split along religious lines, the south (Judah) worshiping at the Jerusalem temple and the north (Israel) worshiping at shrines that Jeroboam installed at his southern (Bethel) and northern (Dan) borders, shrines that proliferated into conveniently local "high places" throughout the country, furnished with conveniently local priests (see 1 Kings 12:26-33 and 13:33-34). Jeroboam knew he had to establish a counter religious presence to rival Jerusalem if he was to keep the loyalty of the people. It was the establishment of these shrines and "high places" that earned him the epithet, "the man who taught Israel to sin." The temple at Jerusalem in Judah maintained the worship of Yahweh, but the worship centers in the north incorporated various indigenous Canaanite idolatries. The northern tribes (Israel) did not exactly repudiate Yahwism, but with access to the Jerusalem temple blocked, their worship tended to accommodate other gods and worship practices, most notably Baal.

Ahab's father, the vigorous Omri,[2] brought Israel out of fifty years of instability marked by two royal assassinations (Nadab and Elah) and a royal suicide (Zimri). As it was about to collapse in chaos, he put the country on its feet again, both economically and politically, and built a new city, Samaria, to challenge the prestige of ancient Jerusalem. Everything was better under Omri. Except. Except that in matters that had to do with God things went from bad to worse. As the country got better and better economically and politically it became worse spiritually — not the last time that a better standard of living would be accompanied by a worse way of life.

Jeroboam's epithet as the man "who taught Israel to sin" was hard-earned, but Omri went him one better, distinguishing himself by doing "more evil than all who were before him" (1 Kings 16:25). His son Ahab "did evil in the sight of the LORD more than all who were before him" (16:30), improving considerably on his father's legacy. In the city his father had built to replace the authority of Jerusalem, his temple to Baal replaced Solomon's temple for the worship of Yahweh. His altar to Baal and image of the sex goddess Asherah were a brazen challenge to the imageless Holy of Holies, this altar and image a shameless offer of religion with all the "benefits" of instant gratification. Ahab's temple, altar, and image make a clear statement: As far as the new nation of

2. The adjective is John Bright's. See *A History of Israel* (Philadelphia: Westminster, 1959), p. 220.

Israel is concerned, the Jerusalem temple and its worship of Yahweh no longer define worship. If the people in Judah want to worship Yahweh, let them do it. But if you live in Israel, Baal is the god to worship.

*   *   *

Suddenly, under Ahab the country is in crisis, a crisis far greater than any enemy army could pose, far greater than any economic disaster could visit. Will Israel live under the blessing and command of Yahweh — who had formed her as a people of God, had delivered her from Egyptian slavery, had given her a land flowing in milk and honey rivers of love and justice — in worshipful awe and wonder? Or will she descend into the orgiastic world of sex and religion, the moral cesspool of self-indulgence seeping from King Ahab's arrogant temple of Baal and obscene image of Asherah into all the villages and fields of the ten tribes?

Elijah's seventeen-word sermon is an altar call.

The Widow

Elijah does go into hiding by the brook Cherith in Gilead, safe from reprisal from Ahab and Jezebel. After they have deciphered the blasphemous implications of his sermon they do go looking for him. And God does take care of Elijah as he had assured him he would. Each morning ravens bring him a breakfast of bread and meat, each evening a supper of bread and meat. And the brook provides living water.

We are in familiar country here. If God could provide bread (manna) and meat (quail) for the Israelites in the Sinai wilderness for a great company of his people, it is no great surprise to find him taking care of his lone prophet in the Gilead wilderness. The ravens are a nice touch. Against the overall background of the Ahab-Jezebel and Baal-Asherah coalition and its signature drought, Elijah enjoys the hospitality of the Lord's "table in the wilderness" (Ps. 78:19), served morning and evening by the elegant ravens. God's providence is never characterized in broad generalities or pious abstractions but always in the particular, in the personal, in the recognition of grace in an unlikely time, at an unlikely place. Who could have anticipated ravens?

And then the brook dries up and providence shows up in a new way. God now directs Elijah to the town of Zarephath in Sidon. This *is* a surprise. Gilead was more or less obvious as a hideout, remote and not easily accessible. Out of reach of Ahab and Jezebel. Zarephath is in Sidon, Jezebel's backyard, an area not only inhabited by the people Jezebel grew up with but teeming with the gods and goddesses she is determined to bring into Israel. This is hostile country, dangerously hostile for a man on the run, a man attempting to live incognito.

But Elijah is not a man to calculate his chances. He knows how to obey orders, even when the orders make no sense (maybe especially when the orders make no sense). He goes where God directs him and finds himself cared for not by Gilead ravens this time but by an even more unlikely hand of providence, a starving widow. She gives him her last meal, a meal that she is getting ready to cook and eat with her son after which the two of them will die together. That is the plan. But it doesn't turn out according to plan. The hospitality the widow shows Elijah is transfigured into the hospitality that Elijah shows the widow and son. Giving begets giving. The little becomes much.

Once we have the entire story of Elijah before us, it will become clear that his life in the wilderness and with the widow, his out-of-the-way life, marginal to everything we assume is important and significant, is foundational to whatever effectiveness he will have when he has the attention of the world. Elijah is as much a prophet in the impoverished widow's home in Zarephath as he was, alone with God's ravens, alongside the wilderness brook Cherith in Gilead, and as he will be, more famously, on Mount Carmel. He is the same man in obscurity as he is in the spotlight.

We are not told how long Elijah spent with the ravens by the brook and with the widow in her impoverished home, but it could have been as long as three years, the time between when Elijah left Ahab pondering the drought sermon and the time Elijah showed up again to arrange for the showdown on Mount Carmel. It wouldn't be either the first or the last time that a long period of seclusion, sustained by providential hospitality, was required to build the "highways to Zion" (Ps. 84:5) in a man or a woman's heart. Herman Melville wrote that his isolating years on a whaling ship were "my Harvard and Yale." Maybe Gilead and Zarephath were Elijah's.

Baal

Elijah's sermon to the assembled congregation of Israel and the 450 prophets of Baal on Mount Carmel is even shorter than the one he earlier had preached to King Ahab — sixteen words in Hebrew, twenty-three in English (1 Kings 18:21). The mountain is his pulpit. Two altars are prepared, a Baal altar and a Yahweh altar with a sacrificial bull placed on each altar. The deal is that the God who answers by fire and consumes the bull will be Israel's God. Elijah's sermon calls for a decision between them. The altar call takes all day (1 Kings 18).

Baal's altar is presided over by 450 Jezebel-hired priests. The action is theater featuring some kind of jerky, hobbling dance, the participants noisily demanding action from heaven — Fire! Rain! The gulf between people and God is leveled out of existence by means of participatory rites. The terrifying majesty of God, his "otherness," is watered down into the religious passions of the worshipers. Desires that inflame the soul are fanned by the dancing, yelling, and blood-letting priests. The transcendence of the deity is reduced to the ecstasy of manipulated emotions.

Sensory participation is featured in Baalism. Images are required — the bolder, the more colorful, the more sensational, the better. Music and dance become the means for drawing persons out of their private diversities and merging them into a mass response. Sexual activity in the cult is frequent since it achieves the primary Baalistic goal so completely — the ecstatic plunge of the whole sensory person into the passion of the religious moment. Sacred prostitution is a common feature in Baalism, magical, homeopathic practices designed to ensure increased fertility and to secure divine power through sexual intimacy.

Prostitutes, male and female (the *qadesh* and *q'desha*), of Canaan are standard accompaniments to the worship of Baal (and Asherah).

"Harlotry" is the stock prophetic criticism of the worship of the people who are assimilated to Baalistic forms (Jer. 3:1ff.; 5:7; 13:27; 23:10; 23:14; Ezek. 16 and 23; Hos. 1:2ff. and 4:12; Amos 2:7; Mic. 1:7). While the prophetic accusation of "harlotry" has a literal reference to the sacred prostitution of the Baal cult, it is also a metaphor that extends its meaning into the entire theology of worship, worship that seeks fulfillment through self-expression, worship that accepts the needs and desires and passions of the worshiper as its baseline. "Harlotry" is worship that says, "I will give you satisfaction. You want religious feelings? I will give them to you. You want your needs fulfilled? I'll do it in the form most arousing to you." A divine will that sets itself in opposition to the sin-tastes and self-preoccupations of humanity is incomprehensible in Baalism and so is impatiently discarded. Baalism reduces worship to the spiritual stature of the worshiper. Its canons are that it should be interesting, relevant, and exciting — that I "get something out of it."

Baal's Mount Carmel altar lacks neither action nor ecstasy. The 450 priests put on quite a show. But the altar call comes up empty.

Yahweh's altar is presided over by the solitary prophet, Elijah. It is a quiet affair, a worship that is centered on the God of the covenant. Elijah prepares the altar and prays briefly and simply. In Yahwism something is *said* — words that call men and women to serve, love, obey, sing, adore, act responsibly, decide. Authentic worship means being present to the living God who penetrates the whole of human life. The proclamation of God's word and our response to God's Spirit touches everything that is involved in being human: mind and body, thinking and feeling, work and family, friends and government, buildings and flowers.

Sensory participation is not excluded — how could it be if the whole person is to be present to God? When the people of God worship there are bodily postures of standing and kneeling and prostration in prayer. Sacred dances and antiphonal singing express community solidarity. Dress and liturgy develop dramatic energies. Solemn silence sensitizes ears to listen. But as rich and varied as the sensory life is, it is always defined and ordered by the word of God. Nothing is done simply for the sake of the sensory experience involved — which eliminates all propagandistic and emotional manipulation.

A frequently used phrase in North American culture that is symptomatic of Baalistic tendencies in worship is "let's have a worship experience." It is the Baalistic perversion of "let us worship God." It is the difference between cultivating something that makes sense to an individual, and acting in response to what makes sense to God. In a "worship experience," a person sees something that excites him or her and goes about putting spiritual wrappings around it. A person experiences something in the realm of dependency, anxiety, love, loss, or joy and a connection is made with the ultimate. Worship becomes a movement from what I see or experience or hear, to prayer or celebration or discussion in a religious setting. Individual feelings trump the word of God.

Biblically formed people of God do not use the term "worship" as a description of experience, such as "I can have a worship experience with God on the golf course." What that means is, "I can have religious feelings reminding me of good things, awesome things, beautiful things nearly any place." Which is true enough. The only thing wrong with the statement is its ignorance, thinking that such experience makes up what the Christian church calls worship.

The biblical usage is very different. It talks of worship as a response to God's word in the context of the community of God's people. Worship in the biblical sources and in liturgical history is not something a person *experiences*, it is something we *do*, regardless of how we feel about it, or whether we feel anything about it at all. The experience develops out of the worship, not the other way around. Isaiah saw, heard, and felt on the day he received his prophetic call while at worship in the temple — but he didn't go there in order to have a "seraphim experience."

At the Mount Carmel Yahweh altar things are very different. Elijah prays briefly. The fire falls. The altar call brings "all the people" to their knees. They make their decision: "Yahweh, he is God; Yahweh, he is God." And then the rain comes.

*   *   *

The one place in the biblical world where we know that "worship experience" is encouraged is in Baalism. When you are terror-stricken you offer a sacrifice; when you are anxious about the crops you make a visit to the temple prostitute; when you are joyful you ingest the wine god. You do what you feel like doing when you feel like doing it. In between, you get on with your ordinary life. Feelings call the tune, feelings of panic, of terror, of desire, of enthusiasm. Baalism offered, then in Canaan and now in North America, a rich array of "worship experiences."

In Yahwism worship is defined and shaped by God's authoritative and clear word. Nothing is dependent on feelings or weather. All is determined by Scripture and Jesus. No person is left to do what he or she simply feels like doing. God has revealed who he is and demands obedience. Worship is the act of attending to that revelation and being obedient to it.

*   *   *

The rout and humiliation of Baal on Mount Carmel that day is total. The long-running rivalry between Baal and Yahweh has ended: Baal is nothing, Yahweh is everything; Baal is an illusion, Yahweh is the real thing. The spell of Baal and his consort Asherah is decisively broken. Yahweh and only Yahweh is the living God. It will take another twenty years or so (under Jehu) to finally clean up the mess, but Carmel is the turning point.

But Jezebel is not a good loser. She refuses to accept the verdict of Mount Carmel: the embarrassment and slaughter of her 450 priests, the item-by-item deconstruction of the elaborate Baal myth. And then, filling that huge emptiness, Yahweh's fire and rain.

She sends word to Elijah that she will kill him. Tomorrow.

Elijah doesn't wait for tomorrow. He escapes south across the Israel-Judah border, to the safety of Beersheba. He is now in the country of Judah with its Jerusalem temple centering the worship of Yahweh. Even if participation in Yahweh worship is less than wholehearted here, at least in Judah death warrants are not issued for Yahweh prophets.

Yahweh

But Elijah needs more than a safe place. He needs to recover his prophetic soul. Mount Carmel had knocked the prophetic wind out of him — the spectacular Yahweh victory had turned out to be no victory at all. After the fire descended from heaven and the drought-ending rain poured from the skies, Elijah, champion of Yahweh, had run all the way from Carmel to the royal palace in Jezreel, triumphantly leading Ahab's chariot, preparing the way for the restoration of Yahwism. Did he expect to be welcomed with shouts of acclamation, palm branches and confetti? Would Jezebel be converted to Yahweh? As it turned out, the Mount Carmel evidence didn't faze Jezebel. Instead of a hero's welcome, Elijah faced assassination. Not what he expected.

But as so often happens on the way of the Lord, he gets something both other and better than he expected. A few miles from Beersheba, out into the wilderness in the vast emptiness of desert, Elijah sits under a large bush fragrant with white flowers, a broom tree, and gives up his reasonable prophetic expectations and his huge prophetic disappointment. He buries them under the broom tree. Now he, too, is ready to die. He offers his readiness to Yahweh and goes to sleep.

But he doesn't die — probably to his disappointment. Yahweh's angel wakes him, feeds him, and sends him on a pilgrimage that restores his prophetic vocation. The angel sends him to Moses country, the same Moses that he will later join in conversation with Jesus in the Transfiguration. The angel sends him to Horeb (Sinai), the mountain of God. There are forty days and nights of slow pilgrimage to Horeb, there are prayers in the cave on Horeb, there is the "still small voice" by means of which Yahweh gives him his prophetic life back — a resurrection from that broom tree cemetery.

*   *   *

Elijah's pilgrimage into Moses country gives his prophetic vocation fresh cogency and restores his prophetic soul so that he can complete the work God gave him. Moses and Elijah are both prophets at critical moments in the life of the people of God, Moses at their formation, Elijah at their reformation. There are numerous parallels between them:[3]

Moses begins the long line of Yahweh's prophets in Israel.
Elijah achieves eminence as the forerunner to John the Baptist, the last of the biblical prophets.

Moses is the prophet to whom the unique name Yahweh is revealed.
Elijah is the prophet who champions the name Yahweh against the Baal cult.

Moses: Yahweh rescues Israel from Egyptian oppression and forms them as his people.
Elijah: Yahweh preserves the faithful members of his people at a dangerously precarious moment, as they teeter on the edge of losing their identity to Baalism.

Moses begins his leadership with a flight eastward to the Midian wilderness to escape the king's wrath.
Elijah begins his leadership with a flight eastward to the Gilead wilderness to escape the king's wrath.

Moses on the run finds hospitality with Jethro's family in Midian.
Elijah on the run finds hospitality with the widow's family in Zarephath.

---

3. Jerome T. Walsh identifies fifteen parallels between Moses and Elijah. See the entry "Elijah" in *The Anchor Bible Commentary* (New York: Doubleday, 1992), vol. 2, pp. 464-65.

Moses and the Israelites are fed with miraculous food in the desert.

Elijah is fed with miraculous food at the brook Cherith and under the broom tree.

Moses and the elders eat a covenant meal on the mountain before Yahweh.

Elijah invites Ahab to "go up the mountain and eat and drink" as an invitation to return to Yahweh as his people have just done.

But mostly the link between Elijah and Moses is the Name. The Name — Yahweh — uniquely sets Israel's God apart from all the no-gods of the culture. The two mountains, Horeb and Carmel, are both Yahweh mountains, mountains on which the Name became the definitively preached text by Moses and Elijah. Elijah, just arrived from Mount Carmel and the defeat of all "other gods," now stands on Mount Horeb on which Moses received the Yahweh commands: No other gods and no graven images.

*   *   *

Having arrived at "Horeb the mount of God" (1 Kings 19:8), Elijah found a cave. Was it the same cave (the "cleft of the rock," Exod. 33:22) in which Moses, after the huge golden calf debacle and disappointment, was assured and reconfirmed in his work by Yahweh? Maybe not, but it is useful to remember that Moses on Mount Horeb experienced a devastating reversal comparable to Elijah's letdown in the wake of Mount Carmel.

*   *   *

Moses' text on Horeb was, in its most concentrated form, Yahweh: being there, being present, bringing into being, or causing to be. The Name cannot be objectivized into an object but must be responded to as personal presence. Being present to the Presence.

Moses preached the Name to the just-saved people of Israel gathered at Mount Horeb. They were not used to this. They had grown up in a country gaudy with gods, stunning god statuary and god temples, with an elaborate priesthood that directed you on how to get the most out of them. Moses had the task of weaning them from all the no-gods they could look at and touch and try to get something from, to a God who cannot be predicted or propitiated, a God completely other than anything they knew from their Egyptian culture. Moses proclaimed a God who was to be obeyed and served. He didn't have an easy congregation. There was a lot of murmuring: "What is this about *serving* God? I thought the gods were there to serve us!"

Four hundred years later Elijah preached the identical text to the people of Israel on Mount Carmel — Yahweh: being there, being present, bringing into being, or causing to be. The Name cannot be objectivized into an object but must be responded to as personal, subjective presence. Being present to the Presence.

There were continuities between the Moses and Elijah congregations. But there was also a difference. Elijah was preaching to the country of the Ten Tribes (Israel) that had broken away from the kingdom that David had united. They now had their own king, their own temple, their own capital. The political rebellion and break from the David dynasty also involved a religious break from the great Yahweh traditions that Moses had established and the great centering Yahweh worship in the Jerusalem temple. These people were immersed in a Canaanite version of that old Egyptian world from which Moses had delivered their ancestors: gods everywhere, Baal and Asherah prominent among them, that could be handled and manipulated. Elijah's prophetic task replicated that of Moses: No other gods, no images.

He didn't find it any easier than did Moses.

On his pilgrimage to Horeb, the mountain of God and of Moses, he recovered his prophetic focus.

* * *

If we have a choice, which we do, of dealing with God or an image of God, we much prefer the image. An image of God is God customized to our requirements. We not only have the pleasure of making the image, using our wonderful imagination and skills in creative ways, but also of controlling it. The image is a god with all the God taken out of it so that we can continue to be our own gods. There are innumerable ways in which we can make a god-image that suits our individual style of spirituality. The possibilities are endless, ranging from the skies above us to the earth around us to the sea under us. It is no wonder that idol-making and idol-worshiping continue to be the most popular religious game in town.

Because it is so satisfying to us, it is difficult to see why there is anything so very wrong with it. It *is* a spiritual act, after all. We are dealing with what has transcendent meaning. We are worshiping, which is the religious act par excellence and therefore always a good thing. Except that at rock bottom there is nothing to it, at least nothing of God to it.

It is both possible and common to embrace the one God, the God revealed in Scripture and in Jesus, and then go off and make an image of him that cuts him down to a size that fits what we want in God. Making an image of God, even the God who is speaking to us from Sinai or the cross, reduces God to our idea of him, or who we want him to be, or a way that we can use him. Once we have an image of God we don't have to deal with God. An image is impersonal, and we don't have to have any relationship with what is impersonal.

*   *   *

The pilgrimage did its work: the slow trudge through the wilderness, retracing paths that Moses had walked four hundred years earlier; time on the mountain to reflect on the great prophetic proclamation of the Name, Yahweh, the name that would free human language from turning God into a thing, reducing God to an idea or cause or verbal tool. The Dutch pastor and scholar Kornelis Miskotte continues to be a wise guide for all of us as we negotiate our way through the rubble of huckstered spiritualities that litter the pilgrimage from Mount Carmel to Mount Horeb. He put his finger on the precise significance of the

Name for the *way* we worship and live our lives: "The God of Israel withdraws himself from all conjuration; he cannot be conjured up with this nameless name [Yahweh] and be made subservient to an ulterior purpose."[4] Yahweh spoke to Elijah and Elijah answered Yahweh. On the mountain and in that cave Yahweh and Elijah got reacquainted.

The most interesting element in the conversation, though, is what is not said: a silence (1 Kings 19:12). Yahweh's gentle, quiet whisper, a "still small voice" (RSV), "sheer silence" (NRSV). The Hebrew phrase *(qol d'mamah daqqah)* is tantalizingly elusive. The suggestive phrases in a poem of St. John of the Cross, "silent music . . . sounding solitude . . . ," catch something of what is conveyed.[5]

The silence is preceded by wind, earthquake, and fire, not unlike the thunder, lightning, fire, smoke, and trumpet blasts that Moses met on this same mountain. Elijah almost certainly expected, after such a Moses prelude, to receive a Moses conclusion in which "God would answer him in thunder" (Exod. 19:19). But instead of thunder, Yahweh met Elijah in a quiet, inarticulate breathing — God's breath, God's life. Instead of a repetition of Moses, there is an anticipation of Jesus, who "breathed on them. . . . 'Receive the Holy Spirit . . .'" (John 20:22). Elijah (incapacitated for fear of Jezebel) and Jesus' disciples (incapacitated for "fear of the Jews") have new life, resurrection life, breathed into them so that they can take up their respective prophetic and apostolic vocations.

*   *   *

Elijah has his breath back, his prophetic breath. He is ready. God sends him off to resume his prophetic vocation by ordaining three men. They will continue his life's work of dismantling the Baal world and re-centering Israel in Yahweh. His work assignment: anoint Hazael as king over Syria; anoint Jehu as king over Israel; anoint Elisha to take his place as prophet. He is on his way again.

4. Kornelis H. Miskotte, *When the Gods Are Silent* (London: Collins, 1967), p. 121.

5. *John of the Cross, Selected Writings,* ed. Kevin Kavanaugh, O.C.D. (New York: Paulist, 1967), p. 223.

He will not see the results of his prophetic work. None of us in this kingdom work ever do. We "plant sequoias."[6]

Naboth

King Ahab had a neighbor, a next-door neighbor as it turned out, Naboth. Naboth's vineyard bordered Ahab's royal palace in the valley of Jezreel. The king and the farmer shared a fence line.

Ahab wanted his neighbor's vineyard for a kitchen garden. He offered to buy it from him. Naboth refused on religious grounds: his land was an inheritance, promised land that was a gift of Yahweh to his people. He did not "own" the land, he was steward of a precious inheritance. Ahab was up against (again!) Yahweh. Ahab went into a sulk.

Jezebel rescued him from his bad mood, cheered him up and told him that she would get the vineyard for him. Which she did. With some rather elaborate staging, she framed Naboth on charges of blasphemy, for which the penalty was death by stoning. With Naboth conveniently dead, Jezebel told her husband that the vineyard was his, free and clear.

Ahab wasted no time. He went immediately to take over the vineyard. But when he arrived, Elijah was there to confront him with the crimes of murder and theft, and to deliver God's gruesome verdict: "where dogs licked up the blood of Naboth, dogs will also lick up your blood" (1 Kings 21:19). The verdict was executed three years later (22:37-38).

*   *   *

The task of the prophet is to say the name God correctly, accurately and locally — *Yahweh,* God alive, God personal, God present. Here.

---

6. The phrase is from Wendell Berry, an American poet-prophet in the lineage of Elijah. See "Manifesto: The Mad Farmer Liberation Front," in his *Collected Poems* (San Francisco: North Point, 1985), p. 151.

Now. Elijah did that — magnificently. But there is more to the way of a prophet than God. There is also the neighbor.

One of the bad habits that we pick up early in our lives is separating things and people into secular and sacred. We assume that the secular is what we are more or less in charge of: our jobs, our time, our money, our opinions, our entertainment, our government, our house and land, our social relations. The sacred is what God has charge of: worship and the Bible, heaven and hell, church and prayers. We then contrive to set aside a sacred place for God, designed, we say, to honor God but really intended to keep God in his place, leaving us free to have the final say in everything else that goes on outside that space.

Prophets will have none of this. They hold that everything, absolutely everything, takes place on sacred ground. God has something to say about every aspect of our lives, the way we feel and act in the so-called privacy of our hearts and homes, the way we make our money and the way we spend it, the politics we embrace, the wars we fight, the catastrophes we endure, the people we hurt and the people we help. Nothing is hid from the scrutiny of God; nothing is exempt from the rule of God; nothing escapes the purposes of God. The ground is holy; people are holy; words are holy: Holy, holy, holy.

Prophets make it difficult for us to evade God or make detours around God after we leave church or temple or synagogue. Prophets insist on receiving God and dealing with God in every nook and cranny of life. As it turns out, in most of those nooks and crannies there are neighbors. For the prophet, God is as real as the next-door neighbor; the neighbor is as real as God. The neighbor, in fact, gets equal — well, maybe not quite equal, but equally serious — billing with God. Elijah brings the same unrelenting intensity to the cause of Naboth as to Yahweh.

*   *   *

In the Naboth story, Queen Jezebel, champion of Baal, takes up the adversarial role that her 450 Baal priests played on Mount Carmel. She received a similar fate: the 450 priests were slaughtered at the brook

Kidron; the queen was eaten by dogs on a street in Jezreel (2 Kings 9:36-37).

When you have a god that is a thing, a god that you can use, an object, neighbors also become things, something to use, objects. With an impersonal god, you end up with an impersonal neighbor. Jezebel certainly did.

The champions of Baal, priests and queen alike, did not have an easy time of it with Elijah. On Mount Carmel Elijah championed Yahweh, the name of God; in the Valley Jezreel Elijah championed Naboth, the name of the neighbor. Elijah was as much a prophet in the valley as he was on the mountain. Elijah lived his life on the margins — marginal to the popular religion of the day, marginal to the power politics of the day. Because he lived on the margins he was unimpressed by what went on in the center: the impressive worship experience put on by the 450 priests of Baal on the mountain, the impressive demonstration of hubristic contempt of a neighbor by the patroness of Baal in the valley. As it turned out, it was from the margins that Elijah re-centered the life of Israel both in worship of their God, Yahweh, and in respect for their neighbors. For people schooled in a biblical imagination, the fascination with numbers as a sign of efficacy, as a demonstration of God's blessing, is strange indeed. Virtually all the men and women who prepared the way of the Lord, which became the way of Jesus, worked at the margins of their societies and cultures. Elijah is conspicuous but in no way unique. The story of Elijah is told from nine site locations. Only one, Mount Carmel, provided a public stage for a crowd of people. All the others are out-of-the-way and marginal.[7]

There was nothing easy-going about Elijah. He was not a popular figure. He never achieved celebrity status. He was decidedly uncongenial to the temperament and disposition of the people with whom he lived. The centuries have not mellowed him. We like leaders, especially religious leaders, who understand our problems — "come alongside

---

7. The marginal eight: the brook Cherith (1 Kings 17:1-7), Zarephath (17:8-24), the broom tree (19:1-8), Horeb (19:9-18), Elisha's farm (9:19-21), Naboth's vineyard in Samaria (21), Elijah's hilltop (2 Kings 1), the Jordan River (2:1-12).

us" is our idiom for it — leaders with a touch of glamour, leaders who look good on posters and television.

The hard granitic reality is that neither Elijah nor his considerable progeny of prophets since, fit into our way of life.

For a people who are accustomed to "fit God" into their lives, or, as we like to say, "make room for God," Elijah is hard to take and easy to dismiss outside the pages of the Bible. But both Elijah's God and Elijah's neighbor are far too large to fit into our lives. If we want anything to do with God, we have to fit into him and the men and women he places alongside us.

Elijah is not "reasonable," accommodating himself to the culture. He is not diplomatic, tactfully negotiating an agreement that allows Ahab or Jezebel or any of us a "say" in the outcome. What he does is haul us unceremoniously into a reality far too large to be accounted for by our explanations and expectations. He plunges us into mystery (Carmel! Horeb! Jezreel!) immense and staggering.

Ahaziah

Ahab was wounded in an ill-advised war with Syria over Ramoth-Gilead, and died that evening in his chariot in a pool of blood. His son Ahaziah became the new king (1 Kings 22). It is of great interest to me that the three children of Ahab and Jezebel that are named in the text (there were many others unnamed) have names compounded with Yahweh: two sons, Ahaz-*iah* ("Yahweh seizes") and *Jeho*-ram ("Yahweh is exalted"), and a daughter, Athal-*iah* (maybe "Yahweh is just," or "Yahweh's robust child" — these etymologies are not certain).

In the naming of his children it seems that Ahab was trying to keep his options open, keeping a foot in the Yahweh camp while going along with Jezebel's Baal zealotry out of marital or political considerations. Grafting the name Yahweh into the names of the three children was a way of keeping a religiously open mind. But it didn't work; the graft didn't take.

In his great altar call on Mount Carmel, Elijah called for a choice:

"How long will you go limping with two different opinions? If the LORD is God, follow him; but if Baal, then follow him" (1 Kings 18:21). "Make up your minds! Enough of this fence-sitting! Choose!"[8] Many of them did. But not all. Judging by the consequences, there must have been a considerable number of foot-dragging, indecisive procrastinators also on the mountain. Ahab's Yahweh-named children Ahaziah, Jehoram, and Athaliah would have been representative. If they were on the mountain that day, it didn't seem to make any difference to their lives.

*   *   *

Ahaziah is the only one of these three children of Ahab who we know had personal dealings with Elijah (2 Kings 1). The story has it that not long after he became king following his father's death, he fell through the window of an upper story room in the palace and was seriously injured. From his sickbed he sent messengers south to Ekron to consult with the priests of Baal where the local Baal god carried the name Baal Zebub, "Lord of the Flies." (The god's proper name among true Baal worshipers was Baal Zebul, which, since "Zebul" means Prince, would be "Baal the Prince." Baal Zebub was a derogatory parody on the name.)

Elijah intercepted the messengers and confronted them: "Is it because there is no God in Israel that you're running off to consult Baal-Zebub, god of Ekron? Don't waste your time. Go back and tell your king, 'You're not going to get out of that bed you are in; you're as good as dead already — Yahweh's decree.'"

So the messengers went back to Ahaziah. The king demanded to know why they hadn't completed their mission, why they had come back. They told him that a man had met them and said, "Is it because there is no God in Israel that you're running off to consult Baal-Zebub,

8. A nearly identical altar-call to the one that Moses, Elijah's great predecessor in the way of the Lord, gave to his congregation: "I have set before you life and death, blessing and curse; therefore choose life . . ." (Deut. 30:19).

god of Ekron? Don't waste your time. Go back and tell your king, 'You're not going to get out of that bed you are in; you're as good as dead already — Yahweh's decree.'"

Ahaziah was curious — and already apprehensive. "Tell me more about this man . . . what was he like?"

"Shaggy. And wearing a leather belt."

"I knew it," said Ahaziah. "That has to be Elijah the Tishbite."

Then and there, Ahaziah had something of a deathbed conversion. Desperate now, and suspecting that Baal-Zebub was a quack, he changed gods on the spot — maybe there was something to his namesake god after all. Maybe it would be worth his while to shop around some, check Yahweh out. He sent a garrison of fifty men to summon Elijah to his sickbed. They had to climb a mountain to get to him. It seems somehow in character that Elijah's hermitage was on top of a mountain — out of the way, out of the traffic, relatively inaccessible. Abraham Heschel comments on Elijah's hilltop hermitage: "Has anything of significance in the realm of spirit been achieved without the protection and the blessings of solitude?"[9]

But the men's effort in climbing that mountain earned them nothing. Elijah refused to come. Worse, Ahaziah's presumption cost them their lives — fire from heaven incinerated them. The king sent another garrison of fifty, but with the same results. And again a third. By now the captain of the garrison is on his knees begging, "Please, respect my life!" This time Elijah, prompted by an angel, went down the mountain and came to Ahaziah's sickbed. But the message was the same, "You're as good as dead already, Yahweh's decree." Not what we think of as a proper pastoral call on the sick and dying.

And that was it. Ahaziah died.

*   *   *

Once having had a taste of intoxicating Baal worship, it is not easy to give it up. Neither did Ahaziah's brother Jehoram, the next king, give it

9. Abraham Heschel, *The Prophets* (New York: Harper and Row, 1962), p. 399.

up; ten years later he was killed by Jehu in a ruthless Baal purge (2 Kings 9:21-26). Ahaziah's mother, Jezebel, didn't give it up; she was killed in that same Jehu purge (9:30-37). And Ahaziah's sister, Athaliah, didn't give it up. Having married into the Davidic royal house in Judah, she became a missionary of Baal in Judah every bit as zealous and murderous as her mother Jezebel, building a Baal temple and installing a Baal priesthood in Jerusalem, almost but not quite replacing Yahweh worship with the Baal cult and then coming within a hair of killing off the entire lineage of the David royal house (11:1-20). And then she was killed (11:1-16). That was the end of the Ahab-Jezebel-Baal-Asherah legacy.

*　　*　　*

There is an addictive quality to Baal. Giving up Baal means that we give up control over God. Giving up Baal means that we no longer have all that vast spiritual paraphernalia at our beck and call. Giving up Baal means that we give up any hope of having influence with God, of being able to get our way with him. Giving up Baal means that we let go of the comforting illusions that allow us to live in guilt-free dishonesty. Giving up Baal means that we can no longer use religion to scare or bribe or bully other people. Giving up Baal means that we have to grow up. And growing up is not an attractive option for men and women who are accustomed to a culture that gives them a free pass to a Disneyesque religion of entertainment and ecstasy.

*　　*　　*

Elijah was "a figure of absolutely primeval force,"[10] but at the same time his was a way along the margins: he took the marginal way. He held no position, lived a solitary life in obscurity, appeared from time to time without fanfare and disappeared from public view without notice. His formative impact on how we as a people of God understand responsi-

10. Gerhard von Rad, *Old Testament Theology* (New York: Harper and Row, 1965), vol. 2, p. 18.

bility and witness in society is inescapable and irreversible. It never goes out of style and by God's sovereign grace is replicated in every generation. The essence of the Elijah way is that it counters the world's way, the culture's way. We need continuous help in staying alert and knowledgeable regarding the conditions in which we cultivate faithful and obedient lives before God, for the ways of the prevailing culture, whether American, Chinese, Polish, or Indonesian — its assumptions, its values, its methods of going about its work — are never on the side of God. Never.

What Elijah did, and what his contemporary prophetic progeny does, is purge our imaginations of this world's assumptions on how life is lived, on what counts in life. Over and over again, God the Holy Spirit uses prophets to separate his people from the lies and illusions they have become accustomed to and put us back on the path of simple faith and obedience and worship of the God and Father of our Lord Jesus Christ, in defiance of all that the world admires and rewards. Elijah and his vast company of prophets, by now centuries deep and worldwide, train us in discerning the difference between the ways of the world and the ways of Jesus, keeping us present to the Presence of God.

CHAPTER 6

Isaiah of Jerusalem: "The Holy"

If Elijah the Tishbite of Gilead is our archetype prophet, Isaiah of Jerusalem is our most comprehensive prophet — our renaissance prophet, if you will, fluent in the language of revelation and bold in the action of salvation that delineates an embodied life of obedient faithfulness to the word of God. When the ways and means by which God works interpenetrate the ways and means by which we work, we have a name for it: *Holy.* The characteristic name for God in Isaiah is "The Holy."

"Holy" is the best word we have for the all-encompassing, all-embracing life of God that transforms us into a uniquely formed and set-apart people. Holy is never a pious abstraction. It is never a quality that can be understood apart from the bodies that we inhabit or the neighborhoods in which we live or apart from the God who made, saves, and blesses us. It is something *lived.* It is the life of God breathed into and invigorating our lives. Leviticus — "be holy: for I the LORD your God am holy" (Lev. 19:2) — insists on a continuity between who God is and the men and women that we become.

When Jesus prays with and for his disciples in his last conversation with them before his crucifixion, he prays just this: "*Holy [hagie]* Father . . . *[s]anctify [hagiason]* them . . . that they also may be *consecrated [hēgiasmenoi]* . . ." (John 17:11, 17, 19 RSV). The triple repetition of "holy" is obscured in our English translation, but it is there: first as an adjective of God ("Holy Father"); then as a verb, the action of God that makes us holy ("sanctify"); and then as a participle describing us as the ones who are made holy ("consecrated") by God's work. "Holy" is among our most precious words. It names the Trinitarian God-vitality, Spirit-vitality, and Jesus-vitality that gradually but surely forms from within the lives of the men and women who pray "Hallowed be ['Holy be,' *hagiasthēto*] thy Name."

But in our culture it is the fate of holiness to be banalized. Holiness is reduced to blandness, the specialty of sectarian groups who reduce life to behaviors and clichés that can be certified as safe: goodness in a straitjacket, truth drained of mystery, beauty emasculated into ceramic knickknacks. Whenever I run up against this, I remember Ellen Glasgow's wonderful line in her autobiography. Of her father, a Presbyterian elder full of rectitude and rigid with duty, she wrote, "He was entirely unselfish, and in his long life never committed a pleasure."

But holiness is in wild and furious opposition to all such banality and blandness. The God-life cannot be domesticated or used — it can only be entered into on its own terms. Holiness does not make God smaller so that he can be used in convenient and manageable projects; it makes us larger so that God can give out life through us, extravagantly, spontaneously. The holy is an interior fire, a passion for living in and for God, a capacity for exuberance in the presence of God. There are springs deep within and around us from which we can drink and sing God.

Thirty years or so ago Frederick Buechner took on the task of reimagining holiness for our generation, and what a magnificent work he has done for us in his novels. Beginning with the unlikely but finally irresistible Leo Bebb, going on to Godric and Brendan, and then with a final flourish, Jacob, Son of Laughter, Buechner immersed us in convincing, contagious stories of the holy that exudes life — stories of lifegiving, life-enhancing, life-deepening holiness.

*   *   *

For Christians, the authoritative source for understanding the holy so that we can participate in the holy is Holy Scripture inspired by Holy

Spirit. Just a little past the midpoint of Holy Scripture we are given a picture of Isaiah at worship in Solomon's temple in Jerusalem (Isa. 6). This midpoint placing has, of course, no exegetical significance, but it does provide an image for the centrality and radiating energy of The Holy throughout our Scriptures. As Isaiah worships, he feels the foundations shake beneath him and hears the angels sing above him:

> Holy, Holy, Holy is the LORD of Hosts,
> the whole earth is full of his glory. (Isa. 6:3)

The scene of worship could not be more magnificent: God enthroned, the temple filled with smoke and glory, the magnificent six-winged seraphim above the throne, the magnificent anthem "Holy, Holy, Holy," the magnificent ordination as the glowing coal from the altar purges Isaiah's lips and launches him into his prophetic vocation. Magnificent, truly.

The seraphim hymn was taken up by John of Patmos's apocalyptic angels singing around God's throne (Rev. 4:8). Reginald Heber made it singable for Scottish Christians in the nineteenth century and for the rest of us ever since.

It is the defining moment in Isaiah's prophetic vocation.

"In the Year That King Uzziah Died . . ."

But before the story of The Holy is told, a warning is posted in bold letters: *Uzziah*. Everyone in Isaiah's world would know what that name meant: "Caution. Danger ahead. Watch your step."

Uzziah was king for fifty-two years in Jerusalem (his story is told in 2 Chron. 26). He was a good king by all accounts — he subdued the Philistines, built up a strong defense system and an impressive and well-equipped military, developed the country economically, and learned the fear of the Lord from his pastor, Zechariah: "And his fame spread far, for he was marvelously helped until he became strong" (2 Chron. 26:15).

Then he did a terrible thing: he desecrated the holy temple. His power went to his head and one day he arrogantly walked into the temple and took it over for his own purposes. He decided to take charge of his own spirituality, manage his own religion, put God to his own uses. He went to the holy altar of incense (the same altar from which one of the seraphim would later take a coal to hallow Isaiah's lips) and proceeded to run things according to his own tastes and desires. The priest Azariah, accompanied by eighty other priests, came after him in alarm to prevent the sacrilege (only priests were permitted to offer sacrifices). Uzziah already had the censer in his hand and was about to make the holy offering. He lost his temper and angrily told Azariah and his priests to get lost. He joined the ranks of those who "close their hearts to pity; with their mouths they speak arrogantly . . . whose portion in life is in *this* world" (Ps. 17:10, 14, italics added). He was king, after all — a very successful king with a long string of accomplishments — and he would deal with God how and when he wanted to deal with him as one sovereign to another.

The desecration had immediate repercussions: Uzziah turned leprous. The dread disease that in the Hebrew mind symbolized sin gave public visibility to the inward profanity.

What in Uzziah's mind was royal prerogative was in fact inexcusable sacrilege. It would be like one of us entering our home church with a can of black spray paint and spraying graffiti on pulpit and Communion table, baptismal font and cross: "Under new management. From now on, I'm in charge here!"

Uzziah, with many honorable years of serving God's people behind him, but now proud and angry and willful, took over the holy temple for his own purposes. Royal vandalism. Violent desecration.

Uzziah spent the rest of his life in isolation, banned by his leprous condition not only from the holy temple but from all contact with the community of holy people. He was still king, but no longer in touch with either temple or people. Judah's king a leper. The government of Judah was in the hands of a man who defiled God's holy temple. The entire society and culture of Judah was living under the shadow of unholiness, of desecration — the social, political, cultural, and religious atmosphere defiled by the king's leprosy; Judah ruled by a leper king.

Uzziah posts a most necessary warning: hanging around the holy is risky business. Holy ground is dangerous ground. The holy is never, never something of God that we can take as if we owned it and use for our own purposes.

*   *   *

A few years ago a grizzly attacked a hiker not far from our home and mauled him badly. The hiker had heard of the wonder and beauty of the mountains of Montana and drove across the country from North Carolina to experience them for himself. Interviewed from his hospital bed, he said, "I'm never coming back to this place!" He didn't know that wonder and beauty can also be dangerous.

A week after that grizzly mauling, Jan and I along with our son and his wife, plus another friend with her two-year-old son, were hiking on that same trail. At the trailhead a notice was posted: "Danger: Grizzly activity on this trail. Hike at your own risk." None of the others knew of the previous week's mauling and I didn't say anything. I relished the spurt of adrenaline. The danger to life heightens the sense of life. The beauty and the wonder in which we were immersed, the love and affection that we shared, were not our secure possessions.

A couple of hours later we reached our destination, a gem-like, glacier-fed lake. We stood at the lakeshore admiring the five waterfalls cascading off the mountain face, listened to and watched a couple of varied thrushes sing and eat bugs. Holy ground. And then I noticed a movement a hundred or so yards up the lakeshore. I took aim with my binoculars: a grizzly and her cub, playfully splashing in the water. I passed the binoculars around; we all had a good look. And then Amy, our daughter-in-law, who was five months pregnant and therefore especially aware of the fragility and preciousness of life, said, "I want to get out of here." And we did get out. Holy ground, but dangerous ground.

Holiness is the most attractive quality, the most intense experience, we ever get out of sheer *life* — authentic, undiluted, firsthand living, not life looked at and enjoyed from a distance. We find ourselves in on the operations of God himself, not talking about them, not reading about them. But at the very moment that we find ourselves in on more than ourselves, we realize we also might very well lose ourselves. We cannot domesticate The Holy. Moses in Midian didn't take a photograph of the burning bush and show his wife Zipporah and children Gershom and Eliezer. Isaiah's singing seraphim were not accompanied by a Handel oratorio that he captured on a CD for later listening at his leisure. John of Patmos didn't reduce his vision of Jesus into charts and use them to entertain religious consumers with sensationalized views on the future.

"Our God is a consuming fire" (Heb. 12:29), not fire to be played with. Holy, Holy, Holy is not Christian needlepoint.

"I Saw the Lord Sitting upon a Throne . . ."

In contrast to Uzziah, who went to the temple to *use* The Holy for his own purposes, Isaiah was in the temple to pray and worship. He wasn't there to get something for himself but to be present to the Presence, The Holy. Isaiah was about to be consecrated to his prophetic vocation at the same Altar of Incense at which Uzziah had become a leper king. The temple was not defined by Uzziah; the times were not defined by Uzziah; the culture didn't take its impress from Uzziah. Uzziah was not the defining presence in Isaiah's life. And how do we know? Because "in the year that king Uzziah died," Isaiah was at prayer, worshiping in the temple that was once desecrated by Uzziah.

The times in which we live are not definitive for our lives. The kings and presidents who lead us don't have the last word (and certainly not the first!) on how we live our lives. Technology does not define our existence. Postmodern does not determine how we live. Psychologism does not account for who we are. The "hard surface of secularity" (Barth's phrase)[1] is a slovenly makeshift attempt to make sense of us and the world around us.

In an unholy place, Isaiah was plunged into the holy. He was given a holy vision, the Lord ruling in holiness, the songs of the holy seraphim filling the air with holy sounds, "Holy, Holy, Holy is the LORD of Hosts, the whole earth is full of his glory."

Midian and Patmos

Isaiah was not the only person, neither first nor last, in Israel and church to see and hear The Holy. His temple vision had precedents; it also had sequels. The Holy is not exclusive to the temple. Isaiah, as we so well know from his writings, lived in a large, expansive world, a world shaped by God's work in the past and a world anticipating God's work in the future.

The Holy must be seen in these expansive terms. I want to construct a stage that has the precedent of Moses on one side, the sequel of St. John on the other, with Isaiah in the middle. Without this large horizon stretched out with Moses and John flanking Isaiah, we run the risk of confining The Holy to what takes place in the sanctuary at a scheduled time.

Moses was surprised by The Holy in Midian. Midian was an austere country and Moses was an exile there. Midian was not an attractive place and Moses was not doing attractive work. A hard country, hard work, a hard life. Moses had been reared in luxury in one of the world's highest cultures and most accomplished civilizations. Moses was used to political power, intellectual conversation, and architectural splendor. And now Moses was in Midian — no books, no temples, no servants, no influence.

And then, without preamble, he found himself immersed in The Holy: God's holy Presence flaming out from a burning bush. Moses addressed by name: "Moses, Moses." Moses answering, "Here am I." Mo-

1. Karl Barth, *Church Dogmatics* (Edinburgh: T&T Clark, 1956), vol. 1, pt. 2, p. 63.

ses called to worship, "Put off your shoes . . . you are standing [on] holy ground" (Exod. 3:5 RSV). Moses addressed by God and given a job to do. There are 104 occurrences of the root word "holy" (*qadosh*) in the Books of Moses.

Holy angel, holy ground, holy God, holy word that forms a holy people and shapes a holy history. And in Midian of all places.

John was surprised by the holy on a prison island, Patmos, a place as barren and unfriendly as Midian. And John, like Moses in Midian, was there in exile. In that place of rejection and severity he was given a holy vision. Instead of Moses' burning bush, John was given Jesus ablaze with The Holy, speaking words that the Holy Spirit used to make a holy people faithful and enduring in unholy times.

The word "holy" (*hagios*) as either noun or adjective occurs twenty-six times in St. John's Revelation. Whatever else we get out of this concluding book in our Scriptures, we know that we are in on something huge and robust, burgeoning blessing, the salvation and glory of God: Holy, Holy, Holy.

Now we have an adequate context for Isaiah's vision: Moses in Midian and John on Patmos bracketing Isaiah in the Jerusalem sanctuary. We need all of Scripture, all of history, all of experience to provide a horizon large enough to take in The Holy. The Holy cannot be cramped into a shoebox. The Holy cannot be perceived through a peephole.

For Isaiah that day, the desecrated temple was bursting its seams with holiness, the desecrated earth was full of glory. *This* is the reality in which we live: Holy, Holy, Holy; Glory, Glory, Glory. No matter what Uzziah does to the sanctuary, no matter what the Assyrians do to the world (they were pillaging the Middle East during Isaiah's time), there is holiness in the place of worship and glory in the land. And holiness in the barren Midian wilderness; holiness in the austere Patmos jailhouse. And yes, holiness in all the defiled churches of North America; holiness in every morally and physically polluted city and state and province. Holiness, because God is still present in creation and history, still creating, still saving. We have to break the ignorant and faithless habit of letting the journalists of the day tell us what is going on. We need at least to give Isaiah equal time: Holy, Holy, Holy.

*   *   *

One summer Jan and I were hiking in the Rocky Mountains of Montana. It was a misty, wet, cold day — not an especially good day for hiking in the mountains. But it had been rainy and wet and cold for weeks and we wanted air, even if it was wet, cold air. We had been slogging along the trail through thick stands of Engleman spruce and Douglas fir for a couple of hours and suddenly came out on a slope that had been burned off in a huge forest fire over sixty years ago when I was ten years old. In all those years it had not grown back.

The sudden openness gave us an immense vista — glacier-cut peaks soaring upward to one side of us, on the other side a valley floor carpeted by golden grain and rivered in meanders of blue. Then we spotted a tiny but bright splash of bird on a dead snag about seventy-five feet away. We looked at it through our binoculars but couldn't identify it. Then, as we looked, it flew — a hummingbird! But one that we had never identified before, a rufous hummingbird. The tiny explosion of bright, coppery orange on that rain-soaked trail was more dramatic than a sunrise. The minuscule bird, framed by mountain and valley, provided a center to the majestic setting. But the delicate, exquisite bird needed a frame that large for us to adequately appreciate its color and flight. Anything less would have cramped the imagination.

Isaiah 6 is a rufous hummingbird in the great exposed wilderness framed by Moses in Midian and John on Patmos.

"And He Touched My Mouth . . ."

Isaiah was not a spectator of the holy, he was a participant in it. The unique thing about the holy is that it cannot be known or understood apart from entering it, apart from being formed by The Holy. It is not a subject we learn from a book or a lecture. We enter in. It takes place in us the same way it took place in Isaiah. Some things don't change. And there are no shortcuts.

It often begins with an overwhelming sense of inadequacy, of sin, of unworthiness: "Woe is me, I am lost. My very speech is defiled and dirty. I don't belong here. I don't fit here. Nothing I know or can do is appropriate here. Get me out of here" (Isa. 6:5). If we take care to insulate ourselves from The Holy and live congruently with our surroundings, it is easy to suppose that we are doing just fine with our lives as they are, thank you. But measuring our lives by the standards set by our dogs and cats and neighbors is a sorry business. It takes The Holy to make me aware of my unholiness. The excess of life makes me aware of my deficit of life. We have been lost ever since we left Eden, wandering the world, looking for home, and getting mighty dirty in the process.

But awareness of sin is not an end in itself, it is an opening to mercy and forgiveness — purification. Our lips are touched with purifying fire (6:6-7). It is our basic, fundamental, most pressing need. Apart from The Holy we think we can improve our lives simply by progressing, getting a little more of this and then of that. But like a badly aimed arrow, the farther we go, the greater the miss. This misdirection is not an occasional lapse. We give evidence against ourselves every time we speak. Sin and impurity are expressed as soon as and whenever we open our mouths, even in our most decorous and polite talk. God responds by purifying our language, making us capable of saying yes to his Yes. The angel, the flaming witness (*seraph* is, literally, a "burning one") to God's holiness, burns the impurities, the sin, the ego from our speech so that we can speak heart to heart. God's primary work in us is not condemnation but forgiveness. "Indeed, God did not send the Son into the world to condemn the world, but in order that the world might be saved through him" (John 3:17). Acceptance, not rejection. Conversation, not a tirade. Holiness no longer outside us, but inside us. If we don't stay around The Holy long enough to first realize and then experience that live coal on our lips, we will spend our lives in tragic ignorance of God and his ways.

With that purifying touch, holy conversation begins. God's word is spoken: "Whom shall I send?" (6:8). God speaks vocationally; there is work to be done. Holiness always involves the word of God: God spoke to Moses at the burning bush; God spoke to John in the Patmos vision; God spoke to Isaiah in the Jerusalem temple. The effusion, the overflow of life that is holiness, is not something to be hoarded but something to be delivered, spread around, spoken and acted. Holiness cannot be reduced to an emotional, devotional experience that we cultivate in order to "feel spiritual." It has command content to it. Holiness is not an experience of sublimity that abstracts us from the world of work; it is an invitation to enter into what God is doing and intending to get done in the world. And it's for everyone — this is not a text targeted to an elite spiritual aristocracy.

The conversation, initiated by the word of God, continues in our answering speech: "Here am I, send me" (6:8). We accept God's invitation, prepare to obey whatever he commands. We pull on our gloves and get ready for work. But it is not an imposed work; God's call is spoken as a question, inviting response; we have the freedom of a yes or a no. However impelling this word is to some of us, it is never a matter of coercion. We are *invited* in.

Isaiah's encounter with and participation in the holiness that originates in God spills over into our lives — it provides a convenient and reliable story against which we can test the authenticity of our own stories. Participation in The Holy is a complex business, but these elements, in various orders and proportions, seem to be normative: the abolition of self-sufficiency ("Woe is me, for I am lost"), the experience of merciful forgiveness (the live coal: "Your guilt is taken away . . ."), God's invitation to servant work ("Whom shall I send?"), and the human response of becoming present to God in faith and obedience ("Here am I, send me!"). I can think of no exceptions in Scripture or church in which these elements are not present, whether explicitly or implicitly.

These elements that shaped Isaiah's life, and ours, in The Holy cannot be removed from their context. We cannot hand over any of the elements to one of the fashionable spiritual technicians of the day and expect him or her to manage them for us. The context is the living God: Holy, Holy, Holy in the temple; and Glory, Glory, Glory in all the earth. Nothing in God or our relations with God can be secularized to our expectations, customized to our conditions, managed for our convenience. We acquire readiness and perceptiveness for the holy by worshiping God, The Holy, and practicing the posture and rudiments of worship wherever we find ourselves — Midian or Patmos or Jerusalem, sitting in a pew or driving a car, reading a book or watching a cloud, writing a letter or picking a wildflower. Wherever we are, whatever we are doing, there is *more*, and the more is God, revealing himself in Jesus by the Spirit, the *Holy* Spirit. This *more* has nothing to do with cosmetics. Holiness is transformative, although rarely sudden. And the *more* is not often obvious, in fact more often obscure. The holy life begins in the times and places and lives that ambition and pride ignores or despises.

But here's the thing: the least hint of holiness has the power to set off this chain reaction of holy living in any one of us. Without question it is dangerous. We most certainly will lose our lives as we have conceived them. But that is only the beginning. The Holy pulls, often only at the far edges of our awareness, at every fiber of our God-created, Jesus-saved being. God, the living God, is what we men and women hunger and thirst for most deeply, and The Holy, seeping (or bursting!) through the containers in which we habitually confine and then label life, whets our appetite.

Holy God and Holy Stump

The Isaianic vision is dazzling, rightly honored, studied, and preached as one of the pivotal scenes in Scripture. But there is far more to the vision than the throne and smoke and glory, more than the seraphim anthem, more than the dramatic purification of Isaiah's tongue by the coal from the altar, more than God's prophet-making question, "Whom shall I send?" There is God instructing Isaiah in just what he is going to be doing as God's prophet, just what he is in for for the rest of his life.

The first part of the vision, God present to Isaiah (vv. 1-8), is extensively celebrated, and rightly so; the second part, God's message to Isaiah (vv. 9-13), is more often than not ignored — and if not ignored, read and commented on in isolation from its place in the vision as a whole.[2] It may be the most under-interpreted, under-attended-to passage in our Scriptures. The glorious seraphim dominate the opening vision; a stump in a field of stumps dominates the vision's conclusion. The concluding sentence and punch line of the vision as a whole is "The holy seed is its stump" (v. 13). Stump — not a word likely to inspire a newly ordained prophet to, as we say, "do great things for God."

The vision of God that Isaiah saw (vv. 1-8) and the message from God that Isaiah received (vv. 9-13) are aspects of the one revelation. It is a single vision. The two parts of the vision, 1-8 and 9-13, cannot be treated in isolation from one another. I want to insist on the unity of Isaiah 6 and honor the continuity between holy God and holy stump. No amount of attention lavished on the seraphim can compensate for inattention to the stump. We ignore the stump at our peril. We will never get The Holy right if we bypass the stump.

The holy God names the content of Isaiah's preaching; the holy stump names the conditions in which the preaching will take place. The holy God in the seraphim-anthemed temple and the holy stump in the devastated land need to be interpreted in tension with one another. So, following Isaiah, we put holy God and holy stump alongside one another and see what happens.

Everything that Isaiah preached and wrote "has Yahweh's holiness at its center."[3] Because this holiness and the consequences of this holiness are in particularly sharp focus in Isaiah 6, I am interested in how Isaiah's experience and participation in The Holy shapes our understanding of the ways and means that are taken up into the way of Jesus and influence us as we follow him. The stump in a field of stumps is absolutely essential to our understanding and participation, quite as much as the Holy, Holy, Holy in the temple.

2. The passage is taken seriously by some theologians, but primarily as a text regarding what Calvin named the "dreadful decrees" that deal with matters of predestination and, particularly, predestination to damnation. See *Institutes of the Christian Religion*, ed. John T. McNeill, trans. Ford Lewis Battles (Philadelphia: Westminster, 1960), vol. 2, p. 955.

3. Walter Brueggemann, *Isaiah 1–39* (Louisville: Westminster/John Knox, 1998), p. 12.

*   *   *

Isaiah is the greatest preacher to be represented in our Scriptures. He is also our most conspicuous failure. For forty years he preached powerful, eloquent, bold sermons. Nobody listened. He preached repentance and the salvation of Jerusalem and Judah. The people did not repent and were taken into exile.

The vision text that Isaiah was given to preach ("Go, and say to this people . . .") was this:

> Hear and hear, but do not understand;
> see and see, but do not perceive. (Isa. 6:9 RSV)

An exceedingly odd text to be given to a preacher. But lest in bewilderment we pass it off too quickly, the text is elaborated: "Make these people blockheads, with fingers in their ears and blindfolds on their eyes, so they won't see a thing, won't hear a word, so they won't have a clue about what's going on, and, yes, so they won't turn around and be made whole" (my translation).

Isaiah was as puzzled by the message as we are. He asked, "How long is this to go on?" God's answer was not reassuring: "Until the cities are emptied out, not a soul left in the cities — houses empty of people, countryside empty of people. Until I, God, get rid of everyone, sending them off, the land totally empty. And even if some should survive, say a tenth, the devastation will start up again. The country will look like a pine and oak forest with every tree cut down — every tree a stump. A huge field of stumps. But there's a holy seed in those stumps" (my translation).

What are we to make of this? Our greatest preacher is given a text to preach that tells his congregation, in effect, "Listen hard, but you aren't going to get it; look hard, but you won't catch on." Isaiah is told to preach to a congregation that is *not* going to hear God's word, *not* going to see what God is doing. And this is not a temporary rhetorical strategy, a shock tactic to get their attention after which he will do his best to get them to see and hear God. This text will define his message across his lifetime.

Isaiah did what he was told to do, and it turned out as he was told it would. A hundred years or so after his last sermon, his country, both literally and figuratively, was a field of stumps.

So with a track record like that, why is Isaiah important? Why do we continue to keep his book in our Bibles, continue to preach the texts that proved so ineffective when he preached them?

Holy God

We begin with the holy God: God, high and lifted up, about whom and to whom the seraphim sing, "Holy, Holy, Holy." *The Holy*. The Holy, as a name for God, emphasizes that God is other, above, majestic. God cannot be understood from below. God cannot be accounted for by what we imagine God might be. God cannot be argued into belief by philosophical reasoning. God cannot be explained or interpreted by notions we have acquired by assembling feelings of reverence from sunsets, spiked with a few stories of miracles, and then legitimated with some comments that we pick up from celebrity interviews. God cannot be subsumed under the categories that we use to classify and order our experience. *Holy* alerts us to an awareness that God "is different, that in his way he is himself, though not far away, but rather near at hand, in the sphere of the present, inflaming and assuaging convention."[4] God *reveals* himself. Because of who God is, *The Holy*, we have to let God tell us who he is. If we insist on using *our* ideas to form our image of God, we will get it all wrong.

Isaiah's vision of God took place in Solomon's temple, a place deliberately and unapologetically empty of any image of God. The extravagant energy and penetrating vitality of The Holy took place in a room designed to shut out any suggestion that we can "work up" holiness on our own, or imagine what it might be like out of the materials supplied by our imaginations. The Holy of Holies, the holy core of the temple, was a vacant place, an emptiness between the two cherubim

4. Kornelis H. Miskotte, *When the Gods Are Silent* (London: Collins, 1967), p. 183.

over the Mercy Seat. Vincent Gillespie and Maggie Ross write that "This 'great speaking absence between the images' signified both Israel's repudiation of earthly representations of the deity and the imageless space into which they sought to come by prayer and devotion. In the New Testament, the empty tomb is similarly eloquent in its absence of presence."[5]

Isaiah's task was to preach God as God revealed himself, in the way and on the terms that God revealed himself. If he were to take the God-ideas and the God-images of his culture, purify them and reassemble them, then use them to appeal to the people's self-interest in getting a God who would serve them, "God" would no longer be *The Holy*. And if Isaiah were to refuse to use the god-desires, the "spiritual hungers," that were common in that culture, they would not know what he was talking about. They almost surely would not see or hear what he had to say or show them. As it was, they didn't.

The Holy is not a marketable God.

Isaiah is told that he is going to spend his life speaking to people who are god-consumers, who go to god garage sales most Saturdays. If Isaiah doesn't preach to them on their terms, everything he says will confuse them — they will neither see nor hear nor understand. So what is he going to do?

To begin with, he is to remember where he received the vision — in the emptiness of the Holy of Holies. And remembering that, what he heard in his assigned sermon text was something like this: "You know now, Isaiah, what you are dealing with — *The Holy*. You are my witness and interpreter. This is not going to be easy. Simply by preaching The Holy you are going to make their eyes glaze over. They won't know what you are talking about. Worse, they will misunderstand what you are talking about and assume that it is totally irrelevant to anything they care about. Ways and means are going to occur to you, be suggested to you, be recommended to you by some of the other prophets

---

5. Vincent Gillespie and Maggie Ross, "The Apophatic Image." Quoted by Belden Lane, *The Solace of Fierce Landscapes* (New York: Oxford University Press, 1998), p. 63.

in town, that are going to be convincing and tempting, ways and means that set aside The Holy for something much more understandable and accessible. The fact is that men and women have no love or taste for The Holy — they want a God who serves them on their terms, not a God they can serve on his terms. Don't be misled: the task of preaching the truth of salvation is not helped by clear communication — clear communication requires using the words and syntax that people are familiar with, that is part of their dailiness. But The Holy is not part of what they are used to. It is obscured by sin, it is a faded memory of the image in which they were created. The preaching of The Holy is not furthered by techniques or strategies. The Holy is not a problem to be solved. And if you compromise in the slightest you will betray me. You will also betray these people. No matter how much they might respond to you, no matter how much they might applaud your preaching, you will end up cheating them of a holy life, a life from Above, a life *healed, restored, ransomed, forgiven* — by *The Holy.*"

Holy Stump

As Isaiah is pulled into the holy life and finds himself involved in holy work, he is at the same time told that nothing much is going to come of it. He is to be a preacher, but a conspicuously unsuccessful preacher. He is going to preach with incredible power and eloquence, and people are going to go to sleep in the middle of his sermons. He will have ready access to all the kings in his lifetime, Jotham, Ahaz, and Hezekiah, will be an insider to the operations of statecraft, and will have his wise and godly counsel ignored. The end result of a lifetime of God-ordained and God-blessed preaching is that the country will be destroyed — "utterly desolate" (6:11). The Assyrians are going to march in and ravage the place. It is going to look like a forest that has been clear-cut by rapacious loggers — ugly, defaced, barren — all the trees cut down and hauled away with nothing left but stumps, an entire country of stumps. This was the sermon that God delivered to him on the day of his ordination: "This is what is going to happen, Isaiah, after a lifetime in my service. This is the end result of your immersion in holiness, your honest confession and cleansed speech, your vocation in holy orders. Stumps. A nation of stumps" (cf. 6:9-13).

The absence of any image of God in the Holy of Holies is going to be matched by the absence of anything human in the country. The apparent emptiness in the sanctuary is going to be matched by an apparent emptiness in the country. And both emptinesses are going to be filled with what only God can do and be, The Holy — the holy presence in the sanctuary and the holy stump in the country.

These parallel emptinesses and fillings need to be studied and assimilated far more than they are, especially by Christians who are intoxicated by success stories and dazzled by evangelical, so-called, patter and sleight-of-hand.

The accuracy of what Isaiah saw and heard in the temple becomes immediately evident as the story continues in chapters 7–9. George Adam Smith, that incomparable preacher and scholar of the Isaiah text, insists on coming to terms with the reality as Isaiah writes it. Commenting on the appearance of Isaiah's son, Immanuel, Smith writes:

> The Child, who is Israel's hope, is born; he receives the Divine name, and that is all of salvation or glory suggested. He grows up not to a throne or the majesty which the seventy-second Psalm pictures — the offerings of Sheba's and Seba's kings, the corn of his land shaking like the fruit of Lebanon, while they of the city flourish like the grass of the earth — but to the foot of privation, to the sight of his country razed by his enemies into one vast common fit only for pasture, to loneliness and suffering. Amid the general desolation his figure vanishes from our sight, and only his name remains to haunt, with its infinite melancholy of what might have been, the thorn-choked vineyards and grass-grown courts of Judah.[6]

6. George Adam Smith, *The Book of Isaiah* (London: Hodder and Stoughton, 1889), vol. 1, p. 117.

Then we come upon the pungent final sentence in God's ordination sermon to Isaiah: "The holy seed is its stump" (6:13).

Oh, really? The word "holy" again, but now applied to a seemingly inappropriate noun. Not the holy angel anthems filling the temple with glorious song, transforming Isaiah's world and Isaiah in the world. Not the holy that blazes out of a desert bush, or explodes into a vision before a prisoner in rocky exile. Not the holy that is evident in Jesus' words and acts that reveal the comprehensive and energetic and gracious life of the Trinity to us.

None of that now. Instead, a squat stump. But there is more to the stump than anyone supposes: "the holy seed is its stump." The stump, unlikely as it seems and against all appearances, is the holy seed from which salvation will grow. Five chapters later in Isaiah we come on this stump again, but now with some elaboration:

> A shoot shall come out from the stump of Jesse,
>   and a branch shall grow out of his roots.
> The Spirit of the LORD shall rest on him,
>   the spirit of wisdom and understanding,
>   the spirit of counsel and might,
>   the spirit of knowledge and the fear of the LORD. (11:1-2)

We know how that eventually turned out: in a word, Jesus. And so we joyfully and gratefully sing the praises of our holy Lord. We can never sing those praises loudly or joyfully enough, but while doing it we must not lose touch with that stump. For very often that stump and nothing but that stump will characterize and dominate our lives. Not for all of us, to be sure, but for many. Never, never forget that holy stump.

The world, the flesh, and the devil are all working full-time to fill our minds and emotions with pictures and longings for a so-called "more" life that is ignorant of The Holy, for abundant life that has nothing to do with God. This godless trinity not only controls the public media and mass advertising as it propagates and glamorizes its lies; it has also infiltrated large parts of the church, interpreting the Christian life for us in such ways that we are trained to avoid or be contemptuous of anything that doesn't promise us gratification. I want to counter these glamorous lies with Isaiah and his holy stump. Does it sound like an oxymoron? Holy . . . stump? But everything in Scripture and the gospel tells us that this is the truth, the reality of Jesus and our lives with and in Jesus. Holy. Life that issues out of death. Beauty that begins in ugliness. The same Holy, Holy, Holy that filled the temple is a holy seed in the field of stumps.

*   *   *

Ten or so miles north of the small Montana town in which I grew up, there is a smaller town that in earlier days was nicknamed Stump Town. The setting of the town was beautiful, nestled under the rock-muscled shoulders of the great Rocky Mountains. But it had the bad luck to get selected as a major railroad switchyard by Jim Hill, who was building the Great Northern Railroad across the continent. Jim Hill was as rapacious and brutal as any of Isaiah's Assyrians. He either bullied or bribed everyone who got in his way as he pushed through his railroad. Railroad beds require huge quantities of railroad ties, and so every tree in this little town was cut for making ties and the stumps left exposed. This village was not good for anything, after all, but to serve the grand railroad-building empire. When I was growing up it was still an ugly place, a shanty-town of hoboes and railroad bums — and stumps. I and my friends referred to it with condescension, and sometimes with contempt: Stump Town.

Thirty years ago my brother became a pastor there; and then ten years ago my son moved there. Between my brother and my son, I began to hear stories told and see scenarios unfold that were full of life and beauty and God, and in which the holy can be discerned. "Stump Town" is no longer a term of scorn. Today it is more like a promise of blessing and beauty and salvation. "The holy seed is its stump."

Isaiah provides an abundance of metaphor and vision so that we are able to recognize the way of The Holy in unlikely circumstances, wilderness circumstances, among neighbors who are deaf and dumb and heartless, in a field of stumps. The Holy, God's unmanageable but irrepressible life, is ever present and hidden within and around us. Unpredictably but most surely it breaks forth into our awareness from time to time: The bush blazes, the heavens open, the temple rocks, the stump puts forth a green shoot. Holy, Holy, Holy.

The Non-Negotiable Holy

All of us, if we only knew it, are on a hunt for the holy, for a life that cannot be reduced to the way we look or what we do or what others think of us. We are sometimes reminded of it by the persistent legends of the Quest for the Holy Grail — the chalice from which, at his last meal with his disciples, Jesus drank with them the wine that became his promise and command, his life in them. It is the holy cup from which we drink the holy life, the life that Jesus set before us when he said, "I came that they may have life, and have it abundantly" (John 10:10). Abundantly. The adverb, *perisson*, — not surprisingly, given his exuberance — became one of St. Paul's favorites. (In various forms it has at least eighteen occurrences.) There are numerous variations on the hunt for The Holy — holy grail, holy places, holy men and women, and, perhaps most wonderfully, Holy Scripture. Many of the quest stories are by now thoroughly secularized, but the quest for something other than and more than muscle and money keeps reappearing in unlikely guises. Quest for The Holy is ingrained in us — biological researchers will probably turn up a quest chromosome in our genetic make-up someday. We are after something — more life than we get simply by eating three meals a day, getting a little exercise, and having a decent job. We're after the God-originated and God-shaped life: a holy life.

*   *   *

All four Gospel writers have Jesus quoting from the second part of the Isaiah vision (and nothing from the first part) to account for the way he taught and for the widespread misunderstanding and stonewalling rejection by so many. Matthew, Mark, and Luke report Jesus early in his teaching using the words of God's message to Isaiah to answer the disciples' question on why he didn't speak so that people could understand what he was saying — "Why do you tell these enigmatic stories (parables)? Why don't you say what you mean?" (cf. Matt. 13:10-15; Mark 4:10-12; Luke 8:9-10). John reports Jesus using the Isaiah passage near the end of his life to account for the blind eyes and hard hearts of the people to whom he preached (John 12:39-40). And St. Paul. After failing to make a dent in the sight, hearing, and hearts of the religious leaders who had come to hear him preach from his place of house arrest in Rome, he remembers and quotes God's words to Isaiah. It's the penultimate story Luke tells of Paul — a failed preacher in the company of the failed Isaiah.

Why did the four Evangelists and Paul find it important to underline the significance of these programmatic words to Isaiah? Why did Jesus and Paul find it necessary to quote Isaiah to account for the brick wall that they hit as they preached and taught the Way? Maybe as a way of telling those of us who are following Jesus that there is no way to eliminate The Holy from the way of Jesus. Maybe as a way of making it clear to insider and outsider alike that, inconvenient as it is, baffling as it is, and disappointing as it is to anyone who was expecting the way to be paved with consumer rewards, The Holy is non-negotiable.

CHAPTER 7

Isaiah of the Exile:
"How Beautiful on the Mountains"

Barn's burnt down —
now
I can see the moon.

MASAHIDE

A Hebrew prophet whose name we don't know preached in Babylon somewhere around the middle of the sixth century B.C. He preached to a congregation whose world had come to an end. As it turned out, the sermons he preached, in the way sermons sometimes do, radically re-shaped the ways the people of God, God's Israel, understood them-selves. He convinced them, against everything that the newspapers and street talk were telling them, that what had happened to them was not a catastrophe but, in fact, *gospel* — a word that in the prophet's preaching took on a life of its own and developed into one of the great words among those who follow Jesus. The sermons then went under-ground, as sermons also have a way of doing.

Approximately 550 years later, "when the time had fully come" (Gal. 4:4 RSV) and God became incarnate in Jesus, the sermons, deeply embedded by then in the imaginations of at least some of the people, provided the precise language for naming and recognizing the actual way in which Jesus, God's Messiah, accomplished the salvation of all humankind and became a "light to the nations" (Isa. 42:6; 49:6).

Exile

Here's the story. A little over a hundred years after the life and preaching of Isaiah of Jerusalem, the Babylonian army, having disposed of the Assyrian military that had threatened Jerusalem for so long, invaded Israel, besieged and then destroyed Jerusalem. They herded ten thousand Hebrews across seven hundred miles of desert to live the rest of their lives in exile.[1] The devastation was not as catastrophic as sometimes envisaged — the Hebrews were not slaves in Babylon and were allowed to continue with some semblance of community life. Some even prospered.[2] All the same, it was remembered as total disaster: the city that the Lord loved "more than all the dwellings of Jacob" (Ps. 87:2) destroyed; the glorious Solomonic temple that for five hundred years had given splendid architectural shape to their worship, smashed; only the "poorest people of the land" (2 Kings 25:12) left behind; King Zedekiah, captured in his futile attempt to escape from his besieged city, shackled and made to watch his sons killed before his eyes — the last thing he saw before those eyes were put out — and then marched off blind, shuffling his way to an eventual grave in Babylon.

A Hebrew poet composed an elaborate and artful lament to keep the awfulness of the event — this catastrophe, this holocaust — incised deeply in the heart-memory of the people. The lament opens with this:

1. The figure is approximate; see 2 Kings 24:14, 16, where the total is considerably more than the 3,023 that Jeremiah reports (Jer. 52:28). Some suggest that Jeremiah's count excluded women and children. Professor William F. Albright suggested that terrific mortality on the route of the march may account for the difference. See Louis Finkelstein, ed., *The Jews: Their History, Culture and Religion* (New York: Harper and Brothers, 1949).

2. See Iain Provan, V. Philips Long, and Tremper Longman III, *A Biblical History of Israel* (Louisville: Westminster/John Knox, 2003), pp. 232-33.

How lonely sits the city
   that was full of people!
How like a widow she has become,
   she that was great among the nations!
She that was a princess among the provinces
   has become a vassal. (Lam. 1:1)

The lament, known among us as the Lamentations of Jeremiah, goes through the disaster, over and over, five distinct times, line by line in excruciating detail: rape, humiliation, mockery, sacrilege, starvation, and worst of all, cannibalism (mothers boiling their babies for supper!). The desperate slaying of innocent children showed complete loss of hope in human worth, the angry murder of priests showed absolute loss of respect for divine will. The worst that can happen to body and spirit, to person and nation, happened here — a nadir of suffering. The lament continues to be chanted still in the prayers of the Jewish community in August of each year (Ninth of Ab in the Hebrew calendar) on the anniversary of the terrible event.

Something over seven hundred years previously, Israel had been delivered in great travail from Egyptian slavery under the leadership of Moses and became a people of God, a "priestly kingdom and a holy nation" (Exod. 19:6). Throughout those seven centuries, stretching from Egyptian Exodus to Babylonian exile, God had used his prophets and priests, judges and kings, to guide and teach Israel to live in believing, obedient faith in the God who revealed himself as Savior, to worship this God with their whole heart and soul and mind and strength, to learn the distinctive "ways and means" that were appropriate to living the life of salvation. It hadn't been easy — there were ups and downs, there were times of blessing and judgment, there was sin and there was righteousness. They had a lot to learn and they were slow learners. But they had survived. They were still a "people of God," a people created, defined, and shaped by God's word.

That was now all over. There was no nation, no "royal priesthood." Their king was a royal wreck, limping blind across the desert sands, the rumble and creak in his ears of the wagons loaded with treasures from the temple of God, hauling off loot to enrich pagan Babylonian temples. As far as they were concerned, their God had abandoned them. Jeremiah, their pastor-prophet at the time of the disaster, had abandoned them, preferring to stay behind in the Jerusalem ruins with riffraff who couldn't even qualify as exiles.

The end of Israel. The end of the "people of God." They had had their chance — many chances! — and there would be no more. How could there be? Every sign, every scrap of evidence of their identity was gone. They were nothing. The disaster far exceeded the wreckage in the land, temple, palace, and people. There was something far deeper with far more extensive implications: humiliation, the deepest conceivable humiliation. The faith of Abraham, the words of Moses, the humanity of David, the fire of Elijah, the "holy, holy, holy" of Isaiah of Jerusalem — all that and more was gone. Absence. Silence. Ashes.

When they arrived in Babylon, the contrast between their failed religion and the successful religion of their captors was stark. They had left behind a city in rubble, a temple in ruins, the taste of their cannibalized babies still in their mouths. They were now living in cities that made Jerusalem look like the country town it was. Wealth and temples now marked the skyline, far surpassing anything of Solomon's that the Queen of Sheba had marveled at. Splendid warriors strolled the streets, a powerful military fast on its way to establishing Babylon as the world's superpower. "It was a vast world in which horizons widened. Just what place was there in it for Yahweh, the erstwhile protector of a ravaged petty state whose ruined temple gaped to the sky on a mountain in Judah?"[3]

If the war between Judah and Babylon was understood as a competition between rival gods and rival ways of life (as many, probably most, would see it), the results were decisive: Babylon's Marduk had beaten Israel's Yahweh, hands down. The end of Israel. The life of faith, as it turned out, was a delicate, lovely, but fragile violet crushed by Babylonian boots, ill-equipped to survive in the "real" world. Nothing. *Nada*. The word has entered our vocabulary through the poetry of

3. John Bright, *The Kingdom of God* (New York: Abingdon, 1953), p. 129.

St. John of the Cross, a Carmelite monk in Spain in the sixteenth century. He himself lived and named for all the rest of us, at least all of us who are willing to abandon our flimsy self-made identities and reject the culture-conditioned straitjacket roles that others make for us, the experience of *nada,* the overwhelming sense of nothing — emptiness, absence, nakedness, silence, night — that takes place between the time that we "put off the old nature" and "put on the new nature."[4]

In the summarizing comments of Rowan Williams, now Archbishop of Canterbury, John,

> simply by his own integrity and faithfulness, unmasked the delusions of the competent and successful religious world. He died in disgrace, after a long history of strained and bitter relations with his order. . . . He gives us a typically long and careful discussion of what might commonly be regarded as "illuminative" experiences — visions, "locutions," clairvoyance — whether imaginative or intellectual, spiritual, supernatural or natural in origin. It is a deliberately devastating catalogue, exhibiting an almost unique sensitivity to the risks of self-deception in the spiritual life. The conclusions are stark: *no* "spiritual" experience whatsoever can provide a clear security, an unambiguous sign of God's favour.[5]

In that "between the times," between the time when most people assumed, even if mindlessly, that "God's in his heaven and all's right with the world" (Robert Browning) and the time that the Nietzschean verdict, YAHWEH IS DEAD, grabbed headlines in the Babylonian Post in the sixth century B.C., a great many of God's so-called "elect" decided that the election had been a fraud and signed on with Marduk, the god associated with consumer prosperity and unbridled militarism.

The Babylonian exile stands unrivaled still as the paradigmatic

---

4. The metaphors of putting off one set of clothes and putting on another, with the implication of a transitional nakedness (nothing, *nada*), are St. Paul's. See Colossians 3:1-17.

5. Rowan Williams, *Christian Spirituality* (Atlanta: John Knox, 1980), pp. 159, 169.

nada for a biblically informed people. Apart from Lamentations we have only a few shreds of witness to what the people went through: a few psalms, Psalm 137 most notably ("By the rivers of Babylon — there we sat down and there we wept . . ."). We have a letter that Jeremiah wrote to the exiles (Jer. 29), urging them to accept their loss and make the best of it by living responsibly: "Quit sitting around feeling sorry for yourselves; don't listen to the lying preachers who are selling you false hopes; build houses, plant gardens, get married, have children, pray for the wholeness of Babylon and do everything you can to develop that wholeness." We also have the great visionary prophecy of Ezekiel, but he was not so much a preacher-pastor, immersing himself in the present conditions of the people, as he was a writer, preparing the imagination of the people for a future of hope. But the few scraps of writing that we do have that report on the exile conditions are enough to show us that exile became the "governing metaphor for all subsequent Judaism . . . the defining abyss of the life and faith of Judah."[6]

Aside from the few psalms, Jeremiah's letter, and the Lamentations, the plunge into the exilic darkness was accompanied by a long silence. It was a silence long enough to expose the silliness of the tinny, huckstering patter of the lying preachers (we know the names of three of them — Zedekiah, Ahab, and Shemaiah — from Jeremiah 29) who were peddling the illusion that things aren't as bad as they seem: "everything is going to turn out just fine, folks." When language is devalued, cheapened by generations of propaganda, silence is the only context in which it can be purified of its pollutants. We don't know how long this silence lasted; something like fifty years is an educated guess.

*　　*　　*

And then, as if out of nowhere, a voice. A powerful, persuasive, convincing voice. The voice of a preacher who put the people on their feet again. The voice of a preacher who gave them a living God, spoke God

---

6. Walter Brueggemann, *Isaiah 40–66* (Louisville: Westminster/John Knox, 1998), pp. 8-9.

into their lives in such a way that they realized that they were still, in spite of all the Babylonian taunts, the people of God. The voice of this preacher using nothing but word and spirit, language and prayer, countered the devastation of exile and replaced it with hope. Largely through the preaching of this one prophet, whose name we never learn, the years of exile, which began as the harbinger of the death of God, became a time of a resurrection.

The voice was not quite out of nowhere. Some in the community could still remember the stories and prayers of their ancestors. But those stories and prayers probably didn't do much to alter the perception of the exiles that Babylon and Marduk, not Israel and Yahweh, defined the world in which they now had to learn to live. A hundred and fifty years before the exile, Isaiah of Jerusalem had preached to the grandparents and great-grandparents of these people. He, too, was good with words, a voice of God's Spirit. But even though he had a prominent Jerusalem pulpit, and over a period of forty years had a succession of four kings in his congregation (Uzziah, Jotham, Ahaz, Hezekiah), he didn't get much of a hearing. The people basically ignored him — they were too absorbed in living life on their own terms.

Instead of letting Isaiah of Jerusalem interpret their lives for them as children of God, they chose to let the ambitions of their leaders and the world-dominating ways of the impressive Assyrians shape their understanding of how to make their way in the world. Isaiah thundered. They closed their ears. Isaiah went down the list of the surrounding nations that they so admired and took their cues from: Assyria, Babylon, Philistia, Moab, Damascus, Ethiopia, Egypt, Tyre. He exposed the insubstantiality of their pretensions. He called down the judgment of God on their idolatries and immoralities. They ignored him. Over and over he called out to them, using language that could wake the dead. Over and over they stuck their fingers in their ears.

But he didn't only thunder judgment. He also quietly and doggedly planted seeds of salvation. He gave them images of God's ways of working behind the scenes, of God going about his salvation work whether they wanted to be in on it or not. The images accumulated in the national psyche. Yahweh at the time he called Isaiah to be the nation's prophet was also frank with him, telling him that no one in his generation was going to listen to his preaching. The nation was going to end up as a vast field of stumps, but (make note of this!) there would be a "holy seed" in the stumps (Isa. 6:13). He went on to elaborate the image of that holy seed: "A shoot shall come out from the stump of Jesse, and a branch shall grow out of his roots" (11:1).

Isaiah introduced more images of hope that would later carry them: Jerusalem as "a quiet habitation" (33:20), the desert that shall blossom "like the crocus" (35:1), a future in which "the ransomed of the LORD shall return" (35:10) and a surviving remnant "take root downward, and bear fruit upward" (37:31). In the disobedient and faithless years following Isaiah's preaching, these seed metaphors and visions went underground, dormant in the Jerusalem dirt.

One hundred and fifty years later under the preaching of our unnamed Prophet of the Exile,[7] the metaphors and visions began to sprout in Babylonian dirt. And five hundred years later still, Jesus brought those seeds to full harvest: "Very truly, I tell you, unless a grain of wheat falls into the earth and dies, it remains just a single grain; but if it dies, it bears much fruit" (John 12:24).

How did this happen? We do not know. We know that it happened. And that it happens. It has happened many times and it continues to happen. Elie Wiesel is a contemporary witness to the fact that the miracle that took place in the Babylonian exile continues to take place.

A number of years ago I was reading the newspaper on a Tuesday

---

7. The general consensus on the authorship of Isaiah is that the named prophet is responsible for chapters 1–39 of the book. An unnamed prophet during the exile picked up where the first Isaiah left off and continued the story (chapters 40–55). For convenience I call him simply the Prophet. Isaiah of Jerusalem preached a message of warning and judgment, unsuccessfully attempting to rouse the people from an idolatrous preoccupation with themselves. Their refusal to listen and repent and obey resulted in the devastation of the exile. Isaiah of the Exile, the Prophet, took up the task of comforting the people and leading them into an obedient life of trust and singing as salvation was worked out among them. A third, also unnamed, prophet is responsible for post-exilic messages (chapters 56–66). Given the three preachers and the stretch of time involved (in round numbers, two hundred years), most readers (this one at least) marvel at how wonderfully and congruently the parts flow together.

morning at my breakfast table. I read a notice that Elie Wiesel would lecture that evening in Baltimore at Goucher College. I had been reading his books for years and had some deep sense of connection with him. I determined to hear him. I rearranged my evening commitments and drove twenty miles to find out more about this person who had for several years interested and intrigued me.

I had read my first novel written by Elie Wiesel, *Night*, five years earlier. It is a powerful, moving story of a Jewish adolescent boy who was taken, with all the other Jews who lived in the small Hungarian village of Sighet, to the Nazi concentration camp at Auschwitz. Later, after a transfer to Buchenwald, the boy watched as his parents and younger sister, along with most of the people he had grown up with, walked into the gas chambers never to come out again. He wrote:

> Never shall I forget that night, the first night in camp, which has turned my life into one long night, seven times cursed and seven times sealed. Never shall I forget that smoke. Never shall I forget the little faces of the children, whose bodies I saw turned into wreaths of smoke beneath a silent blue sky. Never shall I forget those flames which consumed my Faith forever. Never shall I forget that nocturnal silence which deprived me, for all eternity, of the desire to live. Never shall I forget those moments which murdered my God and my soul and turned my dreams to dust. Never shall I forget these things. . . . Never.[8]

I later learned that the novel was mostly autobiography. Wiesel grew up full of the stories and beliefs of Judaism, a joyful boyhood of study and singing and faith. But his adolescent years in Auschwitz and Buchenwald left him with a heart full of ashes; the stories had been torn from his heart, the faith exterminated from his spirit.

He wrote his story over and over, each time in a different novel, but the same story. He changed the setting and characters, rearranged the plot. But always the same story: the Jews — these people who are

8. Elie Wiesel, *Night* (New York: Avon, 1969), p. 9.

so strangely and insistently connected with the idea of God — slaughtered. Six million of them. Murdered on the most civilized continent on the earth; the orders of execution given by persons who had been educated in the great philosophical tradition of Immanuel Kant, who sang Luther's hymns in church on Sunday and listened to the music of Mozart in the evening. Each novel has a similar conclusion: "My eyes were open and I was alone — terribly alone in a world without God and without man. Without love or mercy. I had ceased to be anything but ashes."[9]

I was deeply moved as I read these stories. But two years previous to attending that lecture in Baltimore, I came across another book by the man and read it. This one was different, *very* different. *Souls on Fire* retells the Hasidic legends that Wiesel had grown up on, the remarkable stories of the spiritual leaders in Judaism who emerged in Eastern Europe in the eighteenth century and flourished for a hundred years in the villages and ghettos. *Souls on Fire* was a total surprise. Why on earth would a man who didn't believe in God, a man for whom God was dead, tell stories about persons who were passionate for God? I went on to read *Messengers for God* and discovered him telling Bible stories, the narratives of Abraham and Moses, Joseph and Job. What was going on here?

That is why I was determined to see and hear Wiesel. My curiosity was aroused. What had happened between *Night* and *Souls on Fire*? How was it that this tragic, Lazarus-like figure had moved from telling stories of the death of Jews and the death of God to telling stories about persons who live exuberantly by faith in God?

He walked to the lecture platform that evening in Baltimore, stood behind a music stand podium, and began reading Genesis 15, the story of Abraham. Without small-talk preamble, explanation, or apology, he spent the next hour leading us, a secular audience of seven or eight hundred people, in what was essentially a Bible study. Everything he said could have been transcribed from a Wednesday night prayer meeting in a Baptist church. I copied down this sentence: "Nothing is

9. Wiesel, *Night*, p. 10.

worthwhile compared to this — searching Scripture, asking questions of the text, seeking the truth of God's word." He was passionate, but without theatrics. He was intense without raising his voice. He made frequent references to prayer. He seemed to me a man who was quietly full of faith in the living God.

He said nothing about what had happened or how it had happened, this resurrection from the Auschwitz/Buchenwald *Night*, the graveyard of God and God's people, to now this Baltimore Bible study on the living faith of Abraham. But he was a clear witness to the fact that it *had* happened, that it *does* happen. A person can go through the worst, have every shred of faith pulled away from the soul, leaving it bare and shivering in a world where all the evidence gives proof that God is dead, and still become a person of faith, alive to the living God. I knew that I was in the presence of a person in whom the absence, the emptiness, had, through the years, gradually become a presence — but a presence stripped of illusion and pretension.

Several times during the lecture Wiesel used the word *midrash:* "If we are realistic persons, honest persons, alert persons, then *midrash* will enter our lives." The word means "seeking out." *Midrash* is the activity of a person who *seeks* the meaning of the word of God. *Midrash* comprises the stories told and comments made by persons who *seek* God's truth in Scripture.

The Prophet was the exile preacher into whose life *midrash* had entered. He had sought out the meaning of the preached words of Isaiah of Jerusalem and then re-preached them to the devastated exiles. He took Isaiah of Jerusalem's preaching, his metaphors and images, seriously, then watered and cultivated them in Babylonian dirt, and was on hand to see the seeds sprout and the branch grow: "the root of Jesse shall stand as an ensign to the peoples; him shall the nations *seek* [*yidroshu,* the verbal root of the noun *midrash*], and his dwellings shall be glorious" (Isa. 11:10 RSV). John Calvin is succinct: "To seek God means in every part of scripture to cast all our hopes upon him."[10]

10. John Calvin, *Commentary on Isaiah* (Grand Rapids: Associated Publishers and Authors, n.d.), p. 178.

Isaiah's preached metaphor and vision is the very seed that the Prophet saw sprout from the Babylonian graveyards. It is also the sprouted seed of which Elie Wiesel's life and writings are a witness.

Your God

The only thing we know about the Prophet of the Exile is that he was a magnificent preacher. We don't know a single personal or circumstantial detail about him, only the words that came out of his mouth, words that either he or another wrote down. We don't know where he lived, not a word of his family or how he made a living, not a word regarding his appearance. Not a single word about him, only the words he spoke. And God was the subject of virtually all the words that he spoke. As a prophet he gave voice to God.

We who have grown up in a world in which a voiceless technology dominates our imaginations tend to denigrate what we sometimes designate as *just* words. Words out of a machine. Words isolated from a personal voice, a Babel-like torrent of words severed from anything relational, from a living being — a particular man, a named woman, God revealed in Jesus. When we think in terms of getting things done, we typically think in terms of machines and bombs, size and horsepower and money — impressively effective but at the same time thoroughly impersonal. What are mere words in such company? Words occur, of course, but mostly to provide information and give instruction. When we want to get something *done*, want to make a difference in history, we send a rocket to the moon, drop a bomb on a city, build a skyscraper or stadium, a hospital or school. But as we spend time in the company of the Prophet, that diminishing adjective "just" becomes less and less useful, at least in conjunction with words. In the company of the Prophet we draw near "to the One in whom the word embraces the act itself."[11] Words used as the Prophet used them are not *just* words, they are words *plus* — words that bring into being what they say. They

11. Kornelis H. Miskotte, *When the Gods Are Silent* (London: Collins, 1967), p. 421.

are words in the lineage of Genesis: "Then God said, 'Let there be light'; and there was light" (Gen. 1:3); words in continuity with Jesus, who spoke to the man who was paralyzed, "Stand up," and he stood up (Mark 2:11-12).

This is what the Prophet did: he gave voice to the voice that "spoke, and it came to be" (Ps. 33:9). He said, "Here is your God . . . [Isa. 40:9] — Look! Listen!" And they did. People who were blind to God looked; people who were deaf to God listened. Through the preaching of the Prophet, people who to all appearances were a no-people again became a people of God. And they still are, we among them, living out this people-of-God identity, continuously sustained and deepened by preaching that is designated by the Prophet as gospel (*good news* or *good tidings*).

The Prophet's preaching installed the term "gospel" as a key word in the Hebrew/Christian vocabulary. The Prophet did not coin the word, but he did use it in a new way. In the Semitic world of his time, it was commonly used of reports, whether good or bad, the kind of reporting supplied to us still by journalists. But the Prophet uses the word as far more than a report of world news and neighborhood gossip. He condenses the proclamation of God's active presence in our lives into something concentrated, not only in our hearts but in our history, not just reporting news but "joyfully proclaiming Yahweh's great deeds as confession and in order to awaken religious joy"[12] — gospel. It is more than an announcement. It brings us into a participating awareness of what it proclaims — God himself active and present in his word and we ourselves *involved*, whether we want to be or not. It is a word that contains a message: the news that God acts, not only *is* but *is acting* — right now.

Basar is the Hebrew word. (In Greek it is *euangelizo*, from which we get evangel and evangelist). The Prophet uses the word five times (twice in 40:9; in 41:27; twice in 52:7). Five hundred years later St. Mark

12. O. Schilling, in *Theological Dictionary of the Old Testament*, ed. G. Johannes Botterweck and Helmer Ringgren, trans. John T. Willis, vol. 2 (Grand Rapids: Eerdmans, 1975), p. 315.

will use the word (*euangelion*) as a title to his account of Jesus' life, death, and resurrection. The first words out of Jesus' mouth in Mark's Gospel are the comprehensive words designating the reign of God that Jesus inaugurates, "the kingdom of God." "Gospel" became the word used to name Mark's account of Jesus' life and work that establish God's kingdom on earth (as it is in heaven). Later the same word was used as a title for what Matthew and Luke and John wrote as they retold the same story: God among us, God saving us. St. Paul used the word, both as a noun and a verb, more than any other biblical writer, sixty times (out of the seventy-six instances in the New Testament). But it was the Prophet who got it started, got "gospel" launched in this proclamatory, kerygmatic, God-speaking, God-creating, God-saving sense.

Overuse and misuse drains the word of its Isaianic and apostolic punch. When we use the word as an adjective we virtually obliterate its usefulness (as in gospel quartet, gospel tabernacle, gospel truth). We do better to immerse ourselves in the Prophet's poetry and preaching.

The Prophet's first task was to recover for his companions in exile a sense of the living, present God, the God of their salvation: *Behold, your God!* (Isa. 40:9). For a long time the people of Israel had been dabbling with Canaanite and Assyrian gods, trying first this one, then that. Now, in their exile, they are immersed in Babylonian gods, Babylonian temples, Babylonian god-myths. It is time to take a good, long, worshipful look at the God of their fathers, the God who revealed himself as the "God who is present, the God who is right here and at hand" (*Yahweh*: I am here, I am present to you).

F. Dale Bruner clarifies the uniqueness of *proclaiming* (preaching) the gospel as distinguished from teaching it: "Gospel . . . is the news of God's society and of God's coming with it. . . . [It] focuses on *God's* activity and the announcement of it."[13] Teaching tells us what we need to know and do; it is about us. Preaching tells us who God is and what he does; it is about God. And that is what the Prophet does. He doesn't talk *about* God, explain God, argue for God. Neither does he explain ourselves to ourselves, give counsel on how to survive the exile, pro-

---

13. F. Dale Bruner, *The Christbook, Matthew 1–12* (Waco, Tex.: Word, 1987), p. 130.

vide directions to improve our lives. He *preaches the gospel*: tells us that God is alive, present, and savingly active in places where we are living and among the people with whom we are living. There are implications, of course, for the way we live, but only if we understand that the living reality that concerns us is *God* here and among us. Preaching that is primarily about us is not *gospel* preaching; in fact, it is not preaching at all. That would be bad news, not good news.

The Prophet's sermonic strategy comprises three elements: in unprecedented and still unsurpassed proclamation he provides images of God for the people of God, images that are personal, relational, and that intend our salvation. Interspersed among these images he carries on a running ridicule, mocking the silly business of idolatry that is on such splendid and pretentious display all around them. And finally, so that those images don't blur into just images and the idols don't end up as just cartoon caricatures, he underpins his gospel proclamation with references to their Genesis and Exodus beginnings, the grand creational and historical precedent for what is now taking place in their present exile.

Images of God

The effectiveness of the Prophet's preaching was not in his arguing for the reality of God, not in his warning of the consequences of not following God, but in the way he conveyed the present and alive personal *here-ness* of God. His way of doing this was through a lavish and skillful use of metaphor.

The two most frequently used images are Creator and Savior (Redeemer is a near synonym). God is Creator. Over and over again, from first this angle and then that, the Prophet proclaims God in the act of creation, using imagery that we are familiar with from Genesis. And no wonder. Exile was also "without form and void," but, if they only knew it, God was at this very moment "hovering over the face of the waters" (Gen. 1:2 NKJV). What God did in Genesis, he is doing now. "Look around you — evidence of creation everywhere you look!"

Lift up your eyes on high and see:
  Who created these?

Have you not known? Have you not heard?
The LORD is the everlasting God,
  The Creator of the ends of the earth. (Isa. 40:26, 28)

At least twelve times the work of creation is specifically cited to interpret what God is doing among them at present: Isaiah 40:12-17, 21-31; 41:17-20; 42:1; 43:1; 44:2; 44:24; 45:8, 12-18; 48:7-13; 51:13, 16; 54:5.

Savior (or Redeemer) gets equal billing in the Prophet's preaching. Exile was not only a place of nothing, "darkness . . . upon the face of the deep" (Gen. 1:2 ASV). It was a place of suffering and deprivation. Exile was captivity, and the people needed a Redeemer; exile was a living death and they needed a Savior. The Prophet announces that God is present to be precisely that.

Then all flesh shall know
  that I am the LORD your Savior,
  and your Redeemer, the Mighty One of Jacob. (Isa. 49:26)

The citations of God as Redeemer and Savior are as frequent as the Creator/creation citations: Isaiah 43:1-7, 11-21; 43:25-28; 44:6, 22-24; 45:17-22; 46:12-13; 47:4; 48:17-20; 49:7, 22-26; 51:4-8; 52:3, 7-10; 54:5-8.

God creates. His creation provides the context, the form, in which he works. God saves. His salvation provides the content that accounts for everything that is going on in the world, for everything that is going on in our lives. Karl Barth furnishes the comprehensive discussion that we need to realize the necessary and indissoluble connection between the creation of heaven and earth and "all their multitude" (Gen. 2:1) and the covenant of redemption and salvation that is history: "Turn to me and be saved, all the ends of the earth! For I am God, and there is no other" (Isa. 45:22).

Creation is like the building of a temple, perfectly planned for the life of worship and salvation it is to serve. Creation is the theater; covenant is the salvation that is played out in the theater. Creator and Savior are the outside and inside of Yahweh. The meaning of creation is to prepare a place in which the will of God will be done. Creation is the external basis for the covenant; the covenant is the internal basis of creation.[14]

The Prophet piles up the images of God the Creator and God the Savior, shifts them around, rearranges them, mixes and mingles them: "Did you think creation was over and done with when the mountains were carved, the rivers set flowing, and the Lebanon cedars planted? Did you think that salvation is only a date in the history books and some stories you heard from your grandparents? The Creator is still creating, here in Babylon! The Savior is still saving, here in Babylon!"

Other metaphors are introduced along the way, enriching the imagination, catching nuances. God is Warrior and Shepherd: "the Lord GOD comes with might. . . . He will feed his flock like a shepherd" (Isa. 40:10-11). The strength of a mighty warrior who delivers from oppression is combined with the merciful tenderness of a shepherd who feeds, gathers, and leads his sheep. God is Helper, not only doing the "big" things involved in creation and salvation but present also in personal ways to do what we cannot do for ourselves. Do you feel like a worm in the shadow of the Babylonian temples, an insect, an object of contempt of the Babylonian soldiers? Never mind; "Do not fear, you worm Jacob, you insect Israel! I will help you, says the LORD" (41:14). God is Mother, perhaps the ultimate image for conveying care and intimacy: the mother with a child at her breast that she has brought into the world through much travail. "Can a woman forget her nursing child?" (49:15).

And more, much more. The ears of the exiles were filled with the sounds — a symphony of sounds! — that made their God present. The eyes of the exiles saw God in action, in colorful, kaleidoscopic imagery. God creating, still. God saving, still. And all of it going on at once — impossible to sort the items out, organize them alphabetically, and select what we want — a vast simultaneity in which we are caught up.

---

14. See Karl Barth, *Church Dogmatics* (Edinburgh: T&T Clark, 1958), vol. 3, pt. 1, pp. 228ff.

The Idols

Interspersed with these serious images of the living God of salvation, the Prophet from time to time mocks the no-gods that litter the Babylonian landscape. His ridicule is withering, merciless.

"All those who make no-god idols don't amount to a thing, and what they work at so hard is nothing. Their little puppet-gods see nothing and know nothing — total embarrassments! Who would bother making gods that can't do anything, that can't 'god'? Watch all the no-god worshipers hide their faces in shame. Watch the no-god makers slink off humiliated when their idols fail them. Get them out here in the open. Make them face God-reality.

"The blacksmith makes his no-god, works it over in his forge, hammering it on his anvil — such hard work! He works away, fatigued with hunger and thirst.

"The woodworker draws up plans for his no-god, traces it on a block of wood. He shapes it with chisels and planes into human shape — a beautiful woman, a handsome man, ready to be placed in a chapel. He first cuts down a cedar, or maybe picks out a pine or oak. He lets it grow strong in the forest, nourished by the rain. Then it can serve a double purpose: Part he uses for keeping warm and baking bread; from the other part he makes a god that he worships — carves it into a god shape and prays before it. With half he makes a fire to warm himself and barbecue his supper. He eats his fill and sits back satisfied with his stomach full and his feet warmed by the fire: 'Ah, this is the life.' And he still has half left for a god, made to his personal design — a handy, convenient no-god to worship whenever he's so inclined. Whenever the need strikes him he prays to it, 'Save me. You're my god.'

"Pretty stupid, wouldn't you say? Don't they have eyes in their heads? Are their brains working at all? Doesn't it occur to them to say, 'Half of this tree I used for firewood: I baked bread, roasted meat, and enjoyed a good meal. And now I've used the rest to make an abominable no-god. Here I am praying to a stick of wood!'

"This lover of emptiness, of nothing, is so out of touch with reality, so far gone, that he can't even look at what he's doing, can't even look at the no-god stick of wood in his hand and say, 'This is crazy'" (Isa. 44:9-20 *The Message*).

The Prophet has a good time, it seems, doing this. He is scathingly funny as he lampoons the Babylonian god charade (see also Isa. 40:19-20; 41:5-7, 21-24; 42:17; 45:20-21; 46:1-2, 6-7; 47:12-14). I wonder if any of the Babylonians laughed.

The Exodus

One more thing was necessary. If this recovered sense of "your God" was to work as gospel, the Prophet had to root his salvation preaching in a solid sense of creation and history. Not an idealized creation and not a romanticized history, but *lived* history in a *grounded* creation, the history that the Prophet's congregation, even as he was speaking to them, was living in sixth-century B.C. Babylon.

It would have been possible — it is always possible in the religious life — for the people to "spiritualize" the Prophet's preaching, to internalize it, to privatize it, to make it into a comforting truth, to "ghetto-ize" it. It was possible to compartmentalize God and the Prophet's preaching about God into something quite disconnected from Babylon and the Babylonian conditions in which they were living. But creation and history cannot be reduced to the private or mystical or mental — they are worked out in an arena of public events: Egyptian exodus, Babylonian exile, and Golgotha crucifixion "under Pontius Pilate."

But despite the unrelenting witness of the Scriptures to the contrary, a surprising number of people are uncomfortable with this witness and try their best to spiritualize both creation and history: spiritualize the dirt and mosquitoes out of creation and then sign up for lessons in flower arranging; spiritualize the accidents and train wrecks out of history by reducing them to dates in a textbook. To spiritualize in this sense involves the reinterpretation of life into something that is not compromised by cancerous growths, or difficult neighbors, or corrupt economics. It reduces the vast world of creation and the complex world of salvation to a few memorized Bible verses, a devotional book or two useful for inspiration, and a handful of truths or principles to keep us on the straight and narrow. By hook or crook, spiritualization insists on deconstructing a gospel way of life into a feeling or an idea or a project. Spiritualization succeeds when it sanitizes prayer into pious clichés and cordons Scripture off from the traffic. Spiritualization succeeds to the extent that it avoids dealing with Babylon and the conditions of Babylon. Spiritualizing the gospel means that we love God but not the world that "God so loved."

To guard against this spiritualizing dismissal of the everyday life of Babylonian politics and business and religion, the Prophet preached in such a way that the people would understand that what God was doing with them in their exile had its precedent in what God did in Genesis and Exodus and was parallel with it:

> Was it not you who cut Rahab in pieces,
>   who pierced the dragon?
> Was it not you who dried up the sea,
>   the waters of the great deep;
> who made the depths of the sea a way
>   for the redeemed to cross over?
> So the ransomed of the LORD shall return,
>   and come to Zion with singing. . . . (Isa. 51:9-11)

Rahab names the primordial dragon of the waters of chaos in ancient Semitic storytelling (see Ps. 89:10; Job 9:13; 26:12). Rahab is also used as a metaphor for Egypt, the "dragon" that oppressed Israel for four hundred years (see Isa. 30:7; Ps. 87:4). In the great work of creation, God defeated chaos when he "cut Rahab to pieces." In the great work of salvation he "made the depths of the sea a way for the redeemed to pass over" and defeated the Egyptian oppressor. The Prophet fuses the two dragons into one: God subdues the unruly forces of evil and he works his salvation in Babylon even as the Prophet is preaching to his congregation in exile that "the ransomed of the LORD shall return."

The Prophet preaches vigorously, giving the people image after image, metaphor after metaphor, of God creating, of God saving. He is rousing their imaginations to see again the "circle of earth" on which they stand, to hear again the Exodus story of their redemption that locates them in history. Exodus and exile are parallel — the Israelites had been saved out of those seemingly godless centuries and conditions of Egyptian slavery and they are being saved again out of the devastation and death-of-God conditions of Babylonian exile. What happened before is happening again.

The Prophet is relentless: a holy creation is taking place on Babylonian soil; a holy history (salvation) is taking place on Babylonian streets. But if we have picked up the bad habit of spiritualizing the creation and spiritualizing history, we won't see it. We will have edited "heavens and earth" down to merely earth.

God rules in heaven, true. God is "enthroned upon the cherubim" (Ps. 80:1) and upon "the praises of Israel" (Ps. 22:3), true. God does "not forget the oppressed" (Ps. 10:12), wonderful. God does "not give me up to Sheol" but shows me "the path of life" (Ps. 16:10-11), yes. But God also — never forget it! — "breaks the cedars of Lebanon" and "shakes the wilderness of Kadesh" (Ps. 29:5, 8). He "bowed the heavens, and came down" and "rode on a cherub, and flew" (Ps. 18:9-10). The "horse and rider he has thrown into the sea" (Exod. 15:1).

God works in us, but not in us abstracted from creation and history. God touches the human heart; God also touches the mountains so that they smoke (Ps. 144:5). God's highways are in our hearts (Ps. 84:5), but his way is also "through the sea" (Ps. 77:19). We cannot reduce God to our experience or our understanding of him. Creation is immense; salvation is comprehensive. The Prophet's preaching formed a participating imagination in his congregation that embraced God on his most magnanimous terms.

My Servant

Salvation is on the way! But how will it be accomplished? What are the means? The answer is succinct; it is also surprising: *My servant.*

"Your God" is the leadoff term in the Prophet's assigned task of rebuilding the creation/salvation imagination of his exiled congregation (Isa. 40:9). His vigorous images of God alive, God personal, expand into a magnificent world: saved men and women, women and men saved — from exile! This is impressive, but no real surprise. We more or less expect something like this from the Prophet, Israel's premier preacher of the Gospel of the Way.

But "my servant" is a surprise. As the Prophet describes the means that God uses to build the "way of the LORD" (40:3) out of the Babylonian desert, the "highways" (49:11) that he is constructing, he names "my servant" as the means. George Adam Smith wrote, "Next to Yahweh himself, the Servant turns out to be the most important figure in the prophecy. Does the prophet insist that God is the only source and sufficiency of his people's salvation? It is with equal emphasis that he introduces the Servant as God's agent of choice in his work."[15]

Four songs that feature a servant are embedded by the Prophet in the course of his gospel preaching: Isaiah 42:1-9; 49:1-7; 50:4-9; 52:13–53:12. Servants — menial servants, believe it or not — are God's choice to implement the great act of salvation. We begin with the Prophet himself, who understands himself under the designation "servant." The Prophet who *preached* to his congregation, "Behold your God," also *listened* to God say to him, "Behold *my* servant." Prophetic preaching is useless if it is not accompanied by prophetic listening.

The four songs are employed to make sure that the Prophet, or Israel, or any of the rest of us do not substitute something that seems to us a more appropriate means, something that we think is more in keeping with the glory of God. The servant is called and defined by

15. George Adam Smith, *The Book of Isaiah* (London: Hodder and Stoughton, 1889), vol. 2, p. 253.

God; the servant understands himself exclusively in the terms given by God. George Adam Smith again:

> [N]arrow and imperfect believers are reminded that they must not substitute for faith in God their own ideas of how God ought to work; that they must not limit his operations to their own conception of his past revelations; that God does not always work even by his own precedents; and that many other forces than conventional and religious ones — yea, even forces as destitute of moral or religious character as Cyrus himself seems to be — are also in God's hands and may be used by Him as a means of grace.[16]

As the Prophet lays out the way and ways of the servant in the four songs, he provides enough details to make sure that we do not turn the word into a cliché, a mere label that depersonalizes the richly personal into some colorless abstraction. These songs, as it turns out, are the most distinctive contribution that the Prophet makes to our understanding of the gospel, the way of Jesus. They are arguably also the most difficult aspect of his message to assimilate and live out. Nobody aspires to be a servant. We have a higher opinion of ourselves.

But the Prophet, in far more detail than any prophet before him, embraced the image of the servant in order to identify and elaborate the human ways and means by which God reequips and redefines both himself and his people to participate in the salvation life prepared for them. "Servant" was not a new image, but in the exile it may well have lost a good bit of its punch. But if the image was dead, it was dead only in the way that a seed is dead — seemingly dead but ready to burst into green vitality when the conditions are right. The *nada* of exile supplied those conditions.

Seven hundred and fifty years previous to the exile, when Moses led the people of Israel out of slavery in Egypt, "servant" was a primary image for both Moses ("his servant Moses," Exod. 14:31) and the people

16. Smith, *Book of Isaiah*, p. 174.

he led. They had been slaves in Egypt (a bad thing); now they were servants of Yahweh (a good thing). And now the Prophet of the Exile — might he be the "prophet like Moses" anticipated in Deuteronomy 18:15, 18? — is proclaiming the reality, the presence, the saving activity of Yahweh in the story of Israel's beginnings, its creation as a people of God, and in the story of salvation out of Egyptian slavery, God active again in Babylonian exile.

*   *   *

"Servant" is not a new term to designate the people of God. Early on, the term "servant" formed the core of their self-understanding. The great Red Sea salvation that set Israel free from Egyptian bondage did not make them a free people but servants of another Master: "For it is to me [God] that the people of Israel are servants [*'abadim* = slaves]. They are my servants whom I brought out from the land of Egypt: I am the LORD your God" (Lev. 25:55 ESV). They were free from Egyptian bondage, but they were not free from God. "The point of the exodus is not freedom in the sense of self-determination, but *service*, the service of the loving, redeeming, and delivering God of Israel, rather than the state and its proud king," writes Jon Levenson.[17]

When Moses negotiated the release of the Israelite slaves, he used the word "serve" over and over again. God instructed Moses, "Say to Pharaoh, 'Let my people go, that they may *serve* me'" (Exod. 7:16; 8:1, 20; 9:1, 13; 10:3; all RSV). Pharaoh's servants, fed up with the accumulation of plagues visited on the land, told their master, "Let the men go, that they may *serve* the LORD their God" (Exod. 10:7 RSV). Exasperated, Pharaoh finally gives in and tells Israel, not just once but four times, "Go, *serve* the LORD your God" (Exod. 10:8, 11, 24; 12:31; all RSV). They went. But no sooner were they gone than Pharaoh changed his mind and set out to bring them back. As the Egyptian chariots thundered after them, the Israelites realized that they were trapped at the shore of the

---

17. Jon Levenson, *The Hebrew Bible, the Old Testament, and Historical Criticism* (Louisville: Westminster/John Knox, 1993), p. 144.

Red Sea with no way out. Moses had led them into a blind alley. They fired Moses as their leader ("let us alone") and were ready to return as slaves under Pharaoh: "let us *serve* the Egyptians" (Exod. 14:12). A day later, Moses had them standing on the far shore, shouting and singing — saved! But Moses was still a servant, as were the people he had led. Moses' servant status hadn't changed: "the people believed in the LORD and in his *servant* Moses" (Exod. 14:31).

Both the people and Moses were still slaves. What changed, the only thing that changed, was that they had a different Master, Yahweh the Lord of life instead of Pharaoh the tyrant of death. (The same word in Hebrew, *'ebed,* translates into English as either slave or servant depending on context: if the servitude is forced, you are a slave; if the servitude is chosen, you are a servant. The same goes for the New Testament Greek word *doulos* — either servant or slave).

"Servant" surprises us because it is so incongruent with the *way* itself, the way of salvation, a "highway for our God" (Isa. 40:3). The "way in the wilderness and rivers in the desert" (43:19) is a glorious affair, extravagantly glorious. But the agents God chooses to carry out this glorious work are inglorious servants. Servants have no credentials, no status, no achievements that qualify them for great work.

Is this the way that God wants to give witness to the work of salvation? Is this the way the all-powerful God who "sits above the circle of the earth" expects to be recognized? We might have expected better: freedom fighters, perhaps, battle-hardened warriors, politically savvy statesmen skilled in negotiating terms. And why not throw in a host of angels? Servant is a position without distinction, the lowest rung on the work ladder. And here they are, mere servants — these exiles, these landless, kingless, godless (as so many of them assumed) exiles — the men and women whom even then God was using to accomplish their salvation.

*   *   *

Among a biblically informed people, servant has always been our given identity. We serve God; God does not serve us. God gives the orders, God provides terms of our service; we carry them out. God is a good and merciful master, but God does not serve us.

God's way, always, is to use servants. Servants: men and women without standing, without accomplishment, without influence. The core element in a servant identity is *not* being God, not being in charge, not taking the initiative. Or, to put it positively, a servant enters into what has already been decided by another, what is already going on, alert to the gestures and guidance of the Master (Ps. 123). The servant doesn't know the whole story, doesn't know the end from the beginning. The servant's task is to be competent in the immediate affairs that have to do with what he knows of the desires of his Master. All the while he is also aware that there is far more going on, both good and evil, than he has any knowledge of. He lives, in other words, in a mystery but not in confusion. A good servant is ever eager to trust and obey and honor God as the sovereign who is always personal and present — *Yahweh:* God here and now.

The Four Servant Songs

The four passages designated the "servant songs" are of particular interest as the Prophet identifies the servant and/or servants that God will use to save his people from their Babylonian exile.

It is clear by now that the designation "servant" is fluid (there is a huge consensus among Bible readers on this): Sometimes it is a named person (such as Moses or David). Later, the New Testament writers will present Jesus as the one who understood himself as a servant in terms taken from the four servant songs. Paul identified himself with the same word. But at the same time it includes every last one of us, without qualification or watering down — all the people of God. "Servant" is the highest and most accurate word that can be used of us. We are all servants. Any one of us, pulled at random out of a congregation, in the eyes of God can fulfill the role of servant every bit as well as any of these named ones (Moses and the others). But most servants are unnamed. This is of particular interest to those of us who are interested in

Jesus as the way, wanting to know the *way* in which Jesus is the way we are called to travel.

* * *

The Prophet used the attention-getting "Behold!" to mark the urgency of his gospel-salvation preaching — seven staccato *behold* repetitions: Isaiah 40:9, 10, 15; 41:11, 15, 24, 29 (RSV). "Look at this! Listen to the word of God." When it comes time to introduce the servant songs, he uses the same word: "Behold!" (42:1). "Look at this! Listen to these songs of the servant. You need to pay attention to who God is in your lives" ("Behold, your God!"). It is just as important that you know the ways and means, namely, the *servant* through whom God works in your lives" ("Behold, my servant!"). The first and fourth servant songs begin with the "Behold"; the third song concludes with a double "Behold" — as if to say, *mark this — this is most important!*

* * *

Isaiah 42:1-9. In the first song the servant is "chosen" for a mission: he will "bring forth justice to the nations." A large assignment. But the way he does it is anything but grandiose: he will work quietly and gently, no yelling, no forcing, no bullying. The congruence between end and means is significant. And despite the seeming inadequacy of means, its success is guaranteed — "he will not fail."

Isaiah 49:1-7. The second song describes the servant as "formed . . . in the womb." This is no late-coming desperate attempt to salvage a failing enterprise. This is no last-minute decision. This has been in the works for a long time. All the same, it is not going to be easy: the servant himself feels the uselessness of his work, and God acknowledges that he will be "deeply despised, abhorred by the nations." But the largeness of the assignment is not tailored down to accommodate his inadequacy: "I will give you as a light to the nations." And the outcome is going to be satisfactory: "Kings shall see and . . . prostrate themselves."

Isaiah 50:4-9. The third song reaffirms the servant's work of witness and preaching that is met with scorn and contempt — "I gave my back to those who struck me. . . . I did not hide my face from insult and spitting." But the servant doesn't waver, doesn't flinch — "I have set my face like flint." Victory continues to be assured: "Behold, the Lord GOD helps me" (v. 9 RSV).

Isaiah 52:13–53:12. The fourth song turns out to be the main song to which the first three are the introduction. It continues the witness that the servant is chosen, equipped, and assigned by God to carry out God's work of justice and salvation; it continues to place his work in conditions of rejection and suffering; it continues with the assurance that these unlikely means will nevertheless accomplish their end. But there is a new element that sets this song apart in a remarkable way, a way that turns out to be definitive for our understanding and participating in the gospel, the news that stays news. That definitive way involves sacrificial suffering, suffering with and for others.

*   *   *

This final servant song is in two voices: the opening (52:13-15) and closing (53:11b-12) portions are in the voice of God; the center voice (53:1-11a) is the "we" voice, the persons reporting on the suffering and death of the servant and its meaning for their salvation. This "we" voice is the heart of the song, but it is so excruciatingly counter to what we are used to thinking about what is involved in taking care of what is wrong with us, so offensive to our sense of propriety and justice, that it requires hefty bookends of assurance that this is truly what God intends. At one end, "Behold, my servant shall prosper" (52:13 RSV), and at the other end, "The righteous one, my servant, shall make many righteous" (53:11b). This is the way, this way of sacrificial suffering, by which God deals with what is wrong with Israel — and what is wrong with the world. The substantial prologue (52:13-15) and confident conclusion (53:11b-12) hold the center firmly in place so that we can consider it without wavering.

This servant is the centerpiece of the song: "a root out of dry ground . . . no beauty . . . despised and rejected . . . we esteemed him stricken, smitten by God . . . oppressed . . . cut off out of the land of the living . . . his grave with the wicked" (RSV). A suffering servant.

But here's the thing: this suffering is not presented as tragic, as a misfortune, as an interruption of what should be. The suffering is the *chosen* means of salvation: "carried our sorrows . . . bruised for our iniquities . . . upon him was the chastisement that made us whole . . . laid on him the iniquity of us all . . . stricken for the transgression of my people . . . he makes himself an offering for sin" (RSV). The servant stands in for us, takes our place. Bernd Janowski in a most careful exegetical study of Isaiah 53 distills the essence of the servant's significance in a sentence: "one person, by some action or suffering, takes the 'place' of others who are not willing or able to take it up themselves."[18] What we sometimes name vicarious suffering.

The servant serves God. That goes without saying. But the distinctive thing that comes into focus in the fourth song is that the servant serves God by serving the sinner, by taking the sinner's place, taking the consequences of sin, doing for the sinner what he or she is helpless to do for himself, herself.

This is the gospel way to deal with what is wrong with the world, deal with this multifaceted sin-cancer that is mutilating and disabling us. Variations on what is wrong are multiform: unbelief, missing the mark, evil, rebellion, transgression, willfulness, indifference, violence, arrogance, and on and on and on. But whether the wrong is intentional or inadvertent, the servant neither avoids it in revulsion nor attacks it by force of words or arms. Instead, the servant embraces, accepts, *suffers* in the sense of submitting to the conditions and accepting the consequences. The servant personally *takes* the wrongdoer and the wrong to the altar of sacrifice and makes an offering of him or her or it. The servant says to his brothers and sisters, "Only God can save you. You don't think you can go to him? I'll go for you." Or, at least, "Let me go with you."

---

18. Bernd Janowski, *The Suffering Servant: Isaiah 53 in Jewish and Christian Sources*, ed. Bernd Janowski and Peter Stuhlmacher, trans. Daniel P. Bailey (Grand Rapids: Eerdmans, 2004), pp. 53-54.

*   *   *

A great deal of attention has been and continues to be given to asking and answering the question, "Who is this servant?" Few passages of Scripture have received such a meticulous going over in search of precise knowledge of this person and event that form the core of our understanding of the salvation gospel. The consensus of the Christian church establishes Jesus the Christ, God incarnate, accomplishing salvation definitively both at the foundation ("the Lamb slain from the foundation of the world," Rev. 13:8 KJV) and as the centerpiece of history: Jesus on the cross is the means of salvation.

But while the suffering and death of Jesus is definitive and complete, there is more — and the more has to do with our participation in what Jesus accomplishes in his suffering and death. There is more to the servant than Jesus: there are also his servants. The reluctance of the text itself to provide a definitive servant identification is probably deliberate. Maybe the lines of definition are blurred so that we cannot assign the office exclusively either to an anonymous person in the exile or, supremely, to Jesus. We are in on this too, and cannot disqualify ourselves. The overall pervading concern of the text is that every follower of the gospel shall embrace the identity of servant in the very terms in which the Prophet of the Exile presents it: "I am the servant, just as Moses was the servant (and for those of us who anticipate what's ahead, Jesus is the Servant Complete); each one of you is also the servant." Much as we try to get out of it or find a way around it, there is simply no following of Jesus that does not involve suffering and rejection and death. No exceptions.

At the Exodus Moses was just such a servant in Egypt: When the people were unfaithful at the golden calf and threatened with extinction, he offered himself in "the mystery of vicariousness for Israel but also for God"[19] in their place: "blot me out of the book that you have written" (Exod. 32:32). But not exclusively — many of his followers also took on the identity of servant.

19. Miskotte, *When the Gods Are Silent*, p. 385.

At the time of exile, the Prophet was probably just such a servant in Babylon: "he bore the sin of many, and made intercession for the transgressors" (Isa. 53:12). He broke the vicious cycles of unbelief and disobedience, and not, as Walter Brueggemann reminds us, "by force, by power, by assertion, for such vigorous assertion only escalates and evokes more from the other side. The servant, this nobody with no resources, breaks the cycles of death and hurt precisely by a life of vulnerability, goes into the violence, and ends its tyranny."[20] But not exclusively — many in his congregation also embraced the servant life.

And Jesus. All the New Testament writers understand Jesus to have lived out in the full light of day details that they discerned in the fragments and suggestions in the exilic language of Isaiah 53: the suffering, the humiliation, the silence before his accusers, the lamb [of God] led to the slaughter, the cruel stripes, the judgment before Pilate and Caiaphas, the death, the godforsakenness. Jesus embraced each detail of the servant to which the Prophet gives witness. What Moses and his followers did in part, what the Prophet and his congregation did in part, Jesus did whole, complete. Jesus was at one and the same time God and servant. He brought all the elements of God's proclamation together, and the way he did it was as a servant "for us and for our salvation." This is a huge mystery that defies comprehension, but the mystery doesn't prevent participation.

But neither did Jesus do it exclusively. He did it uniquely, to be sure, for there is nothing we can do to either add to or take away from what Jesus did and does. The cross on Golgotha, the place where all this Isaiah 53 imagery comes into focus, is unrepeatable — but cross *bearing* is not. The uniqueness that is Jesus does not exclude us from participation in his servant ways. We can — we *must* — participate in Jesus' work the way Jesus did it and does it and only in the way Jesus did and does it, obedient and joyful servants as we follow our servant Savior who "came not to be served but to serve, and to give his life a ransom for many" (Mark 10:45).

Is not this what we do when we offer *our* "bodies as a living sacri-

---

20. Brueggemann, *Isaiah 40–66*, p. 147.

fice" (Rom. 12:1)? Do we not become partners in his servant ways when we "bear one another's burdens" (Gal. 6:2)?

*   *   *

The gospel that the Prophet preached in the obscurity and anonymity of the exile finally found its most prominent pulpit on Golgotha and Jesus as its preacher. But however prominent that pulpit and however powerful that preacher, the way of the servant has rarely, maybe never, been a well-traveled way in the Christian community.

This sacrificial-suffering-servant way of dealing with what is wrong in people, with what is wrong in the world, is so different from the ways to which our culture accustoms us. The standard operating procedures practiced outside the orbit of Scripture and Jesus attempt to get rid of, or at least minimize, whatever is wrong with the world primarily by means of teaching and making: *teach* people what is right, or *make* them do what is right. The professor and the policeman represent these two ways, education and law enforcement. We send people to school to *teach* them to live rightly and responsibly; if that doesn't work we *make* them do it through a system of rewards and punishments, even it means locking them up in a cell.

Neither way seems to make much difference. The way of teaching as given form in schools and universities is not flourishingly successful. Scoundrels and betrayers, thieves and cheats, suicides and abusers, flourish in the best of professions and businesses. As literacy abounds, sin does much more abound. Neither does the way of coercion as given form in jails and prisons seem to make much difference. We remove a small percentage of wrongdoers from the streets for a time, but even then our prison population seems at times to rival our school attendance. We distribute guns and bombs to any and all who will agree to use them to serve "God and country" and proceed to threaten or kill any who "disturb the peace" whether at home or abroad. None of it seems to make much of a dent in diminishing the sheer quantity of wrong.

Isaiah 53 is the final nail in the coffin that buries all the false expectations, all the devil's seductions, all the pious revisions of the biblical story that make Jesus and his followers into American success stories.

Meanwhile that Golgotha pulpit still centers history. And that Preacher still speaks the only word that will save the world.

Beauty

One word requires comment before we are done with the Prophet of the Exile, the word "beautiful." The Prophet uses the word only once, but it is the single word that most accurately and thoroughly gathers up everything that the Prophet has been setting before us. It requires comment because the cogency of the word given the conditions obtaining in Babylon at the time — godless arrogance, exilic despair, glorious God and suffering servant, salvation and god-delusions, what you see and hear and what you can't see and hear, what has been going on, is going on, and will go on — is not at all obvious. The Prophet's word for all this is "beautiful." Yes, this requires comment.

Beauty is commonly trivialized in our culture, whether secular or ecclesial. It is reduced to decoration, equated with the insipidities of "pretty" or "nice." But beauty is not an add-on, not an extra, not a frill. Beauty is fundamental. Beauty is not what we indulge ourselves in after we have taken care of the serious business of making a living, or getting saved, or winning the lottery. It is evidence of and witness to the inherent wholeness and goodness of who God is and the way God works. It is life in excess of what we can manage or control. It arrives through a sustained and adorational attentiveness to all that we encounter on the way: a forced march across a desert, a rock, a flower, the dragon Rahab, a face, a rustle in the trees, the "cup of staggering," a storm crashing through the mountains, wounding and bruising of all sorts, an old man's gesture, a lamb led to the slaughter, a child's play, an altar call, a good death, wings like eagles, the Scriptures, Jesus.

My wife and I spent a few hours in a museum in North Carolina that was holding an exhibition of the work of Auguste Rodin. Once Rodin's sculptures invade your imagination, it is impossible to look at a man walking or a woman loving and shrug him or her off as trivial or insignificant. In whatever pose or action Rodin found people, he saw what can only be called, I think, beauty, and the beauty gave witness to something ecstatic, something more, to sheer life itself.

I learned from the program notes that he would often instruct his students, "Don't look for a good-looking model, some perfectly proportioned specimen — take anyone you come across. They are all beautiful."

This is a beauty that escapes all the dictionary definitions. It involves a re-working, a re-shaping of all the words that we commonly use to make our way satisfactorily through the shopping malls, keeping our sin-distorted identities intact. All our biblical words, in fact, require this — insist on being redefined in terms of the detailed working out of a life of faithful obedience that is given its full and final form in Jesus. "Beautiful," says the Prophet, are the "feet of him who brings good tidings" (Isa. 52:7 RSV), the feet of the messenger who is proclaiming the gospel of salvation accomplished by the suffering servant.

But it most certainly is not the kind of beauty we are accustomed to: "his appearance was so marred, beyond human semblance . . . no form or comeliness that we should look at him, and no beauty that we should desire him" (52:14 and 53:2 RSV). Beauty in the very person and circumstance where we saw "no beauty." This is a beauty that defies our stereotyped ideas of beauty, but once we take it in and begin living it, it goes far beyond all the travel posters and fashion plates and glamour poses. The Prophet is schooling us in a theological aesthetic that is in contrast to virtually everything in both Babylon and North America.

With all this so plainly before us, why do so many stubbornly refuse any use of the word "beauty" that diverges even slightly from the godblessamerica template? We need this Prophet to feed our imaginations with insight and competence in beauty that is not *prettiness* but the *form* that the fullness of the Godhead takes in bearing the sins of many in the Shekinah as it comes into view in the neighborhood. If we insist on taking instruction in beauty from the designers of machines and the hairdressers in beauty salons, we will never have the slightest idea of what makes the feet of that messenger on the mountains *beautiful*.

*   *   *

The distinctive thing about beauty is that it *reveals*, reveals the depths of what is just beneath the surface, and connects the remote with the present. But "revelation" is a meaningless word to those who think they are in control of all seeing, hearing, touching, smelling, and tasting. "Taste and see that the LORD is good" — is *beautiful* (Ps. 34:8). (The Hebrew word *tob* can be translated as either "good" or "beautiful.") But the sentence is nonsense to anyone who has pre-decided that "Lord" is a nonsense word. Beauty that is salvation is virtually unrecognizable to those who are indifferent to transcendence, to the organic connections between above and below, between far and near. Ugly is the verdict of those who refuse to follow the Way. It is hardly surprising that the Prophet's contemporaries failed to see the lineaments of the Savior in the servant, saw him instead "as one from whom men hide their faces . . . and we esteemed him not." Many of our contemporaries do the same.

Beauty does not impose anything that makes either God or us, God's world or our circumstances, look better or seem better. The beauty is already there: by means of prayer or love or worship (all mysteries) we perceive truth, reality, goodness, salvation — God. Beauty gives form to the coinherence (to use the vocabulary of Charles Williams). It doesn't explain anything. It reveals what is implicit in every detail of creation and salvation, what has been there all along: in a dragonfly, in an accident, in a tornado, in Jerusalem, in Babylon. There it is: *beautiful*. We recognize it as organic to who God is and the way God works — not an intrusion, not a violation. God employs servants in many guises to show us what is going on — artists, pastors, architects, teachers, poets, writers, gardeners, cooks, composers, playwrights, sculptors, mothers and fathers, children, grandchildren — to reveal what is right there before us, the inside and outside, the there and the here so that we can be participants in it. Beauty.

Beauty is the result of the formless taking on form, of God making heaven and earth from the "without form and void." Where we once saw "darkness on the face of the deep" we now see light streaming out of those deeps: a light God called good (*tob* again: beautiful!). It names the gathering of the shards and splinters of broken lives, sin-smashed souls, the patient entering into the mess of chaos and bringing together a new creation that *leaves nothing out*, that "bears the sins of many" and uses them as the stuff of salvation.

Sin is not redeemed by scrubbing it out of existence but by taking it in as a sacrifice that makes "many to be accounted righteous." This is obviously what Jesus did. We, of course, are not Jesus; we cannot do this in and of ourselves. But we can participate in what Jesus does with the sins of the world, the sins in the church, the sins in our family, as he takes and suffers them. We can enter the way of Jesus' cross and become participants in Jesus' reconciliation of the world. Salvation is not escape from what is wrong but a deep, reconciling embrace of all that is wrong.

This is a radical shift from condemning sin and sinners — an ugly business at best. We no longer stand around as amused or disapproving spectators of the sins or troubles of others but become fellow-sufferers and participants in the sacrificial life of Jesus as he takes the sins of our children, the sins of our presidents, the sins of our pastors, the sins of our friends, our sins — names in the newspaper, men and women in the neighborhood.

What I want to insist on is that if we want to keep company with Isaiah 53 we have to radically revise our imaginations and memories in order to take this in: to see sacrifice, offering, weakness, and suffering as essential, not an option, to salvation. This is most difficult to grasp — difficult for the Hebrews in Babylon, difficult for Christians in North America. There is a fathomless mystery at the heart of this: making right by means of another (Another — Jesus!). Aspects of the mystery are refracted through a cluster of words — intercessions, forgiveness, atonement, sacrifice, expiation — all words organic to one another. Salvation: Jesus on the cross, his body and blood in the Eucharist, the bread and wine in me, Christ in me. And all of this going on every day in me and my family, as I visit in the neighborhood, write letters and books, go to work, prepare meals, do the laundry. This is the action — salvation! — at the heart of everything in creation, history, and community. This is what makes a holy world, a holy people, a holy time. There are a few who knowingly and willingly participate. *How beautiful. . . .*

*   *   *

The plain intent of the Prophet's gospel as he forms it in the conjunction of "your God" and "my servant," and then preaches it with such exuberance by the Messenger on the mountains as beautiful, is that there can be no violence or propaganda on the way of the Lord. Life on the way is never violent. Sin is not rejected, it is *borne,* carried in an act of intercession. We enter the world of Isaiah 53 and take our stand with Jesus alongside the sinner, the other, the outsider. We in some impossible-to-define way become surety for others. But no coercion of any kind in practicing the commands or following in the steps of the Master. No invective, no denunciation, no threats. Every raised voice, every curl of a sneering lip, every impatient dismissal is banished from the way.

People on the way need to take this with total seriousness, for we live in a culture saturated with pragmatism. Pragmatism, interpreted in the terms of North American culture, assumes that any means is legitimate if it has a chance of accomplishing a good purpose, whether your purpose is raising kids, saving souls, winning a game, or making a lot of money to give to the poor. The social/political/religious results of violation of this Isaiah 53 and cross-of-Jesus way are appalling: hate escalates into killing, defamation splinters into schism, judgmental criticism hardens into alienation.

If we decide to follow Jesus and live as servants, we cannot do it in the world's way. Not merely must not, *cannot.* The servant is an agent of beauty not by getting rid of the ugly but by following the Servant in discerning, reading, praying salvation into form and fullness right here where we are now.

*   *   *

There is little danger that we will misunderstand what the Prophet is preaching and writing. He is very clear, very detailed, very exact regarding his two primary concerns, your God and my servant. God is the source and servant is the means, but both are inextricably bound together in bringing about salvation. The great danger is not incomprehension but inattention, distraction. And so the Prophet in addition to saying what he has to say, repeatedly calls us to *pay attention* to what he has placed before us so artfully and urgently.

His characteristic word for getting our attention is the exclamation, "Behold!" He used it first in his inaugural sermon, "Behold your God" (Isa. 40:9). The Prophet of the Exile uses the word more frequently than any other Hebrew prophet. The word functions as an interjection, calling attention to what follows: "Attention! Don't miss this! Stop. . . . Look. . . . Listen." There is a lot more to seeing than distinguishing cats from dogs, getting across the street without getting hit by a truck, locating the items on your shopping list while pushing a cart down the aisle in the supermarket, reading the fine print in a contract. There is a lot more to hearing than picking up a telephone, listening to the radio, being soothed into sleep by your mother's lullaby, or sitting through a sermon without going to sleep.

And there is a lot more to "your God" than what you can read in a book. A lot more to "my servant" than the most careful and disciplined exegetical study will give you.

*   *   *

Every sunflower and oak, every dachshund and elephant, every young girl's lithe form and every old man's worn face, has an interior, a depth, a meaning. There is always more, much more than, as we say, meets the eye. There is far more to seeing than a functioning iris and retina. Imagination is required to see all that is involved in what is right before our eyes, to see the surface but also to penetrate beneath the surface. Appearances both conceal and reveal: imagination is our means of discerning one from the other so that we get the whole picture.

Likewise every verb and adverb, every noun and adjective, every interjection and copula, is in living relationship with every other word said and sung by voices past numbering. There is far more to hearing than an eardrum free of wax buildup. *Memory* is required to make sense of even the simplest sentence. Language is vast and intricate and *living*. *Memory* is our means of keeping the complexities of syllables and syntax coherent, of bringing together the voices of the entire membership, of getting the whole story, of hearing the voice across the room but also the voices from across miles and centuries.

Imagination so that we can discern what is beneath the surface and respond appropriately to the life presented to us in this place.

Memory so that we can stay in touch with conversations and sounds previous to and beyond those that are coming into our ears at this moment.

Without imagination and memory we are reduced to surface and immediacy, we live in a cramped prison cell of the five senses and of the immediate moment. But when imagination and memory are healthily active, the prison door springs open and we walk out into a large, multi-dimensioned world that continues to expand exponentially. "Beauty" is the word of witness that we use to identify this world, this world that is both outer and inner, both present and other. When we become aware of and then participate in the coming together, the wholeness, the intricacies of what is implicit always and everywhere, we exclaim, "How beautiful!"

When the Prophet breaks out with his exclamation "How beautiful," we recognize the text with which he began:

> Get you up to a high mountain,
>   O Zion, herald of good tidings;
> lift up your voice with strength,
>   O Jerusalem, herald of good tidings,
>   lift it up, fear not;
> say to the cities of Judah,
>   "Behold, your God!" (Isa. 40:9 RSV)

Now, as he fills out and intensifies the theme of his opening sermon, well on his way now toward the completion of his message, we recognize that we are in familiar territory, for he essentially repeats that earlier text with slight variations:

How beautiful upon the mountains
> are the feet of him who brings good tidings,
who publishes peace, who brings tidings of good,
> who publishes salvation,
> who says to Zion, "Your God reigns." (Isa. 52:7 RSV)

The Prophet's lead-off sermon in chapter 40 features the exclamatory "Behold your God!" (v. 9). This develops into a summarizing exclamation in the final servant song, "How beautiful" (52:7). *Behold* and *How beautiful* reverberate back and forth across those decades of exile. Look at what is going on here, he is saying. Do you see the coherence, the radiancy of all that has been going on among us in our exile? Oh, friends, don't miss this!

The Prophet began his preaching by designating God's message as a gospel, and the one who preached it from a "high mountain" as the "herald of good tidings," the *m'basser* (Isa. 40:9). These gospel messages have been accumulating line by line, page by page. This *m'basser*, this Messenger who "publishes salvation," has shown how deeply implicated we all are, servant and servants, in this great work of salvation. The Prophet obviously intends that all who travel this way, this highway, have, even if anonymous, a highly significant part in what is being proclaimed. Along with the jubilant proclamations, the comfort and hope and salvation, there has been much darkness and death, much deprivation and despair. As the vision expands into the finale, the fourth song (chapter 53) and its sequel (chapters 54–55), all the details — exilic despair, Babylonian god-delusions, God-compassion, holy salvation — come into a holy radiance, a gospel: *how beautiful!*

*   *   *

We sink ourselves into Jesus' metaphor, the way, and discern these complex strands of association, lest we reduce Jesus' metaphor to a cliché or simplify it into a slogan. Abraham and Moses, David and Elijah, Isaiah of Jerusalem and Isaiah of the Exile — the way of faith and word, imperfection and marginality, the holy and the beautiful. Jesus took them all, personalized them all, formed all the elements into a single, coherent, accessible way.

It is not possible to have a Christian gospel apart from Jesus and his predecessors, Jesus and his place, Jesus and his person. The gospel is not an idea or a plan or a vision: it works exclusively in creation and incarnation, in things and in place. And in Jesus, who makes sure that we understand everything that he brought together as local and now, personal and relational — always. Dis-incarnation (exchanging a life for an idea, substituting an abstraction for a metaphor) is the work of the devil.

Years ago I came across these words of Saul Bellow, one of our finest novelists, and copied them out (but failed to note the source) regarding "the gray net of abstraction covering the world in order to simplify and explain it . . . that must be countered . . . by insisting on the particularity of detail and the immediacy of place, giving us access to life firsthand so that we are not 'bossed by ideas.'"

All this and more, far more, is contained in Jesus' words, "I am the Way."

II

OTHER WAYS

. . . we move in a prodigy of reckonings,
sustaining in the toil of a journey
the rarity of our desire.

WENDELL BERRY, "BOONE,"
FROM *Collected Poems*

A few years ago my wife started reading *Winnie the Pooh* to me. She had read it to our children thirty-five years ago, and I had overheard parts of it. But she thought it would be good if I got it whole and firsthand before it was too late.

One evening while she was reading, I was watching the autumn light leak out of the mountain lake that is our front yard and letting the words of the story drift through my consciousness. And then, I was fully awake: the blurred world in which I teach and write on Christian spiritual theology came into crisp focus. I saw the people I was working with in a fresh way.

Jan had just completed chapter 8: the childlike animals had been assembled by Christopher Robin for an adventure — they were off to discover the North Pole. It is a meandering tale in which everyone takes everything with complete seriousness, although no one understands much of what is going on. Each character contributes something essential to the quest. The world is large with meaning and no one is left out. But neither is any one sure what the North Pole is, not even Christopher Robin, who proposed the expedition.

Along the way little Roo falls into a stream and needs rescuing. Everyone pitches in. Pooh picks up a pole and fishes him out. The emergency over, the animals talk it over while Pooh stands there with the pole in his hands. Christopher Robin then says,

> "Pooh . . . where did you find that pole?"
> Pooh looked at the pole in his hands.
> "I just found it," he said. "I thought it ought to be useful. I just picked it up."
> "Pooh," said Christopher Robin solemnly, "the expedition is over. You have found the North Pole!"
> "Oh!" said Pooh.

The animals go on with their desultory, haphazard conversation for a while until Christopher Robin finally gets them back to attending to the North Pole that Pooh had discovered.

They stuck the pole in the ground, and Christopher Robin tied a message onto it,

North Pole
Discovered by Pooh
Pooh Found It.

Then they all went home again. . . .

What I "saw" as I was listening to Jan read was the culture in which I live, peopled with engaging characters out looking for a vaguely defined spirituality (the North Pole). Every once in a while one of them picks up something and someone says, "That's it!" Sure enough, it does look like "it." And someone, usually a spiritual authority (Christopher Robin), hangs a sign on it: "Spirituality." And then everyone goes home again, until the next expedition is proposed.

People are attracted to "spirituality" in increasing numbers in our part of the world. Fresh expeditions for the "North Pole" set out almost daily from most places in the country. (The East Pole and the West Pole are also options.) As I listened to the story that late autumn evening, I recognized many of the characters whom I love and admire so much but am not content to leave as they are: I want to honor every detail of their winsome charm, but I also want to show them both what and where the North Pole is. I want to lead them to Jesus.

The way of Jesus is not the only way to live. There are innumerable other ways. The other ways attract many, many persons — far more than the way of Jesus ever did. The other ways compete with the way of Jesus and often replace the way of Jesus. I want to observe some of the other ways that attracted so many followers in the time of Jesus and contrast them with the way of Jesus. I want to train our eyes and ears to see and hear precisely what is distinctive in the Jesus way so that we can make the daily — hourly! — discernments required to keep us faithfully and obediently in and on the way of Jesus. In our schools and businesses, in our entertainment industry and in our professions — and, yes, our churches — we are immersed in a world of ways and means that either blatantly or subtly erodes or perverts the ways of Jesus, often in the name of Jesus. Sometimes it does this by suggesting seductive detours around the way of Jesus; sometimes by maliciously false signpostings away from the way of the cross into the "broad way that leads to destruction." Directionless and distracted men and women standing around in the company of Christopher Robin and friends, especially Pooh, "a bear of very little brain," are particularly vulnerable to misdirection.

My working assignment in this meaning-hungry, spirit-thirsty, God-curious world is to teach and preach the Holy Scriptures as the revelation of Life, the life defined and created by Jesus. But I don't find it easy. I live in a culture that is largely either indifferent to or ignorant of Jesus. I would like to recover clarity and urgency in the way of Jesus for my generation.

In Part One, The Jesus Way, I began with Jesus and then followed up by using Abraham, Moses, David, Elijah, Isaiah of Jerusalem, and Isaiah of the Exile to show the multilayered and richly textured ways of the men and women whom God used to "prepare the way of the Lord." The preparations were extensive, stretching over nearly two thousand years. When they were complete — in Paul's words, "when the time had fully come" — Jesus became the way, God's way to us and our way to God. ("The way up and the way down is the same way.")

Surprisingly, considering the extensive and patiently elaborate preparation across those two thousand years, not many recognized what was going on. Not many left what they were doing and followed Jesus. Jesus didn't take the world by storm. Spirituality was in the air those days. The marketplace was crowded and noisy. There were options galore. Most people, despite the presence of God incarnate in their midst, the Word made flesh actually walking through their neighborhoods, followed, whether mindlessly or intentionally, other ways.

They still do. As in first century Palestine, so in twenty-first-century North America. We, too, are saturated with well-advertised and well-lighted ways for living. In order to clarify precisely what is unique and urgent in the way of Jesus it is useful to look at some of the other ways that were available then. In the time of Jesus these other ways were developed in ignorance or indifference to Jesus. When looked at closely they don't seem very different from today's other ways.

So: other ways. For a start, the way of Herod.

CHAPTER 8

The Way of Herod

When I was twelve years old my family moved from our small Montana town to Seattle — to me, a very big city. I was thrilled to be in a famous city, a big city. There were skyscrapers and buses and six-lane highways. Very soon I was off on my own each Saturday, exploring the city, very much aware that I was exploring the *big* city. Big and large were defining values in my adolescent imagination. Most Saturdays in that twelfth year of my life I took the bus downtown and basked in borrowed fame. I wandered along the waterfront, absorbing the atmosphere of the big ships. I rubbed shoulders with the people on the streets, intoxicated with the sounds of the four or five languages being spoken all around me — more people on one Saturday in Seattle than lived in the entire state of Montana.

One detail in my Saturday adventures that in retrospect seems significant was my weekly ascent by elevator to the top of the Smith Tower, then the tallest building in Seattle and by far the tallest building I had ever seen. For eighty years (but no longer!) it was the tallest building west of Chicago. Twenty-five cents lifted me to the observation floor at the top and a look over the city and its hills: Whidbey Island, Puget Sound and its ferries, the Olympic Mountains to the west, the Cascades to the east, the great volcanic thrusts of Rainier and Baker, the teeming buzz of cars and people below.

It wasn't the height as such and it wasn't the scenery — Rainier and Baker and the Olympics; it was that I was on the tallest building in the west, the Smith, and in the biggest city in the northwest, Seattle. Somehow I became tall and big and important in that company. I had grown up climbing in the Rocky Mountains and was no stranger to heights — breathtaking vistas of mountain ranges and lakes and rivers spread out before me. I had climbed mountains from which I could see almost to Chicago if I looked hard enough. But I never felt important in those mountains. If anything I felt small, worshipful, embraced by something large, but not large myself.

But on the top of the Smith Tower in Seattle I felt large and important. My adolescent imagination was being trained by Herod. I was immersed in a Herodian world where size and wealth define the human condition. It took me a long time to get over it. I still live in that world but am no longer impressed. In the intervening years, with many lapses along the way, I have become wary of the Herodian world. As I have deliberately cultivated a biblical imagination held together in Jesus, I have been furnished with images that counter Seattle and the Smith Tower, Babel and its tower, Egypt and its pyramids, Babylon and its temple to Marduk. Images of wanting more, of being on top, of exercising power, of becoming important — all of which so easily and frequently become a cover for sin. In the Palestine of Jesus' day, the central figure in this pantheon of bigness and power and importance was Herod. Jesus was the primary, but mostly ignored (as he still is), counter-figure.

Given my adolescent infatuation with the Smith Tower, I know that I would have been impressed with Herod if I had lived in the first century. Herod was the biggest name in Palestine. He was the richest man in the world. He employed more people than anyone in the country. You couldn't walk out of your house without hearing the name Herod. You couldn't walk down any road without coming on one of his massive building operations. Herod, Herod, Herod.

*   *   *

Jesus was born and Herod died in approximately the same year. The contrast between Jesus' life and Herod's death could hardly be more stark: Jesus was born in a shelter for animals in a small village. It was probably a cave with a wide opening, the usual habitat for sheep and goats and cows in that country.

We don't know the exact place of Jesus' birth, only the name of the village, Bethlehem. An old cave was selected seventeen hundred years or so ago, probably by Helena, mother of the Roman Emperor Constantine, and marked out as the place where Mary gave birth to our Savior. A clumsy church has been built over the spot, a church that looks more like a fortress than a sanctuary. The site location is a guess at best, but year after year people by the thousands stream into the place and climb down into the cave. Some of them worship.

Jan and I were there a number of years ago, crowded into the shadowy, cramped quarters under the church that was marked out as Jesus' birthplace. About thirty men were there in a group just ahead of us. They were worshiping, singing robustly in a language we didn't know. But we did recognize some of the tunes — they were obviously singing about and to Jesus. They were so energetic and emotionally present we assumed they were a group of pentecostal preachers.

Later we talked with one of them who had a little English and learned that they were Polish priests on pilgrimage. The priest was guarded and brief in his conversation with us. This was before the iron curtain had fallen and there might be communist informers in the vicinity who would be suspicious of any conversation priests would have with westerners. We experienced that wonderful sense of recognition and delight in discovering a kindred spirit, a living Christian witness, in a stranger. The moment was heightened by the sense of danger and secrecy on his part. I remembered Herod's paranoia surrounding the birth of Jesus and thought that not much had changed in two thousand years.

Not very long after Jesus' birth — a few months maybe, a year or two at most — Herod was buried about three miles southeast of Bethlehem in his massive mountain palace fortification, Herodium.

Jesus' birth was a quiet affair, out-of-the-way, affectionately attended by his parents, a few young shepherds, some visiting religion scholars (the famous magi), and a donkey, a cow, and two sheep, if our Christmas crèches have it right. When we were first married, Jan taught first grade in a nearly all African-American school in Baltimore. One day one of her little girls, Betty Ann Galloway, exclaimed, "Holy Cow!" Jan said, "Betty Ann, cows aren't holy." Betty Ann said, "Well, they kneeled at the manger when Jesus was born." Yes. We add homely details to that obscure birth and birthplace. It penetrates our imaginations and we recreate it in our homes and churches with thousands of personal variations. We love remembering that birth. We continue to embroider it with affectionate details and songs.

But Herod's burial was neither obscure nor quiet. And certainly not affectionate. The place of his burial tomb reached high above the flat desert, a Herod-constructed mountain. There is a modest natural hill nearby, but nothing approaching the size that Herod required; so he had his mountain built higher and higher, moving huge quantities of dirt and rock so that eventually it loomed high on the desert horizon, with his elaborate palace constructed on the pinnacle — a stunning piece of architecture, breathtakingly elegant. Herod didn't intend to disappear into the grave forgotten when he died. This was an in-your-face burial place, designed to keep people aware and impressed with his power and importance and fame forever. And people do continue to come and be impressed, but the numbers are meager compared to those who come to Bethlehem and worship.

From the Mount of Olives, a mile east of Jerusalem, looking south, Herod's burial mountain castle, Herodium, is still prominent on the horizon, while Jesus' birth cave is obscured by the lumpy church building. Nobody ever worships at Herodium.

Herod's burial was a lavish affair, with thousands in the procession. During the last years of his life his proclivities to cruelty accelerated. He became a virtual monster, hated by everyone, massacring at whim. Executions were routine. Twice, when he had to be away on dangerous political business, he arranged with a confidante that if for any reason he failed to return, his favorite wife, Mariamne (he had ten wives), was to be killed — he couldn't stand to think of anyone else having her. He was passionately in love with her, but it was a typically Herodian kind of love, love of a possession, not a person. He returned safely from his trips both times and so the marital murder was never carried out. But later, suspecting infidelity, he went ahead and killed her anyway. He also killed his uncle Joseph, his mother-in-law Alexandra, and three of his sons: Aristobulus, Alexander, and Antipater. The famous quip from Caesar Augustus back in Rome, a close personal friend of Herod's, would have served as an apt epitaph over his grave: "I would rather be Herod's pig than his son."[1]

Herod knew that when he died there would be celebrations all over the country. As the time of his death approached — he was seventy years old and desperately ill — he made plans to ensure widespread lamentation. He ordered the arrest of Jewish elders from a number of villages across Palestine. They were jailed in the Jericho racetrack (the Hippodrome), with instructions to have them killed as soon as he died. That way there would be loud lamentation all over the country at the time of his death. Fortunately his orders were not carried out. There was plenty of pomp and ceremony, but no tears.

That cave in Bethlehem and the palace-fortress of Herodium contrast two ways of getting on in the world that are still with us: the way of Jesus and the way of Herod.

Jesus and Herod

The way of Herod set the standard for the way to get things done in the world into which Jesus was born. At that pivot point in our calendars marked by Jesus' birth and Herod's death, Rome was well established as a world empire, the dominant military and political presence of the age. Herod reproduced that world of power, conspicuous consumption, and display on a smaller scale in Palestine. In reproducing it he was in no way inferior to Rome; in some ways he out-did Rome. Every

---

1. A pun in Greek: *hys* = pig; *huios* = son. See F. Dale Bruner, *The Christbook, Matthew 1–12* (Waco, Tex.: Word, 1987), p. 50.

one of his palace complexes — he built seven of them — was larger than what any of the Caesars had in Rome.

It is impossible, at least for me, not to be impressed with Herod. He ruled Palestine for thirty-four years. Politically he was able to manipulate power-hungry Rome, the many factions of religious Jews, and the swelling numbers of secularizing Hellenist Jews into a semblance of order and prosperity. He was not a religious man, but he turned out to be a relentlessly aggressive propagandist for Greek and Roman culture, using it as a means to political power: art and architecture, literary works and dramatic productions, athletic prowess and performance. His building projects were absolutely stunning — amphitheaters, hippodromes, palaces, shrines, fortifications, aqueducts, forums, roads, new and restored cities, fountains, and, his crowning achievement, the rebuilt Jerusalem temple. Everywhere you go even now in Palestine/Israel you see the evidence of Herod's building projects.

And here is the astonishing thing: Jesus ignored the whole business. Jesus spent his life walking down roads and through towns dominated by Herod's policies, buildings shaped by Herod's power, communities at the mercy of Herod's whims. And he never gave them the time of day.

Our astonishment increases when we realize that, in one ironic sense, Jesus had virtually the same agenda as Herod: Jesus set out to establish a comprehensive way of life that would shape the behavior and capture the imaginations of all the people of the world. Jesus had no intention of working out a private righteousness with a few people, withdrawing from the mainstream of worldly life and creating little enclaves of love in which people could cultivate peace with God through study and prayer and good works. He had his eyes on the world: God so loved *the world*. . . . Go into all *the world*.

Jesus launched his public ministry by saying, "The time is fulfilled, and the kingdom of God has come near" (Mark 1:15). Time's up, we're inaugurating a new government. *Kingdom.* When Jesus uses the word "kingdom," and he uses it repeatedly and prominently, he is speaking in the largest and most comprehensive of terms. Nothing we do or feel or say is excluded from "kingdom." And if this is *God's* kingdom, which it most certainly is, it means that everything that goes on is under God's rule, is penetrated by God's rule, is judged by God's rule, is included in God's rule — every one of my personal thoughts and feelings and actions, yes; but also the stock market in New York, the famine in the Sudan, your first grandchild born last night in Atlanta, the poverty in Calcutta, the suicide bombings in Tel Aviv and New York and Baghdad, the abortions in Dallas, the Wednesday-night prayer meetings in Syracuse, the bank mergers being negotiated in Chicago, Mexican migrants picking avocados in California — everything, absolutely everything, large and small: the kingdom of God in which Jesus is king.

What we need to get a feel for is the sheer *scale* in which Jesus is working, the largest scale imaginable — kingdom. His intention at the very outset was to establish a kingdom on earth, beginning in Palestine, but not confined to Palestine. It still is.

So we cannot help but notice that right before his eyes there was a man who had done what he himself was setting out to do. Herod, working against formidable odds in his thirty-four-year reign, had done the kingdom thing magnificently: his skilled brokering of power, his shrewd acquisition of immense wealth, his use of Greek theater and athletic contests to shape people's thinking and values, his architectural splendor giving everyone a sense that their king was all-powerful and majestic. He had gathered a very diverse population of Jews and Romans, pagans and Greeks, feuding sects and uncongenial political parties, and hammered out a kind of working unity among them.

So why didn't Jesus learn from Herod? Why didn't Jesus take Herod as his mentor in getting on in the world? In the world into which Jesus was born, no one had done this kingdom thing better. It's true that Herod was not interested in God, but everything else was intact. All Jesus had to do was adopt and then adapt Herod's political style, his skills, his tested principles, and put them to work under the rule of God. It's true that Herod had no morals to speak of, but Jesus was perfectly capable of supplying those out of his own deep sense of righteousness. The fact is that in the Palestine where Jesus was born, grew up, and called men and women to follow him in a way of life that he was defining as a kingdom life, Herod was the accomplished master at fashioning a kingdom — thinking big and then working out the concrete details that would bring it into reality and include everyone in it.

But Jesus did not do that. He lived as if Herod had never existed. The only time we know of that he mentioned the name was in connection with Herod's son, Antipas, when he warned his disciples of the "yeast of Herod" (Mark 8:15). Another time, but without even using his name, he brushed him off as a non-entity, "that fox" (Luke 13:31). Jesus ignored the world of power and accomplishment that was brilliantly on display all around him. He chose to work on the margins of society, with unimportant people, giving particular attention to the weak, the disturbed, the powerless.

He chose as his base of operations the small town of Capernaum on the north shore of the Sea of Galilee. It was not exactly out of the way, for a major trade route passed through the vicinity. But it was not important politically. Two other small towns, Chorazin and Bethsaida, along with Capernaum, formed what we now call the "evangelical triangle." These towns served as Jesus' primary places for teaching and preaching, as he called and trained followers to represent and give witness to the kingdom that he was inaugurating.

These three towns — the archaeological excavations show this — were true communities, small enough so that probably everyone knew everyone else. The houses were all joined around a central courtyard; the synagogue was the most prominent building. Extended families lived together, adding rooms as children grew up and married and then had their own children, as many of the Amish do today. Virtually everything took place in a web of intimate personal relationships. Morals, meals, celebrations, marketing, business, politics, worship. Nothing was impersonal. Everyone knew your name.

Two architectural features define these towns: first, the interconnected houses, this maze of built-on, built-together houses (commonly called "insula"); and second, the synagogue. This architecture tells us two things: these people had a lot to do with one another as named persons — neighbors; and they had a lot to do with God. As you went about your life and work, you couldn't avoid people you knew and people who knew you. And you couldn't avoid dealing with God.

Herod's architecture stood in sharp contrast: buildings designed to collect crowds — theaters and amphitheaters, athletic arenas, massive fortifications, and palaces into which masses of people were gathered. And all of them built by hundreds of imported workers. Herod built cities that were primarily secular and impersonal. (The Jerusalem temple was one exception, but the motivation for building it was secular — a religious sop thrown to the Jews to keep them quiet while he went about his secularizing mission.)

The insula and the synagogue together provided the settings in which Jesus formed the membership and trained the citizenry in the ways and means of living and serving in his world-encompassing kingdom of God.

*   *   *

There were two large cities in Galilee at the time: Sepphoris, the capital of Galilee, just three miles north of Jesus' home town of Nazareth, and Tiberias, built on the southwestern shore of the Sea of Galilee, an administrative and commercial center. Both were impressive cities. Sepphoris was an old city. Soon after Herod died there was a rebel revolt. The Roman governor Varus took care of the problem by burning the place to the ground. Herod's son, Antipas, who was contemporary with Jesus, lost no time rebuilding it in the elaborate and extravagant style (it included a theater that seated three thousand) that he apparently acquired through the genes of his father. Some speculate that Jesus, with his father Joseph, may well have been part of the workforce that rebuilt the city.

It is easy to imagine Jesus in his youth and early adult years, walking a road across the compact hill country of lower Galilee from his home in Nazareth through Sepphoris to Cana. Several years later, Herod Antipas built Tiberias from scratch, complete with a royal palace, a stadium, and market. There were also baths that incorporated the natural hot springs of the area. It was a prosperous administrative and commercial center in Jesus' time.

The two cities provided architectural, commercial, and political panache to Galilee. They were centers of influence. For the people of Galilee, Sepphoris and Tiberias were where the action was. Both cities were within sight of the places and roads that we know Jesus frequented. Neither city is mentioned in the stories of Jesus. There is only a passing reference to "boats from Tiberias" carrying people who were looking for Jesus (John 6:23).

What I want to insist upon in this is that Jesus did not work out his way of life in the intensely personal and God-oriented small towns of Capernaum, Chorazin, and Bethsaida simply because he didn't know any better, because that was the only world he knew. No, he *chose* them. He had equal access to Sepphoris and Tiberias and, over on the coast, Caesarea, where the Herod way set the tone for how the people tended to live.

"It is not enough," observes N. T. Wright, "to say one's prayers in private, maintain high personal morality, and then go to work to rebuild the tower of Babel. The substance and structure of the different aspects of our world need to be interrogated in the light of the unique achievement of Jesus."[2]

On the virtual doorstep of the Herodian option, attractively on display and easily accessible in Sepphoris and Tiberius, Jesus said "Follow me." At least some of what that means is, "Do it the way I am doing it. Follow me into a network of souls, a web of personal relationships. And follow me to the place where these people gather to worship God."

The Pharisees

Herod was impressive; Herod was effective; Herod was successful. But Herod was also secular and godless. No matter how good he was at bringing prosperity and peace to their land, there were many Jews who would have nothing to do with him. For these Jews there was no life

2. Quoted by Philip W. Eaton, *SPU Response* (Seattle: Seattle Pacific University Publications, Summer 2005), p. 7.

worth living, no matter how prosperous or secure, that did not honor God. These were the Pharisees.

*   *   *

About three hundred years before Herod died and Jesus was born, the Greeks, led by Alexander the Great, emerged as the new world empire by conquering the Persians. The Persians had treated the Jews benevolently, letting them worship in their own ways. But the Greeks were not content with conquering militarily. They were crusaders for a way of life marked by intelligence and beauty and pleasure. Power was not enough for them, money was not enough for them. They were missionaries for something we might designate humanism. They wanted to convert men and women to a life in which the mind and body were celebrated and developed to their full potential. We send out missionaries to save men and women from their sins through Jesus Christ; they sent out missionaries to civilize men and women through learning and art, drama and athletics. They were aggressive, persistent, passionate, persuasive, and highly successful.

They had most impressive conversion statistics. A hundred years or so after Alexander's Hellenizing blitzkrieg, the Middle Eastern world had become Greek — Greek language, Greek schools, Greek theater, Greek art, Greek games and athletic contests, and Greek gods who required little or nothing of anyone but supplied a magnificent and colorfully textured background to the Greek enterprise, placing the proud person of excellence at the center of the world stage. Greek gods functioned more or less as stage scenery in a drama that explored the human condition.

This mass evangelism campaign was wildly successful virtually everywhere. Many Jews in Palestine took up the new Greek ways with considerable enthusiasm. The pro-Greek party was strong and attracting adherents daily. Many Jewish leaders of influence were pro-Greek.

But the Hellenizing campaign also hit a hard core of resistance in Palestine. A significant number of Jews commonly referred to as "the devout" (*chasidim*) refused to be converted. They understood themselves as a people of the God who had revealed himself, making a covenant with them and giving them commands. As Jews, they had no faith in the human as such. Their faith was in God, a jealous God who fiercely rejected manmade substitutes or alternatives to his revealed justice and love, his mercy and salvation. To put the human in place of God as the Greeks were so zealously doing was outrageously blasphemous to Jews.

Greeks were not used to taking no for an answer. So convinced were they that human civilization, not God's salvation, was the basis for living right and well that they began to put pressure on the Jews. The more the Jews resisted, the more the Greeks pushed.

Meanwhile, the expansionist Romans were threatening the Greek empire. The Romans had taken large parts of what is now western Turkey and cut off valuable natural resources. The Romans were threatening their military power on most fronts. As the Greeks saw their empire crumbling they took to robbing temples (Jerusalem and elsewhere) for money, and imposing Hellenism to try to create political unity. It was no longer a zeal for Greek culture, as such. They were desperate to maintain power.

Finally the Greeks began to use force, enacting legislation to forbid Sabbath-keeping, circumcision, and the temple sacrifices, going so far as to kill those who wouldn't accept the Greek ways, and beefing up the political infrastructure against the Roman threat. If they had to they would impose this wonderful Greek civilization, this transformative Greek program for turning men and women into the best the human being is capable of becoming.

It was this pressure and persecution that catalyzed the merely "devout" into an opposition party: the Pharisees. The Pharisees opposed the foreign Greek-led program of Hellenization but also the fast-growing pro-Greek party among the Jews. "Pharisee" means "the separated one," separated in the sense of being separated from sinful and evil ways, pagan ways, *Greek* ways. They defied Greek pressure to impose a political unity and assimilate them to Greek values and standards. They defied demands to repudiate God's covenant with them, defied all suggestions that keeping God's commandments was a form of moral or spiritual slavery, defied the brainwashing propaganda that more energy given to God meant less energy available for being truly human.

The pressure on Jews to abandon their foolish God-fearing ways and embrace the wise, human-centered Greek ways exploded in a volcanic insurrection of armed revolt that soon spread throughout the land. The forces of dissent were a long time in formation, seething beneath the overlay of Greek-imposed culture, but the Greek king Antiochus IV Epiphanes set off the insurgency volcano. He had been putting pressure on the Jews for thirty years (he came to power in 198 B.C.), but their stubborn recalcitrance finally provoked him to move in with force. He outlawed Sabbath-keeping and circumcision on pain of death. In December of 167 B.C. an altar was built in the Jerusalem temple and a heathen sacrifice offered to Olympian Zeus on it (the "abomination that desolates" referred to in Daniel 11:31 and 12:11).

Antiochus Epiphanes went on to order sacrifices to heathen gods in all the villages. When the king's officer arrived in the village of Modein to enforce compliance, it was the last straw for Mattathias, who was priest there. He refused the order to sacrifice. When another Jew stepped in to offer the sacrifice, Mattathias killed the priest and then the king's officer. In a finishing flourish, he destroyed the altar. He then fled with his five sons into the caves and hiding places in the desert, soon joined by many of the people, devout Jews, their peculiar identity sharpened and energized by the persecution, ready to fight for their freedom to worship their God. He organized them in guerrilla warfare and went all over the country, destroying altars, killing lapsed Jews, circumcising children, and preaching open resistance to Antiochus Epiphanes' decrees.

There were many martyrs. Mattathias died the following spring, but his five sons, with Judas Maccabeus (the "hammer") in the lead, took over. The Maccabean war was on.[3] After a rocky start, Judas and

3. For details on the Maccabean War, see Jonathan Goldstein's translation and commentaries in the Anchor Bible Commentary, volumes 41 and 41A (Garden City, N.Y.: Doubleday, 1976 and 1984). For the entire period from Antiochus Epiphanes to Herod see Emil Schurer, *The History of the Jewish People in the Age of Jesus Christ*, revised and edited by Geza Vermes and Fergus Millar (Edinburgh: T&T Clark, 1973).

his brothers, followed by their descendants, achieved a somewhat precarious but still significant political and religious independence. For the first time since the Babylonian exile (586 B.C.), the Jews were out from under the thumb of a foreign power. They survived until the Roman general Pompey marched into Jerusalem in 63 B.C. That was the end of Jewish independence.

A few years later (it was 37 B.C.) the Romans appointed Herod as king over Judah.

*　　*　　*

The 150 years between Antiochus Epiphanes and Herod the Great were tumultuous to say the least. All through it, though, the Pharisees played a prominent role. The Pharisees preserved and reinforced uncompromised Jewish identity that the Greeks were determined to wipe out against cultural and political forces both within and without. The Pharisees were incredibly courageous and fiercely devout. Pharisees were Jews at their passionate and loyal best. They were a party of the people, a grassroots movement, thousands of ordinary Jews who refused to respond to the Greek evangelistic altar call to turn from an oppressive life under Moses and instead embrace freedom and beauty and intelligence — to be really human for the first time in their history.

Because the Greek pressure was so total and all-encompassing, the Pharisee response was equally total and all-encompassing. It had to be. They couldn't afford to compromise on a single thread of detail, lest that loose thread begin to unravel the rich tapestry of a life committed to a radical, uncompromising, and believing obedience. Rules accumulated to keep the separation intact. Customs developed to keep the identity sharp. By the time the Pharisees come into the story as it is told in our New Testament, two unfortunate things had happened.

One, this accumulation of rules and customs had become a rigid exterior armor among many of the Pharisees. Jewish identity had been preserved, but after a couple hundred years the identity had become more external than internal. They had become religious crustaceans: all their bone structure was on the outside.

And two, the Pharisees had become small-minded, obsessively concerned with all the minute details of personal behavior. They started out doing something necessary: challenging the bullying arrogance of the Greek mind. They had a vision of God and God's law far larger than anything the Greek missionaries could ever imagine. They countered the grandiosity of the Greek vision of civilization with God's throne, "established in the heavens." But by the time Jesus showed up, they had somehow lost the vision of the kingdom of God and had become obsessively concerned with every conceivable item of dress or behavior that went into being a Jew — arguing and defining detail by detail what it meant to be a Jew. They had become obsessive over every detail of identity about themselves: the Jew.

Imagine yourself moving into a house with a huge picture window overlooking a grand view across a wide expanse of water enclosed by a range of snow-capped mountains. You have a ringside seat before wild storms and cloud formations, the entire spectrum of sun-illuminated colors in the rocks and trees and wildflowers and water. You are captivated by the view. Several times a day you interrupt your work and stand before this window to take in the majesty and the beauty, thrilled with the botanical and meteorological fireworks. One afternoon you notice some bird droppings on the window glass, get a bucket of water and a towel, and clean it. A couple of days later a rainstorm leaves the window streaked, and the bucket comes out again. Another day visitors come with a tribe of small dirty-fingered children. The moment they leave you see all the smudge-marks on the glass. They are hardly out the door before you have the bucket out. You are so proud of that window, and it's such a large window. But it's incredible how many different ways foreign objects can attach themselves to that window, obscuring the vision, distracting from the contemplative beauty. Keeping that window clean develops into an obsessive-compulsive neurosis. You accumulate ladders and buckets and squeegees. You construct a scaffolding both inside and out to make it possible to get to all the difficult corners and heights. You have the cleanest window in North America — but it's now been years since you looked through it. You've become a Pharisee.

Because of this slow change from an interior passion to an exterior performance and the shift of attention from the majesty of God to housecleaning for God, the Pharisees at the time of Jesus were not, as a group, very attractive. All the same, they represented the best of Judaism. They at least were in touch with their heritage; they knew they were Jews first and always; they studied their Scriptures and knew them inside and out; and they were proud heirs to this vigorous and fierce preservation of Jewish identity. The gospel story is brightened by the names of three Pharisees: Nicodemus, Joseph of Arimathea, and Gamaliel.

Jesus and the Pharisees

If Jesus had been looking for allies, a group to align himself with in his kingdom work, the Pharisees were the obvious choice. They had the best track record in Palestine. They had historically proven their sincerity and loyalty to the demands and promises of God wonderfully. They were the strongest and most determined party of resistance to the ways of the world, represented in Herod. In the years preceding Jesus' birth, Herod had taken on himself the mantle of Antiochus IV Epiphanes and vigorously held revival meetings all over the country, with Hellenistic altar calls calling for conversions to the Greek gospel of civilization. Think of Herod as the Billy Graham of the Greek gospel, holding mass crusades in his many amphitheaters around Palestine. In retrospect, it is apparent that Herod cared little for Greek culture. His Hellenizing campaign was a front for raw political power. What the Pharisees had stood for against Antiochus they stood for still, two hundred years later, against Herod and all that he represented.

The Pharisees had become a little rigid through the years, true. They needed some reforming, some livening up, yes. But they could very well serve as a solid base to work from.

But Jesus no more took his cue from the intensity of the Pharisees than he did from the grandiosity of Herod. There was much to admire in the Pharisees. Every Jew owed a debt of gratitude to the Pharisees for keeping Jewish identity alive. I don't think we appreciate the Pharisees nearly enough. They need to be honored far more than has been common among Christians. All the same, it is obvious that Jesus did not work out of a Pharisee context. Our sense of the singularity, the originality, the radicalness of Jesus' way is reinforced when we observe that Jesus, besides rejecting the way of Herod, at the same time rejected the way of life that was most deliberately counter to Herod, the way of the Pharisees.

*   *   *

Imagine yourself as a man or woman in the first century who had grown up in the ways and means of Herod. Then you meet Jesus. You have always been intrigued by Jesus from afar. And then one day you hear Jesus say, "Follow me." You take him up on it and start following. What would you notice? I think that the first thing I would have noticed is that I was immediately plunged into a world of relationships — an intricate, shimmering web of real persons and God. I would have left a world of size and numbers, huge and beautiful buildings, famous gods and Roman celebrities and lavish spectacles, noise and violence and crowds, and walked into a far more modest and quieter world of personal names, personal encounters, personal conversations, personal meetings, and a personal God.

Likewise, if I had grown up with my imagination nourished on the heroics of Judas Maccabeus and his brothers (the martyrdoms, the great cause of Jewish freedom), been impressed by the backbone given to the movement by the Pharisees, heard Jesus say "Follow me," taken him up on it and started following, I think the first thing I would have noticed is his use of language. Jesus' characteristic way of talking was in story. Jesus told stories — parables, we call them — and used metaphors.

A story is the use of words that creates involvement and relationship. Stories take the stuff of our everyday lived life and carry us into the actions that constitute our experience: the people we love or hate, the jobs we do well or badly, the way parents and children behave, decisions that we face. If the storyteller is good, we often hear or notice something that is going on right now as we live our lives today, but that we had missed. Now that we see it, we can live into it better — enjoy a plea-sure more deeply, be wary of a danger more vigilantly, grasp an oppor-tunity that we were unaware of, appreciate a person we hadn't thought was worth spending any time with.

Sometimes a storyteller will recast what it means to be a man or a woman to make us see ourselves and the people around us in such a different way that we get a fresh burst of energy to go back to the same old thing but in a brand new way. We had concluded that we were at a boring dead end. But the storyteller reveals love or conflict or values in a way that engages us at an entirely different level. Storytellers imagine alternate ways of living, wake up our imaginations to who we and who our neighbors are in fresh ways. We are stimulated to live more in-tensely, with more awareness.

Pharisees didn't use language that way. They used language to de-fine and defend. They were famous for their rules and regulations. They discussed endlessly the rights and wrongs of various behaviors. They studied Scripture and pored over the meaning of each syllable and punctuation mark, worrying the text like a dog with a bone. They used language *seriously*. And colorlessly. They couldn't waste time tell-ing stories. That would be frivolous. Their Hebrew and biblical back-ground was rich in stories, and in the years to come they would re-cover their stories. But at the time of Jesus they had far more important things to do than tell stories. They had to give people no-nonsense in-structions on what to do, and when, and where.

The contrast in the two ways of using language became about as clear as it can get when one day a man asked Jesus to define "neighbor." Pharisees loved definitions. Jesus answered him with a story, the story of the Samaritan (Luke 10). If Jesus had answered the question along the lines in which it was asked, the two men could have split the hairs of a definition far into the night. But Jesus didn't do that. He told a story. The story pulled the man into *becoming* a living flesh and blood neighbor (or not), not bloodlessly defining the neighbor.

And Jesus used metaphor. He told us that we are salt and light. He told us that he was bread and a door. Much of the time people had no idea what he was talking about. The literal-minded Pharisees had a particularly hard time. Nicodemus was typical: "What do you mean 'born again'? That's impossible. Talk sense, please."

A metaphor is, literally, a lie. It is simply not true. You are not salt. If I sprinkle you on my breakfast eggs their taste is not improved. I am not light. If I walk into a dark room, nothing is illuminated. God is not a rock. Geologists don't examine rocks looking for fossil evidence of God, or write learned papers arguing for the pre-Cambrian revelation of God.

So why do we speak in metaphors? Why was Jesus so fond of metaphors? Why is the Bible so profuse in metaphor? When we first ask these questions, it does seem odd, for metaphors are not precise. A metaphor can almost always be understood in several different ways. If Jesus was interested primarily in precision he certainly would not have gone around saying things such as "I am the vine, you are the branches" (John 15:5) or "Feed my lambs" (John 21:15).

But after some reflection we realize that a metaphor does a couple of remarkable things that are at the heart of both language itself and the gospel. One is that a metaphor requires participation. When Jesus says, "I am the good shepherd" (John 10:14), our imaginations go into action. A picture forms in our mind, associations spring up, the phrase lives. A metaphor is a compressed story, and as the metaphor embeds itself in our consciousness it begins to tell a story that involves us. It is hard to maintain passivity in the presence of metaphor. Metaphor makes it difficult to continue as a bystander, coolly watching the action. Metaphor pulls us into an involved participation in what the writer or speaker of the metaphor is about.

And metaphor involves us in a web of meanings. In this world of God's creation and salvation, everything is connected. The world is not a vast flea market of stuff from the basements and attics and closets of homes and towns all over the world that we sort through to find what might suit us just now at this time of our lives. It is more like a complex and intricate organism — a creation and a covenant in which there is meaning and purpose everywhere we look, in everything we touch, in every sound we hear. Metaphor is a word that actively involves us in that intricate, organic connectedness that is inherent in God's creation and covenant. Everything has something to do with everything else. Pruning vines and branches and feeding lambs is part of the same world in which Jesus is revealing God to us and working out our salvation.

The Pharisees, in their commitment to keep the truth exact and keep separated from the world's ways, used a language that was as impersonal and controlled as possible. Jesus, no less committed to the truth and no less concerned about the dangers of the world, used language that was intensely personal and relational and participatory. He used stories that prod us to realize that we are involved in a plot teeming with characters through whom God is working out our salvation and the salvation of the world; he used metaphors that get us into the action, thinking and praying with all our soul, and mind, and strength in the stuff of family and finance, caring for the earth and protesting injustice, worshiping God and repenting of our sins.

$$*\qquad*\qquad*$$

When Jesus says "Follow me," and we follow, he rescues us from the ways that Herod used to depersonalize people so that he could use them to serve his ambition, reduce them to mere functions. And Jesus rescues us from the Pharisee way that depersonalizes language so that it can be precise and pure in order to define an identity that is separate from the ambiguities of the world's ways, that avoids personal participation with others who may well contaminate us, that achieves truth by using language that avoids personal involvement and separates its users not only from what is wrong in the world but also from the entirety of God's creation and covenant.

Praying on the Way with Mary

Following Jesus necessarily means getting his ways and means into our everyday lives. It is not enough simply to recognize and approve his ways and get started in the right direction. Jesus' ways are meant to be embraced by our imaginations and assimilated into our habits. This takes place only as we *pray* our following of him. It cannot be imposed from without, cannot be copied. It must be shaped from within. This shaping takes place in prayer. The practice of prayer is the primary way that Jesus' way comes to permeate our entire lives so that we walk spontaneously and speak rhythmically in the fluidity and fluency of holiness.

Left to ourselves we are a fragmented and distracted people, jerky and spasmodic. Sin does that to us. The cultural forces of both Herod and the Pharisees in their quite different ways exacerbate the debilitating effects of sin by depersonalizing our values and our language. The more object-like, the more thing-like, the more impersonal we become, the more disengaged we are from our God-created humanity and from the God-created people around us, the more we need prayer. Prayer, as the Spirit prays within us, recovers our original place in creation, making us capable of ambition-free work in the world (Rom. 8:19-26). It involves us in the grand reconciliation going on in Christ setting us free for relational intimacies with family and friends (Col. 1:15-23). When Jesus entered the land of Herod and the Pharisees from that Bethlehem stable, "Everything," in W. H. Auden's penetrating words, "became a You and nothing was an It."[4]

For a start, as we set ourselves to Jesus' way of converting It to You, countering the depersonalizing effects of Herod in the work world and the Pharisees in the personal world, I commend Mary's prayer, a prayer that anchors this re-shaping work of the Spirit deep within us so that we acquire the ways and means of Jesus as we follow Jesus the Way.

When the angel Gabriel announced to Mary that she was to become pregnant and the mother of Jesus in that first-century world where Herod was trying to make everybody a good Greek and the Pharisees were doing their best to make them good Jews, Mary prayed,

> Behold, I am the handmaid of the Lord;
> let it be to me according to your word. (Luke 1:38)

4. W. H. Auden, *For the Time Being* (a Christmas Oratorio), in *Collected Poems*, ed. Edward Mendelson (New York: Random House, 1976), p. 308.

*　　*　　*

I am going to make a huge guess right here: I am guessing that this prayer was not only formative for Mary, but also formative for Jesus. As Mary taught Jesus to pray, she very likely taught him this prayer. The prayer life of Jesus was formed, as the lives of all praying Jews were formed in the first century, by the Psalms — those 150 prayers that gather everything in our lives into a responsive believing and obedience to God. But this prayer that formed Mary in her mother-hood of our Savior was also formative for Jesus as he lived and defined the way. The formative effect of this prayer on Jesus, even as he was in the womb, is confirmed by the nearly identical prayer of Jesus in Gethsemane on the eve of his death: "not my will but yours be done" (Luke 22:42).

I think Jesus prayed the prayer his mother taught him all the days of his life. It was praying this prayer, or something similar to it, that kept him from adopting Herod's ways. It was praying this prayer that prevented him from taking up the Pharisee agenda. I can't think of a better way to get this into ourselves than by praying it ourselves: "Behold, I am the handmaiden of the Lord; let it be to me according to your word."

*　　*　　*

One noun and one verb structure the prayer: the noun identifies Mary, the verb pulls her into God's action.

The noun is servant, or slave — *doulē*. We pray ourselves into our truest, deepest identity. We are servants. Mary has just received her call to the most honored vocation imaginable in the kingdom of God: mother of our Lord, the person who will bring God incarnate into this waiting world. And yet she understands herself as the servant of God, *doulē*. The more exalted we become, the more prominent the position in which we are placed, and the more important we become in the economy of the kingdom of God, the more subservient we become. "Servant" was a prayed identity for Mary. And it was a prayed identity for Jesus. Mother and Son alike prayed themselves into becoming servants.

Day by day, week by week, month by month, as Jesus' identity as God among us was filled out detail by detail, he prayed each detail into the form of a servant. His daily, persistent praying kept every notice and recognition that came his way, every gesture he made, expressive and revelatory of God and God's salvation.

> You know that the rulers of the Gentiles lord it over them, and their great ones are tyrants over them. It will not be so among you; but whoever wishes to be great among you must be your servant, and whoever wishes to be first among you must be your slave; just as the Son of man came not to be served but to serve, and to give his life a ransom for many. (Matt. 20:25-28)

By means of the verb, Mary prays God's action into her life: "let it be to me according to your word." The action is not anything that Mary will do on her own. It is what God will do in Mary. It is that to which she submits. She embraces the action of God.

Jesus obviously also used this verb in his prayers for his entire life. He was God being revealed, speaking truth, inviting disciples, rebuking sin, forgiving sin. Personal speech. Intimate relations. And what we end up with is incarnation — all of God in all of Jesus.

When we pray, we cannot be too careful about our verbs. Are our prayers a means for putting us in charge of kingdom affairs, or making us the person through whom God can reveal himself and bring his will into being in this world? Are our prayers assertive and demanding: "O God, make me like Herod and I'll do great things for you!"? Are our prayers self-serving, separating ourselves from others: "O God, I thank thee that I am not like this tax collector"?

Or are our prayers acts of submission that shape a life of willing obedience in the kingdom of God: "Let it be to me according to your word"?

CHAPTER 9

The Way of Caiaphas

The mere mention of the name Caiaphas triggers an avalanche of associations, all of them negative: religion as privilege, religion as exploitation, religion as a rich man's club — an in-group of wealthy insiders — religion as a commodity, religion as oppression.

Herod enters the story of Jesus at the beginning, at Jesus' birth. Herod tried to kill him but didn't succeed. He massacred many, many babies, but Jesus escaped the massacre. Caiaphas enters the story of Jesus near the end, with Jesus on trial for his life. He was part of a conspiratorial plot to kill Jesus, and the plot succeeded. Jesus was killed.

The two men operated in quite different worlds: Herod was a politician, working out of a world of Roman paganism and raw power; Caiaphas was a priest, working out of a Jewish world of worship and belief in God. Herod was a leader in the secular world; Caiaphas was a leader in the religious world. Both were very good at what they did. Both held the top jobs in their respective realms. And both were against Jesus. Both saw their worlds of influence threatened by Jesus. Killing Jesus was a fixed policy with both of them. If archaeologists ever turn up a document that contains their vision statements — something that I'm told all good leaders formulate — it's a good bet they would be identical, clear and to the point: Kill Jesus.

*   *   *

We don't know much about Caiaphas, virtually nothing compared to the extensive data that we have on Herod. We know nothing about him personally, except that he held a position of prominence in a Jerusalem family of chief priests, and that he was associated with the party of the Sadducees, the rival party of the Pharisees. We know that this Jerusalem priestly family had its power base in the temple. We know that Caiaphas's father-in-law, Annas, had been the high priest ten years previously and that he had successfully kept the position in the family.

The Sadducees were affluent and aristocratic, interested in making it big by associating with the important people in government and culture, in contrast to the rival Pharisees, who were made up of the common people and far more interested in being the best Jews they could be in a world flooded with anti-Jewish values and strategies. By virtue of his family, his position, and the Sadducean world that he inhabited, we know that Caiaphas was aristocratic and privileged — a religious professional who made a more than comfortable living from his profession.

Excavations in Jerusalem in 1971 and 1972 by Israeli archaeologists uncovered a number of luxurious homes from the time of Caiaphas — large, two and three stories, with water installations (cisterns, baths, and pools) and mosaic floors, houses occupied by Jerusalem's wealthiest families. Some of the excavators appear fairly confident that they have found the house of Caiaphas.[1] If they are right, we can't help but be impressed by the lavish style of life in which the high priest indulged himself. Caiaiphas was a priest at the top of his profession, a "high" priest — and he occupied this position at a time in history when the Jerusalem chief priests were slotted into the highest social echelon of that society. Caiaphas was the most prominent and powerful religious leader in Palestine during the years that Jesus was making his way around the country telling people, "Follow me."

---

1. Helen K. Bond, *Caiaphas: Friend of Rome and Judge of Jesus?* (Louisville: Westminster/John Knox, 2004), pp. 157-58.

*   *   *

A priest is a key person in most societies in the world. And here is the reason. The core of our being as men and women is the "image of God." We are created by God for God. We carry the stamp of God in the very fibers of our body and soul. Our relationship with God is the most important thing about us. We have physical needs of food and clothing and housing and healing; we have social needs of family and friends and neighbors; we have security needs for protection and stability; we have emotional needs for love and recognition and comfort; we have intellectual needs to know and understand.

We are complex and multi-faceted creatures. The variations among us are staggering. No one of us is quite like another. We serve one another by mutually helping to meet these needs: farmers and teachers and physicians and soldiers and lawyers and writers and merchants and artists and builders and bankers. But at the center of all these needs and permeating them all is our need for God. Priests are persons who help us deal with this God need. They don't do it for us, any more than a grocer digests our food for us. But they are part of the divine economy.

And we do need help. We don't live very long before we find that we would rather be our own gods. We like to have God in the background, a kind of safety net for the times when we fall off our self-made god-tightrope, but when things are going well and the sun is shining and all our other needs are being met we are not really inclined to deal with God.

As a matter of fact, things don't always go well and the sun doesn't shine every day and our other needs don't always get met to our satisfaction. In the midst of all these dissatisfactions and frustrations, our fundamental *neediness,* we find ourselves looking for help at the center, our core being, our need for God. More than in all other needs, some of us (eventually, most of us) finally realize we don't know what we are doing. We need help. We need a priest. We need someone to tell us what is going on and provide wise direction.

A priest stands in the middle between us and God, between God and us. The priest presents God to us: tells us who God is, the way he acts, the truth that he reveals, and invites us to receive this God, believe in him, obey and trust and worship him. And the priest presents us to God: presents our sin and guilt, our work and our thanksgiving, our failures and pretensions, our sickness and our ignorance, and asks God to receive us, forgive us, guide us, save us. The priest offers God to us, all of God, everything that God is and does — a gift to us. The priest offers us to God, everything that we are and do — a gift to God. There is no coercion either way; the priest clears a vast field of freedom, in which God freely gives and we receive, in which we freely give and God receives. Just as God is most himself in this meeting, we are most ourselves.

The action over which the priest presides, this back-and-forthness, this giving and receiving, this receiving and giving, is worship, and the heart of the action as the exchange takes place is sacrifice.

Here is how it works. A place of worship is prepared. The place is set aside as a meeting place between God and us. Something is constructed to give witness to the presence of the invisible God — a stone, a tent, a temple. An altar is set up to focus attention on the exchange that is to take place.

At this altar men and women bring an offering. It is to be the very best that we have. It can be a goat, a lamb, a dove, cup of flour, or a crust of bread. How much or how little doesn't matter, but it does have to be the best we can offer. As we bring our offering we are saying, "This is the best we have, this is the best we can do; but it isn't good enough, it doesn't satisfy my need to be whole and saved, it hasn't worked. Here it is, God, it's your turn. See what you can make of it."

A vivid scene etched in two lines of Psalm 5 puts this action on display. The psalm pivots on an act of sacrifice:

> O LORD, in the morning thou dost hear my voice,
> in the morning I prepare a sacrifice for thee, and watch.
>
> (Ps. 5:3 RSV)

The psalmist places his offering on the altar: the sacrificial animal or loaf of bread or cup of barley meal. The priest starts a fire under it.

The psalmist watches: "I prepare a sacrifice for thee and watch." What does he see? He watches the offering burn up, the smoke ascend to God and become invisible as it is transformed into forgiveness and grace and blessing and healing and eternal life. When the sacrifice is finally consumed and the transaction is complete, the priest pronounces absolution, benediction, salvation.

This is what priests do; this is what Caiaphas was appointed to do. But sometimes priests, impatient with being servants of God and God's people, insist on taking control of the relationship, managing God's business and our salvation. When that happens we have the scandal of the bad priest. We end up with Caiaphas.

Because of priests like Caiaphas, priests who are self-serving instead of God-serving and other-serving, reformers, both political and religious, begin by getting rid of priests. Professions in religion do seem to be particularly vulnerable to corruption. But in the biblical tradition priesthood as such is not dismissed. It is, rather, completed in Jesus. And the function of priest — being on hand to assist and help, to guide and instruct the community — continues under various terms: bishop, deacon, pastor, minister.

When Martin Luther made the priesthood of all believers one of the foundation stones in his work of reforming the church, he didn't, as many other reformers have tried to do, intend to eliminate priesthood as such. He was democratizing a priesthood that had been debased into a religious bureaucracy. He was designating every one of us to responsibilities of being priests to one another: guiding, praying for, encouraging — but not taking over, not interfering. Stubborn and rampant consumerist individualism — everyone for himself, herself, and the devil take the hindmost — is alien to the Christian life. We need our brothers and sisters; our brothers and sisters need us, and they need us as men and women *of God*. That is the context in which Peter told his congregation that they were a "holy priesthood" (1 Peter 2:5, 9). Jesus is our high priest. Jesus makes the sacrifice that establishes our intimate relationship with God but also in community with relationships with one another. No merely human priest is permitted to interfere with that intimacy (the magisterial Letter to the Hebrews makes that clear). But neither are we permitted to assume that we can go it alone in the way of Jesus.

*   *   *

Page after page after page in our Bibles is given over to training our imaginations in just this kind of meeting. All that altar building in Genesis, the elaborate instructions for constructing the tabernacle and priests' robes in Exodus, the meticulous working out of various sacrifices for various needs in Leviticus, the exactness and detail provided in Kings for building the Solomonic temple, the care given in Chronicles to providing adequate personnel and sufficient preparation for services of worship, the precise refocusing of sacrificial worship on Jesus himself in the four Gospels, the stunning recasting and re-understanding in Hebrews of Jesus as the ultimate priest, and then that glorious finale in the Revelation in which this entire world of sacrificial worship is brought together and reproduced in heaven.

This is what priests do; this is what Caiaphas was appointed to do.

*   *   *

Surprisingly, given the glorious context in which this work takes place and the eternal and holy significance of each detail, priests do not emerge from the pages of Scripture with very good press. Melchizedek is the first priest to be presented in the biblical story, but we know virtually nothing about him — a shadowy figure in the Abraham narrative. But a good shadow, nothing ominous. A mystery, but an inviting mystery.

Aaron is the first priest we see in action, and he bungles the work terribly, making that infamous golden calf and leading the people in the kind of worship that separates them from God instead of bringing them to God.

Old Eli comes into view as a fat old man with about as much sense of God and care for people as a rhinoceros. His two priest sons, Hophni and Phinehas, were drunks with the sexual morals of tomcats.

When Jeremiah was trying his best to speak God's word to his people, it was a Jerusalem high priest, Pashur son of Immer, who made life miserable for him, beating him up and putting him in jail (Jer. 20).

There were also good priests: Samuel and Ahimelech and Abiathar and Zadok. And the high priest Joshua (son of Jehozadak), who teamed up with Zerubbabel to rebuild Israel after the exile (in the book of Zechariah).

Priests are at their best when we don't notice them. The moment we begin to notice, we become wary. When he or she, whether laity or clergy, pretends to do God's work for us, an alarm sounds. There have been thousands upon thousands of good priests whose names we will never know; their anonymity suggests their authenticity. George Herbert's poem "Aaron" is exemplary of sound priesthood. George Herbert, himself a priest, wrote his poem "Aaron" as witness to good priesthood, both biblical and contemporary.[2]

Holines on the Head,
Light and perfections on the Brest,
Harmonious bells below, raising the Dead,
To lead them unto life and rest.
Thus are true Aarons drest.

Profanenes in my Head,
Defects and darkenes in my brest,
A Noise of Passions ringing mee for Dead
Unto a place, where there is no rest,
Poore Preist thus am I drest.

Onely another Head
I have, another hart and brest,
Another Musique, making live not dead,
Without whom I could have no rest,
In him I am well drest.

2. In *Major Poets of the Earlier Seventeenth Century,* ed. Barbara K. Lewalski and Andrew J. Sabol (New York: Odyssey, 1973), p. 363.

Christ is my onely *Head*
My alone onely hart and *Brest*,
My onely Musick, striking mee even *Dead*,
That to the old man I may *Rest*,
And be in him new *Drest*.

So Holy in my *Head*,
Perfect and light in my deare *Brest*,
My Doctrine tun'd by *Christ*, (who is not *Dead*
But lives in mee, while I doe *Rest*)
Come people; *Aaron's Drest*.

But that is not the way Caiaphas was dressed. When Caiaphas appears on the scene at the trial of Jesus, he was anything but anonymous. The priesthood among Aaron's descendants had for at least two hundred and thirty years been getting worse and worse and worse. Caiaphas was no exception.

After the return from exile (around 520 B.C.) the Jews had been under the political rule of first the Persians, then the Greeks, and finally the Romans. In the absence of their own political leader (their last king, Jehoiachin, died in the Babylonian exile), the religious leader — the high priest — became the most prominent and powerful person in the Jewish community. And this is as it should be. The Jews were defined as God's people; their identity was totally wrapped up in God and his covenant and commandments and worship. The Jerusalem temple, presided over by the high priest, was the nerve center for Jews, even though Persian and Greek and Roman kings and governors ran the country.

But then things began going bad in the priesthood. Ambitious and calculating men bartered and bargained and sometimes bought outright the position of high priest from the occupying government. Things went from bad to worse when the high priest Jason's machinations (in 174 B.C.) turned into an auction, the position going to the highest bidder. The high priesthood hit bottom a few years later in the period of the Maccabees.

The Maccabean revolt had established an independent Jewish state once more. It was a brilliant period, truly, with amazing stories of courage and bravery and passion. John Hyrcanus — son of the last of the original Maccabean brothers, Simon, and the grandson of old Mattathias who galvanized his five sons into freedom fighters — ruled brilliantly for thirty years. But he did one thing that was outrageous. He was king of the newly independent state of Israel. Now he also set himself up as high priest. He was not the first Maccabee to do it — his uncle Jonathan and father Simon had set the precedent. But in his thirty-year reign, John Hyrcanus (134-104 B.C.) secularized the office even further. He was a powerful and brilliant political leader, and now that he had hijacked the high priesthood, the office was completely absorbed into politics. He had no interest in a revealing God or a worshiping people. He was a priest who was not a priest.

John Hyrcanus had started out as a Pharisee, that party of the people who were so passionate and intense about preserving their identity as God's people. But when the Pharisees found fault with his secularizing ways, he switched parties and became a Sadducee, the party that traced its identity back to David's high priest, Zadok ("Sadducee" is derived from the name Zadok). He was now a self-appointed high priest. He took over the badly deteriorated priesthood from the priestly party of Sadducees. By the time he was done, he had thoroughly secularized the office. The high priesthood never recovered.

By the time Caiaphas became high priest in A.D. 18, there was little concern for God among the tightly knit Jerusalem Sadducean priesthood. They were wealthy and powerful, thoroughly Hellenized and cozy with the Romans. Their wealth came from the temple: they ran the temple and had a monopoly on the temple sacrifices and the temple taxes. The Romans let them do it because they depended upon them to keep the peace.

Caiaphas must have been better at what he did than most: Herod was appointed king by Rome in 37 B.C. He immediately brought in an undistinguished priest from Babylon, Ananel, to serve as high priest, a priest he could keep in his back pocket. The era of the Maccabean priest-king was over. Herod downgraded the office of high priest to a bureaucratic desk job to eliminate any possible rivalry to his rule.[3] From 37 B.C. (the beginning of Herod's rule) to the destruction of the temple in A.D. 70, there were twenty-eight high priests. Caiaphas held the office for eighteen years (A.D. 18-36). The average tenure of the others was a little over three years.

Leaders survived in those days by getting along well with Rome. Caiaphas, working in partnership with his father-in-law Annas, expertly cultivated the Roman connection. As a result Caiaphas lived pretty high on the hog, making a good living out of religion.

Given the prominence of the way of Caiaphas, Jesus needed to make sure that his own followers did not misunderstand what was involved in following him. Following Jesus is not a path to privilege. It is not a way to get what you want. It is not the inside track to a higher standard of living. In both Judaism and the church there have always been a lot of people who expect everything to turn out wonderfully when they commit themselves to God's ways, worship faithfully, study their Bibles, witness to their friends, and give generously. But it is following Caiaphas that gets you that kind of life, not following Jesus. Jesus makes that explicit when he says, "If any want to become my followers, let them deny themselves and take up their cross . . ." (Matt. 16:24).

Jesus and Caiaphas

When we come across a person like Caiaphas it is easy to be harshly critical of religion as such, but especially institutional religion. Religion as a way of getting ahead in the world. Religion as form and business and show and influence. Religion as a way of helping you to become your own god so that you don't have to deal with the God of Abraham, Isaac, and Jacob, the God and Father of our Lord Jesus Christ.

The widespread interest in what is often termed "spirituality" is in some ways a result of disillusionment and frustration with institutional

3. James C. VanderKam, *From Joshua to Caiaphas: High Priests After the Exile* (Minneapolis: Fortress, 2004), p. 395.

religion. Much of this new spirituality avoids all the trappings of liturgy and finance, fundraising campaigns and buildings, ecclesiastical bureaucracies and councils making hair-splitting decisions on theology, legislating and domesticating the Spirit. This new spirituality sets itself in opposition to all that. It encourages us to explore our higher consciousness, cultivate beauty and awareness, find friends of like mind with whom we can converse and pray and travel. Spirituality is an inward journey to the depths of our souls. Spirituality is dismissive of doctrines and building campaigns and formal worship and theologians.

There is something to be said for this, but not much. It is true that the world of religion is responsible for an enormous amount of cruelty and oppression, war and prejudice and hate, pomp and circumstance. Being religious does not translate across the board into being good or trustworthy. Religion is one of the best covers for sin of almost all kinds. Pride, anger, lust, and greed are vermin that flourish under the floorboards of religion. Those of us who are identified with institutions or vocations in religion can't be too vigilant. The devil does some of his best work behind stained glass.

We live at a time when there is a lot of this anti-institutionalism in the air. "I love Jesus but I hate the church" is a theme that keeps reappearing with variations in many settings.

So it is interesting to note that Jesus, who in abridged form is quite popular with the non-church crowd, was not anti-institutional. Jesus said "Follow me," and then regularly led his followers into the two primary religious institutional structures of his day: the synagogue and the temple. Neither institution was without its inadequacies, faults, and failures. The temple especially was shot through with corruption, venality, injustice, discrimination. Caiaphas and his henchmen had installed vendors in the temple courts, controlled taxation, made huge profits on the sacrificial animals, and presided over the daily prayers and the great festivals.

The temple was immense and beautiful. Herod the Great had constructed it a number of years earlier to impress and court the Jews, and it *was* impressive. This is the building that Jesus' disciples were looking at when they said, "Look, Teacher, what large stones and what large buildings!" (Mark 13:1). This was the center of Jewish life, this massive, architecturally stunning temple, built on the grand scale for which Herod was famous, the Jerusalem temple from which Caiaphas exercised power and acquired his wealth.

Jesus didn't seem to be impressed. He dismissed the comment of his disciples by telling them that this immense temple complex was going to end up a pile of rubble (Mark 13:2). All the same, he didn't boycott the place. He didn't avoid either synagogue or temple. He regularly joined in the prayers in the small-town synagogues scattered around Galilee. He made regular pilgrimages with thousands of his countrymen at the great appointed times of festival worship in the Jerusalem temple: Passover, Pentecost, Tabernacles, Dedication.

Those who followed Jesus, followed him into those buildings, those religious institutions. After his ascension, they continued to frequent both temple (until its destruction in A.D. 70) and synagogue. I don't think we are going to find much support in Jesus for the contemporary preference for the golf course as a place of worship over First Baptist Church. Given the stories that the four Gospel writers have written for us, it doesn't seem likely that, if Jesus showed up today and we were invited to follow him, we would find ourselves taking a Sunday morning stroll out of the city: away from asphalted parking lots, away from church buildings filled with people more interested in gossip than gospel, away from city noise and smells to a quiet meadow and a quiet stream for a morning of meditation among the wildflowers.

We sometimes say, thoughtlessly I think, that the church is not a building. It's people. I'm not so sure. Synagogues and temples, cathedrals, chapels, and storefront meeting halls provide continuity in place and community for Jesus to work his will among his people. A place, a building, collects stories and develops associations that give local depth and breadth and continuity to our experience of following Jesus. We must not try to be more spiritual than Jesus in this business. Following Jesus means following him into sacred buildings that have a lot of sinners in them, some of them very conspicuous sinners. Jesus doesn't seem to mind.

A spirituality that has no institutional structure or support very soon becomes self-indulgent and subjective and one-generational. A wise and learned student of these things, Baron Friedrich von Hügel thought long and hard about this and insisted that institutional religion is absolutely necessary, being an aspect of the incarnational core that is characteristic of the Christian faith.

Using some of von Hügel's imagery, we can construct what for me is a useful analogy. The Christian life is like a tree: beginning underground and invisible in a root system embedded in dirt and millions of microorganisms. Nobody ever sees that depth-dimension of the tree's life, but neither does anyone doubt that it is there. The evidence of its life is in the leaves, immersed in the invisibilities of air and receiving life from above. What connects the roots in that soil that you can't see to the air above that you can't see is a thin, delicate membrane that girdles the trunk of the tree. That membrane is called the cambium, and the flow of life from roots to leaves goes through it. But neither do you see the cambium. It is covered with very visible but thoroughly dead bark. The rough, dead bark protects the hidden, delicate, living cambium. The *life* of the tree (roots, cambium, air) is invisible.

Religious institutions are to the spiritual life what bark is to the cambium. What you see is dead bark but the dead bark protects the life. The more intimate and personal an activity is — sex or meals, for instance — the more likely we are to develop rituals and conventions to protect it from profanation or disease or destruction. The most intimate, personal, and intensely alive of all human activities is the life of the spirit, our worship and prayer and meditation, believing and obeying. But without the protection of ritual and doctrine and authority, Christian spirituality is vulnerable to reduction and desecration. It is also important to note that while the bark both hides and protects the cambium, it does not create it. The bark is dead. And neither do religious institutions create life — the life comes from invisibilities below and above, soil and air, all the operations of the Trinity.[4]

---

4. For a wise elaboration of the necessity and place of the institutional in matters of the spiritual life, see Friedrich von Hügel, *The Mystical Element of Religion*, vol. 1 (London: J. M. Dent and Sons, fourth impression 1961), pp. 50-82.

When Jesus says "Follow me" and we follow, people are going to continue to see us entering our churches and working for our mission organizations. But most of who we are becoming as we follow Jesus — our Spirit-formed life — they won't see. They won't see and we won't see the massive invisibilities in which we are sinking our roots, the endless atmosphere above us, also unseen, from which we receive the light of life, our lives reaching, reaching, reaching to the depths, reaching across the horizon, reaching to the heights.

The Essenes

There was a group of people in Jesus' day who did refuse to enter the Jerusalem temple because it was such a corrupt place, a center of so much godless ambition and pride. They go under the label Essenes.

They comprise one of the more interesting groups in the time of Jesus. We've always known of their existence but not very much of what they believed or did except that they were very radical; they vehemently rejected the Jewish religious establishment of the day (the Caiaphas crowd) and practiced an ascetic life. But in 1947 on the northwest shore of the Dead Sea, a large number of ancient scrolls (the "Dead Sea Scrolls") were discovered. The breakaway sectarian community (the "Qumran community") that copied and wrote the scrolls was excavated. It didn't take long for scholars to make a connection between the Essenes and this Dead Sea community at Qumran. The discoveries threw an international spotlight on these people and brought hundreds of details into the light of day.

The story of the discoveries begins with three Bedouin shepherds going about their work in the shadows of the cave-riddled cliffs above the Dead Sea. One of the shepherds amused himself by throwing rocks up into the mouths of the caves. One of those throws brought the sound of breaking pottery. The next day another of the shepherds, curious about the sound of breakage that he had heard, climbed up and examined the cave. He found ten pottery jars and three scrolls. Later, four more were found, making seven scrolls from that first cave. In the years that have followed, more than eight hundred manuscripts have been found in eleven different caves, the Bedouins proving to be by far the best finders.[5]

The story of the Essenes, especially now that it has been illuminated by the Dead Sea Scrolls and Qumran discoveries, is important to all who follow Jesus today because these people provided one of the most attractive options to first-century Jews who were fed up with institutional religion and who were committed to preparing the way for the Messiah. Variations on this Essene way continue to be attractive to many Christians, so they are worth looking at in some detail.

There were two streams of Essene life. One stream was represented in semi-communal gatherings in towns and villages all over Palestine and as far away as Egypt. Men and women lived together for mutual support and encouragement in protest against the official Jerusalem temple leadership, and practiced baptism as a rite of purification. One estimate is that there were about four thousand of them.[6] Another stream, more radical and focused, flowed into the community at Qumran, the site that has been excavated a few hundred yards from the Dead Sea. There were probably no more than one or two hundred members at any one time. This is the Essene community that we know most about.

*   *   *

The Essenes got their start in the early years of the Maccabean establishment of a Jewish free state (second century B.C.). We don't know the story of how the Essenes came into being in detail, but scholarly detective work, piecing together materials from the Dead Sea Scrolls, provides a possible scenario. As already mentioned, we know that one of the Maccabean brothers, having established an independent state,

5. The story has been told many times, but perhaps most succinctly by James C. VanderKam, *The Dead Sea Scrolls Today* (Grand Rapids: Eerdmans, 1994), pp. 1-24.

6. William Fairweather, *From the Exile to the Advent* (Edinburgh: T&T Clark, 1894), p. 159.

was now king of the newly free nation. But not content with the dramatically achieved political freedom and independence, he also made himself the high priest — a priest-king. We don't know which brother. Most scholars think it was either Jonathan or Simon.

This callous and illicit usurping of the high priesthood by the king may have been the incident that resulted in the formation of the Essenes as a sect. The blasphemous act by the priest-king outraged one of the priests in the temple. The outraged priest is referred to not by name but by title: the Teacher of Righteousness. Neither is the Maccabean king named, but referred to as the Wicked Priest. The priesthood had been in decline for a considerable time already, corrupted into a position of power and privilege, with no concern for God, no concern for people's lives before God, a corruption and desecration that continued into the time of Jesus in the high priesthood of Caiaphas.

The Teacher of Righteousness pulled out of the temple and led a group of followers the forty or so miles to Qumran near the Dead Sea, a place of desolate isolation. There they established their community — a protest and alternative to the corrupt and illegal machinations of the priest-king and the blasphemous goings-on in the temple. They constructed their desert monastery in the pure, uncontaminated air of the wild and lived there under strict rule. No city sounds, no city smells, no city crowds.

They became an alternate world to the Jerusalem world, with its buying and selling, fornication and adultery, ambition and theft, violence and crime, poverty and greed, beggars and whores — all the stuff that a big city inevitably collects. And they became an alternate world to the temple; throwing out the bag and baggage of the sacrificial system that was so prone to corruption, they gave themselves to copying, commenting upon, and studying the Scriptures, preparing for the coming of Messiah. And they got away from the dissolute priest-king, the Wicked Priest, a high priest who was not a priest, presiding over a temple that used religion as a cover for living comfortably and self-indulgently.

The Essenes crafted a simple, focused, morally pure, scripturally exact life that contrasted in almost every way with the world of the Jerusalem temple. The Essenes were a spiritual elite who set themselves up to prepare the conditions propitious for the arrival of Messiah. They were the green berets of the kingdom, the special forces. They were a highly trained, highly disciplined, single-minded community of men who had no sympathy with sloth or sloppiness or sin.

Isaiah 40 gave them their text:

In the wilderness prepare the way of the LORD,
make straight in the desert a highway for our God. (40:3)

The generic word for wilderness in the Hebrew language is *midbar*. But there is another word for wilderness, *'arabah*, that refers specifically to the wilderness area where the Jordan River flows into the Dead Sea and is absorbed in that lifeless salt solution in which nothing lives. This is the word that the Prophet of the Exile used: *'arabah*. Under the leadership of the Teacher of Righteousness, these people went to that exact wilderness (the *'arabah*) to prepare the way of the Lord. Messiah was coming but he wasn't going to come to an unprepared people — a people who were milling around in corrupt and corrupting religion, with its mixture of good and bad, serious and silly, contaminated with unavoidable filth and sin on every street corner. And he certainly wouldn't come to a temple that was led by the Wicked Priest. How could Messiah ever come to a place and people presided over by the Wicked Priest?

So this sect of Essenes packed up, shook the dust off of their feet, left their compromised friends, and emigrated to the desert to make a highway for their God. They embraced an austere, strictly ordered life of prayer and study and moral discipline. They put themselves under a common discipline that kept an eye on every detail of their lives, down to such mundane particulars as not spitting and not interrupting another person in conversation. There was a long period of probation — what monks today call a postulancy or novitiate. They had to prove themselves capable of this rigorous life for a year or two before they were admitted into full membership.

The Qumran community was very likely all male and celibate.

(This was a distinctive feature of the Qumran settlement, for we know that the Essenes who lived in the various camps in Palestine lived with their families.) They were completely self-sufficient, providing their own food and clothing and shelter. They were scrupulously careful about all matters of purity — ritual washing, the Mikvah, was a feature of their daily life. They ate their meals in common. One of their most prominent activities was copying out Scripture and commenting on it. This work resulted in the now famous Dead Sea Scrolls.

They had a strong sense of the end time: Messiah was coming, and their task was to prepare for that coming. One of their documents, the War Scroll, describes in detail the warfare of the Sons of Light against the Sons of Darkness that they believed would inaugurate the messianic age. They maintained a lively interest in current events and identified likely contenders in the end-of-the-world conflict. But they didn't participate in history. They understood their work to be a matter of purifying themselves and making a way for the Messiah to come and put things right. At some point the skies would be full of angels, a cosmic war would break out, and the Messiah would come down, cleanse his temple, and make short work of the Wicked Priest. They became a sect obsessed with predicting exactly what God was going to do and controlling the purity of the community. They were a sect in the classic sense: no mystery and no ambiguity. They were in control.

There are many who think that John the Baptist may very well have been a part of this Qumran community in the desert before he left and embarked on his public prophetic work of preparing for Jesus. Several details suggest it. For instance, John's parents were old when he was conceived and born, so it is possible that they died when he was still a child. We know that it was the practice of this Essene desert community to take in young orphan boys and raise them, training them in the way of the Lord. The text in Luke on John tells us that "The child grew and became strong in spirit, and he was in the wilderness until the day he appeared publicly to Israel" (Luke 1:80). The conjunction of the words "child" and "wilderness" suggests it is certainly possible that John was one of the young boys that the community had taken in.

There are other details. John's words from Isaiah, "Prepare the way of the Lord," was an Essene text. Preparation for the Messiah was the heart of the life of the Essenes; preparation for the Messiah was the focus of John's preaching. John's austere clothing and diet — plain and simple — is reminiscent of the Essene ascetic life. The baptisms that characterized John's prophetic work sound Essenian. The Qumran community had a baptistry prominently placed in their building. The location of John's first public appearance may have been at the Jordan near the Dead Sea, not far from the Qumran site.

None of this, of course, is certain, but it does set John's ministry as the one announcing Messiah Jesus firmly in a context of urgency and serious moral commitment, in contrast to the venal and exploitive religion — "You brood of vipers!" (Matt. 3:7-12) — that had its head-quarters in the temple. Given the context set by the Essenes, when Jesus said "Follow me," we know that there was already in place a well-established group that nurtured messianic expectations with the kind of moral seriousness and spiritual intensity that vigorously opposed the Caiaphas-led religion of the day. And they had proven staying power. They had been at prayer and study for two hundred years or so by the time John and Jesus appeared. John's preaching was widely popular. When Mark tells us that "people from the whole Judean countryside and all the people of Jerusalem" were going down to the Jordan to get baptized (Mark 1:5), we have to imagine quite a crowd.

John's preaching of a baptism of repentance got people's attention. Would some of them have seen a parallel between the cryptic Dead Sea Scrolls' identification of the Wicked Priest from the Maccabean era and their own high priest Caiaphas? It would have been odd if they didn't. It is not difficult for us to see it. Just as Herod mirrored the political atrocities of Antiochus IV Epiphanes, Caiaphas reproduced the religious blasphemies of the Maccabean priest-king.

The popularity of John is strong evidence that he had awakened a hunger among the people of Jesus' day for a way of life that was marked by moral clarity and decisive actions. A lot of people must have been fed up with the sloppiness and self-indulgence of the Caiaphas establishment religion and also the claustrophobic obsessiveness of the Pharisees. They were ready for some fire, a way of life before God that made life large and deep, with purpose, and that had some continuity with the kind of lives lived by Abraham and Moses and David and Jeremiah.

Jesus and the Essenes

But there was also this: Jesus was obviously not an Essene. Jesus frequented the temple and the corrupt, high-priest-dominated temple celebrations. Jesus prophesied judgment on the temple but he didn't boycott it. Jesus was not scrupulous about purity. He associated freely with common prostitutes and the venal, money-grabbing tax-collectors. He touched ritually unclean people like lepers, and when the ritually unclean woman touched him, he commended her faith and healed her.

"Follow me" on Jesus' lips didn't mean going to the desert and joining an exclusive, self-contained sect. Jesus obviously wasn't gathering followers from the moral and spiritual upper-class of society. Jesus wasn't recruiting tried and true, tested and proven fighters, highly disciplined troops for the eschatological warfare that was imminent. He was openly inviting the hurt, the diseased, the rejects — the sick and the sinners.

Any time we interpret Jesus' invitational command "Follow me" as recruitment into a select spiritual company, we totally miss what he was doing. Any time we target our invitations to the people we assume are especially useful to the kingdom — the prominent, the wealthy, men and women with proven leadership abilities and skills that can benefit the kingdom — we are ignoring the way Jesus went about it.

Most of us, at least at times, are mightily tempted by the Essene strategy. We want a church, an organization, that is committed and serious, that has a well-thought-out strategy and a clear goal of where it is going — like the Essenes.

But Jesus was not an Essene. He said "Follow me" and ended up with a lot of losers. And these losers ended up, through no virtue or talent of their own, becoming saints. Jesus wasn't after the best but the worst. He came to seek and to save the lost.

*　　*　　*

As we pay attention to the way of Jesus in detail, it is necessary to be aware of the context in which he worked, to see the alternatives that people were pursuing all around him. The way of Jesus certainly doesn't mean pursuing a relation with God consisting in a comfortable life, as Caiaphas did. But neither does it mean entering an ascetic regimen, isolated from the wider community, self-defined as the special vanguard on the front lines of what God is doing in this world.[7]

When we follow Jesus, it means that we don't know exactly what it means, at least in detail. We follow him, letting him pick the roads, set the timetables, tell us what we need to know but only when we need to know it. Caiaphas knew exactly what he wanted and where he was going, and he had a pretty good idea of how to get there. He was a master at getting what he wanted in religion. The Essenes knew exactly what was required to bring in the Messiah. They had their timetables worked out and an agenda of what needed to be done to be the supporting cast.

When Jesus says "Follow me" and we follow, we don't know where we will go next or what we will do next. That is why we follow the one who does know.

Praying on the Way with Thomas

We have a prayer wonderfully suited for cultivating this posture of open trust, for developing within ourselves this not-knowing that is such an important precondition for being led into a world that we don't know. It is Thomas's prayer, prayed when the resurrected Jesus appeared to him, a succinct five-word prayer: "My Lord and my God!"

---

7. I distinguish sectarian communities, like the Essenes, from the many contemplative and intentional communities that understand themselves as organic to the larger church, offering themselves in prayerful intercession and renewal on behalf of their brothers and sisters at large.

(John 20:28). A basic prayer in all matters dealing with the ways and means of following Jesus.

Karl Barth observed that this prayer was prayed at "one of the peaks of the New Testament message."[8] The prayer is a surprised exclamation that Jesus, so recently dead and buried, is alive and present to him. Thomas didn't expect this. He had no idea that anything like this was involved in following Jesus. He thought that following Jesus was over and done with. He was now left to do life on his own. When the other disciples gave their witness that Jesus was alive again after his brutal crucifixion, he had refused to accept it. He had been one of those people who had followed Jesus to Jerusalem, he had denied himself, he had taken up the way of the cross as he had been commanded to do. But then he dropped out. He had seen with his own eyes that following Jesus was a dead end. He saw the nails go into Jesus' hands and fasten him to the cross. He saw that spear rip open Jesus' side and the blood pour out. He concluded that it was all over. This was the end of the road. No more following Jesus.

When Jesus appeared to his disciples on the evening of the resurrection, Thomas wasn't there. Why wasn't he there? He wasn't there because he wasn't following Jesus. The other disciples weren't showing up all that well either. They were scared to death of Caiaphas's henchmen and had bolted the doors. But they were disciples. They were followers and so they were there. But Thomas wasn't there. He had wanted to see where following Jesus would lead, and with his own eyes he had seen that it didn't lead anywhere. He wanted evidence. He wanted his hands on the controls. And he had all the evidence that he needed. There was nothing to it.

If there was anything more to it, Thomas would require a map, a map for following Jesus — to see with his own eyes the holes where the nails had been and touch those holes, to put his hand in the spear-opened side, to have the crucifixion-become-resurrection all laid out before him.

8. Karl Barth, *Church Dogmatics*, trans. G. T. Thomson (Edinburgh: T&T Clark, 1936), vol. 1, pt. 1, p. 365.

Thomas at that moment was a prime candidate for membership in the flourishing Qumran community down by the Dead Sea, a religious group that had the Scriptures all figured out. This was a community that knew where it was going and exactly what it had to do to get there.

A week later, the disciples were together again. This time Thomas was with them. He hadn't gone to Qumran. And then Jesus was among them again. Thomas was all eyes. Jesus was gracious to him, and offered the "evidence" of the holes in his hand and the gash in his side. And then the prayer burst from Thomas: "My Lord and my God!"

Thomas's prayer keeps us ready for what comes next; it keeps us alert to the Jesus who rules our life as Lord and commands our worship as God when we are least expecting it. Following Jesus is not a skill we acquire so that we can be useful to the kingdom (the Essene way). Following Jesus is not a privilege we are let into so that the kingdom can be useful to us (the Caiaphas way). It is obedience ("my Lord!"). And it is worship ("my God!").

No matter how much we know, we don't know enough to know what Jesus is going to do next. And no matter how familiar we are with the traditions and customs and privileges that go with being on God's side, we aren't familiar enough to know how Jesus fits into it.

No religious skills that any of us acquire will ever produce resurrection, and no spiritual strategies that we work out will ever produce resurrection. Following Jesus doesn't get us where we want to go. It gets us to where Jesus goes, where we meet him in resurrection surprise: "My Lord and my God!"

CHAPTER 10

The Way of Josephus

As we get out of bed each morning and set out afresh to follow Jesus, we need constant re-immersion into the ways of the Way — how Jesus did it and continues to do it as the Holy Spirit forms Christ in us. Jesus' way, as it turns out, is absolutely unique. That uniqueness gets more sharply etched as we set Jesus alongside the prevailing other ways that Jesus countered so decisively by the radically unique way he lived his life: Herod and the Pharisees, Caiaphas and the Essenes, and now Josephus and the Zealots. These other ways are widely praised and practiced still, two thousand years later. We frequently find ourselves at crossroads that are in sharp contrast to the profoundly distinctive way of Jesus. We have to make decisions.

*   *   *

There is much to be impressed with in Josephus but virtually nothing to admire. The man is emphatically impressive but, once we have the whole story, despicable. Josephus enters the Christian story seven years after the resurrection of Jesus. His name doesn't occur in the Bible, and so he is not as familiar to us as his well-known predecessors, Herod and Caiaphas, who occupied key positions marked by Jesus' birth and death. But he was vigorously active in the world in which Jesus' followers were being formed into a resurrection community.

Josephus grew up in a world in which Peter was the church's lead preacher and pastor and Paul was traveling all over the Mediterranean basin starting churches. He was active in diplomatic and military affairs in Jewish/Roman Palestine at the same time that Paul was writing letters of counsel and encouragement to congregations who were learning how to live in the kingdom of God. He was writing hugely verbose books of history at the same time that the Gospels, slim and austere in comparison, were being circulated among Christians under the names of the canonical evangelists Matthew, Mark, Luke, and John. While the church was struggling for survival, Josephus came into his own and occupied prominent and assured positions. The first half of his life was lived in Palestine among the Jews, the second half of his life in Rome among the Romans.

*   *   *

Josephus was born about seven years after Jesus rose from the grave and ascended into heaven. The church was in its early years of formation. We have the story of the fledgling resurrection community in the Acts of the Apostles. The name Josephus does not appear in that book. The name of Jesus occurs only once, and that almost as an aside, in the books that Josephus wrote.

We wouldn't expect Luke to have mentioned Josephus, for even though he was a contemporary his name had not yet hit the headlines in the days that Luke was writing.[1] But that Josephus only mentions Jesus in passing is odd, for he was obsessively meticulous in writing down everything that was going on in first-century Palestine, especially if it had to do with religion. Josephus and the people of the Chris-

---

1. I am assuming that Luke-Acts was written previous to the fall of Jerusalem in A.D. 70. Joseph Fitzmyer argues for a later date, somewhere around A.D. 80-85. If that is so, the absence of Josephus in the Acts strikes us as strange. See Joseph Fitzmyer, S.J., *The Gospel according to Luke I–IX* (Garden City, N.Y.: Doubleday, 1979), p. 57.

tian church were contemporaries, growing up side by side in the same neighborhood. The church had a seven-year head start on Josephus — he was born in A.D. 37 — but that's not much.

Josephus was a very religious person in his growing-up years. In his late teens (from age sixteen to nineteen) he studied and more or less tried out the options before him — Pharisees, Sadducees, and Essenes — and went to the desert for three years to study with a hermit named Bannus. For a young man eager to explore the religious options available to him, it is curious that Josephus doesn't mention Christians as one of the groups he personally sampled. After experimenting with all these groups, he opted to be a Pharisee. There is no evidence that he took any interest in this exciting, joyful Christian movement that after an agonizingly slow start would turn the world upside down (Acts 17:6) and only the barest hint that he so much as noticed that the church was even there. It was not a factor in his life.

Later, when he started writing books, he mentions three names that show he knew something of the movement, for he refers briefly to John the Baptist, Jesus, and James the Righteous. There is debate among Josephus scholars on the authenticity of the reference to Jesus. Some are sure it is a forgery inserted by a Christian copyist, others just as sure that it came from Josephus' hand.[2] Either way, there is no evidence that he took the Christian community seriously. If he did notice it, he brushed it off.

*   *   *

Revolution was in the air in those days. Armed revolution. The Jews were getting pretty fed up with oppressive Roman rule, which was becoming more oppressive by the year. The country was now crawling with all kinds of sects and groups that wanted to get rid of Rome by force. Roman officials and Sadducean priests cozy with the Romans

2. For summaries of the various arguments, see G. A. Williamson, *The World of Josephus* (Boston: Little, Brown, and Co., 1964), pp. 308-10; and Mireille Hadas-Lebel, *Flavius Josephus*, trans. Richard Miller (New York: Macmillan, 1993), pp. 224-29.

were frequent targets. On a crowded street in a spaghetti of shoulders and elbows, a dagger could easily be slipped between your ribs and no one would know who did it.

"Zealot" was the more or less generic name for these sectarian groups, although strictly speaking "Zealot" referred to a single party. But we commonly use the term now in an inclusive sense — anyone and everyone who wanted to get rid of Rome and was ready to use violence to do it. There were variations on the theme — but the way the theme was played out always involved violence: get rid of the Romans and Roman sympathizers. Jesus had at least one of them in his band of twelve, Simon the Zealot. There is some conjecture that Judas Iscariot (*ish-sicarii,* "a man of the Sicarii" [*sica* = dagger; the Sicarii assassinated with a concealed dagger] or "daggerman")[3] might have had ties to the Sicarii, one of the many revolutionary zealot groups.

The Jerusalem Talmud mentions no fewer than twenty-four sects who were committed to armed revolt against Rome.[4] They had hideouts in the hills with stashes of swords and spears and daggers. They talked and conspired, worked behind the scenes secretly, anonymously. Occasionally, a leader would emerge into the open and stage a revolt against Rome. But Rome was always too much for them. The revolts were quickly squashed. During Jesus' lifetime, the Zealots had a stronghold at Gamala, only ten miles from the village of Capernaum, which was home base for Jesus as he taught, preached, and gathered recruits for the kingdom of God.

When Jesus went public with his ministry, it was understandable that many people would confuse him with the Zealots — he was, after all, from Galilee, a Zealot stronghold, and he was proclaiming the overthrow of this world and the inauguration of a new kingdom. He accepted messianic epithets used by Zealots. He sure *sounded* like he could be a Zealot. But it didn't take long for those who followed him to

3. This and other possible interpretations are provided by Fitzmyer, *The Gospel According to Luke,* p. 620.

4. David Noel Freedman, ed., *The Anchor Bible Dictionary* (New York: Doubleday, 1992), vol. 3, p. 984.

realize that whatever else this might be, it was not zealotry. Jesus blessed the poor in spirit, commanded love for enemies, approved paying taxes to Caesar, collected all kinds of people around him who would be of absolutely no use in a war. There were women and children, the weak and the infirm — in Paul's assessment, not many wise, not many powerful, not many of noble birth (1 Cor. 1:26).

But when Jesus rode down the Mount of Olives into Jerusalem on Passover week, it looked as if it might happen after all. All those people yelling and singing and shouting "Blessed is he who comes in the name of the Lord!"

For the Roman garrison stationed at the Antonia Fortress in Jerusalem it probably didn't seem like much of a threat: a lot of women and children, palm branches instead of swords, an atmosphere of frolic, Jesus riding not a prancing horse but a plodding donkey. That doesn't mean the Romans weren't ready. They were used to dealing with Zealots, and Passover Week provided a popular stage for anti-Roman riots. During Jesus' lifetime, the Roman garrisons had put down outbreaks much worse than this and crucified hundreds and hundreds of Zealots. They were ready, but I can't believe they were very worried.

The final and convincing proof that Jesus was not a Zealot was that after his crucifixion there was no revolt, no violence. No looting. No killing. Nothing.

*   *   *

Josephus got an early start in making his way in the first-century, post-resurrection world in which the church was being formed. He was bright and talented. After his self-schooling in the various streams of Judaism in his late teens and early twenties, he acquired a reputation for precocity among the Jewish leadership in Jerusalem. When some Jewish priests were arrested by the Roman procurator Felix and shipped off to Rome in chains, Josephus was picked to go to Rome on a diplomatic mission to negotiate their release. He was just over twenty-six years old. To be noticed and selected for such a delicate and important mission at such a young age suggests that there must have been something decidedly charismatic about him. The mission was a success. He negotiated the release of the priests. His abilities were confirmed. It turned out that it was not only his fellow Jews in Palestine who were impressed by him, for one of the elements in his diplomatic success was that he was able to make friends with and enlist the help of Nero's mistress, Poppaea Sabina.

This diplomatic coup took place in the year A.D. 64. During the time Josephus was in Rome negotiating the release of Jewish priests, cultivating the influence of Poppaea Sabina and others, St. Paul may well have been in prison in the same city, a prisoner of Nero, who was soon to kill him. It is a fascinating conjunction of two very famous and very different Jews — Josephus, the rising star in Judaism, and Paul, the vigorous missionary in the newly forming Christian church; Josephus, on familiar terms with Nero's court and getting Jewish priests out of prison, and Paul, in Nero's prison and soon to be killed (or maybe just recently killed — the chronology is not exact; Paul was probably executed between A.D. 63 and 64).

And then Josephus, his diplomatic mission completed, was back in Palestine, and Paul, his missionary travels over, dead and buried. Meanwhile, things were heating up in Palestine — increasing outbreaks of Zealot violence against Rome, and Rome responding with a major offensive. Young Josephus, twenty-nine years old now, fresh from his diplomatic victory in Rome, was appointed by the Jewish Council as the Governor-General of Galilee to deal with the revolutionary unrest and the military threat from Rome.

Galilee was crawling with Zealots and Zealot-like groups, challenging the presence of Roman forces, goading and provoking them. Josephus' assignment was to pacify, if possible, the region to avoid a major Roman military confrontation, but also to organize an army if hostilities broke out. He managed to raise an army of 100,000 young men. Galilee was the front line of defense against the Roman forces that were coming from the north. Josephus had his hands full. He was finally unsuccessful in quieting the several insurgent forces that roamed Galilee, and with the arrival of Vespasian, the famous Roman general, serious war broke out. Vespasian's goal was Jerusalem. He was going to settle the Jewish question once and for all. But first he had to get through Galilee.

Josephus and his upstart army were seriously outclassed by Vespasian's veterans. It was ragged order against serried ranks. Even though inexperienced (as far as we know) in war, Josephus had a natural aptitude for cunning and strategy and intrigue as he countered the superior forces of the accomplished General Vespasian. The name Josephus was on everyone's lips (not always approvingly). But he finally met his match at Jotapata, a supposedly impregnable walled city in the hills of Galilee only a few miles from Nazareth. General Vespasian set siege to the small, walled city, and even though Josephus ingeniously and masterfully kept him off for a considerable time, after forty-seven days of battering, the Romans finally penetrated the walls. Forty thousand Galileans were killed and the city and its fortifications burned to the ground. The date was July, A.D. 67.

And then Josephus did something that turned him from hero to villain in a single day. Thirty-seven years after Judas betrayed his leader Jesus to the Jewish leadership in Jerusalem, Josephus betrayed his Jewish nation to Rome. He entered Jotapata with a reputation as perhaps the brightest and best young Jew in Palestine; he left the town as its most infamous traitor. He occupies a place in Jewish history equivalent to Judas Iscariot in the Christian story, and Benedict Arnold in American history. Here is how it happened.

As Vespasian broke through the walls of Jotapata, Josephus jumped into a pit to escape and then found that it was connected by a tunnel to a cave. When he entered the cave he found forty upper-class citizens of the town ahead of him, well-provisioned with food and water. Meanwhile, Vespasian was ransacking the city, searching among the corpses, looking for the famous, brilliant, charismatic Josephus. Josephus was not found for three days, but on the third day a woman was captured and told where Josephus and his companions were hiding.

Vespasian sent emissaries, promising safe passage if they would come out. Josephus was a star, and Vespasian wanted to be able to exhibit him as a war trophy. Josephus was ready to strike a bargain with the emissaries, but the forty others in the cave wouldn't hear of it —

that would be a disgrace, total dishonor. They insisted on suicide. Josephus made an eloquent speech against suicide. They were not convinced, and came at him brandishing their swords, ready to kill him, disgusted that he would choose life over honor, choose to buckle under to pagan Rome rather than die as a free Jew, loyal to the law of Moses. Josephus, always quick with words, offered a compromise. Suicide was wrong. But death in battle was honorable. So they would draw lots and kill each other in turn; the last one would kill himself. That satisfied them: forty murders but only one suicide. They drew lots, and went at it; one after another, each in turn offering his neck to the sword of the next in line. When thirty-nine had been killed, it was the fortieth man's turn to give his life to the cause. Josephus by some stratagem had manipulated the lots so that he got the last one. It was up to Josephus to complete the cycle: he would kill the fortieth man and then kill himself. The two men agreed that there had been enough killing. They left the cave and gave themselves up to the Romans.

Vespasian spared his life and made him a prisoner. And then Josephus outdid himself. He requested a private meeting with Vespasian and Titus (Titus was Vespasian's son). When he had them to himself, he slipped into the role of a holy prophet and proceeded to prophesy that Vespasian would soon be Caesar and Emperor of Rome: "You suppose, sir, that in capturing me you have merely secured a prisoner, but I come as a messenger of the greatness that awaits you ... sent by God himself. . . . You, Vespasian, are Caesar and Emperor, you and your son here."[5] Vespasian, initially skeptical, gradually became convinced. The predictions began to go to his head. He kept Josephus prisoner for two years, probably in Caesarea, where Paul had previously been imprisoned, likewise for two years (probably A.D. 58-60). But he was treated well. When Vespasian's campaign in Jerusalem became mired in the maniacal and suicidal zealotry of the defenders of temple and city, he released Josephus from prison, brought him to Jerusalem,

5. Josephus, *The Jewish War*, trans. G. A. Williamson (Baltimore: Penguin, 1959), p. 203.

and enlisted him to plead with his fellow Jews: submit to Rome; save your lives; save the holy temple.

Repeatedly Josephus addressed the Jewish forces: "Rome only wants what is best for you; save what is left to be saved." His biographer, Geoffrey Williamson, sets the scene: "Time and time again he had ridden round beleaguered Jerusalem in dangerous proximity to the walls, explaining to the deluded defenders the hopelessness of further resistance, and pleading with them while the tears ran down his face to yield to the merciful Roman whose one desire was to end the agony."[6] The Jews treated him with contempt. The man who had so recently been their champion was now treated with invective and curses. While he was giving one of his impassioned speeches, someone threw a stone, hitting him in the head and knocking him out. They thought he was killed, but he recovered and was soon at it again, Vespasian's mouthpiece, every speech reinforcing his identity among his countrymen as the cowardly betrayer of the Jews.

Complete destruction followed. The city and temple were leveled to the ground as Jesus, forty years earlier, had said they would be: "Not one stone will be left here upon another; all will be thrown down" (Mark 13:2).

*   *   *

Vespasian became so fond of Josephus that he adopted him, giving him a Roman name, Flavius Josephus (his birth name was Joseph ben Mattathias). After the completion of the Jewish War and the destruction of temple and city, he went on to live in Rome. He was thirty-five years old. He divorced his third wife and mother of his children and married his fourth, an aristocratic and wealthy woman from Crete. (His first wife had been killed at Jotapata; his second wife had left him.) He became an honorary citizen of the Empire and lived the rest of his life on a comfortable pension in an imperial palace in Rome. He was the personal friend and confidant of three emperors running —

6. Williamson, *The World of Josephus*, p. 285.

Vespasian, Titus, Domitian — and outlived them all. He died in about A.D. 100 at the age of sixty-three.

The Jewish War marked the midpoint of his life. For his final thirty years in Rome he was a writer. He wrote extraordinary books. His first was a history of the war in which he had played such an important part (*The Jewish War*), and his most famous was an expansive re-writing of Jewish history (*Antiquities of the Jews*).[7] But all through his writings there was an underlying message — Jews needed to give up being so Jewish: "The future of the world is with Rome; don't be so stuffy and bullheaded; get with the program, be a real Jew, be a Roman Jew." He became, in short, a propagandist for Rome.

Josephus was a Jew when it was opportune to be a Jew. Josephus was a Roman when it was opportune to be a Roman. Josephus was the consummate opportunist. But it was always Josephus first and foremost. Josephus, Josephus, Josephus.

Jesus and Josephus

All through these years the church was in formation. The Holy Spirit descended on 120 men and women on the day of Pentecost and the Christian church was on its way, following the resurrected Jesus. These people realized that Jesus was alive, more alive than ever, alive in them, and they set out to follow him. Luke, an early convert to the resurrection community, wrote the story that Josephus could have written if he had been looking in the right place, listening to the right people. But he was not in the right place and he was not listening to the right people. Josephus was exploiting his natural charisma, using his talent and charms to get the most out of whatever situation he found himself in. Josephus was a celebrity, most himself when he was on stage with the spotlight on him. He had no morals, no scruples, no principles, no

---

7. There were two more books: *A Life*, an apologetic defense of his conduct in the Jewish War, countering accusations that he had betrayed the Jews; and *Against Apion*, a counterblast to anti-Semitic invective.

character. "Deny yourself" was not in his vocabulary. He was one hundred percent for Josephus.

We know that the first century in Palestine was dog-eat-dog — guerrilla warfare, random assassinations, military and paramilitary groups, conspiracies. Violence permeated the society. The only reason there was any order at all was because of the massive Roman military presence. Always under the surface there was this seething ferment of violent revolt.

It is important to have a sense of this as we put ourselves in the company of the early church as they followed Jesus. They experienced some of this violence from the outset. The crucifixion of Jesus set the conditions in which the church was formed. The newly formed church was first mocked, and then its leaders were arrested and put in prison. Peter and John were brought before Caiaphas for questioning, the same Caiaphas who had so recently arranged for the crucifixion of Jesus. Caiaphas this time was flanked by his father-in-law, Annas, and his sons John and Alexander — the formidable and infamous high-priestly family (Acts 4:1-12). Peter and John were supposed to be impressed — and intimidated.

But they weren't impressed, so they were soon back in prison again, this time to be let out by an angel and in the process picking up the support of the eminent Jewish teacher Rabbi Gamaliel (Acts 5:17-42).

Not long after this, Stephen was killed (Acts 7), the first of many Christian martyrs. He preached Jesus' death and resurrection by embracing a death that would be succeeded by resurrection. Christians were being hunted down right and left.

Paul, in his pre-Christian days, was in the front ranks of the Jesus-opposition, a leader in the violence, on the rampage against Christians, throwing them in prison left and right (Acts 9).

And then the name Herod surfaces again. This time it is Herod's grandson, Herod Agrippa I. This Herod turned out to be as murderous as his long-dead grandpa. He killed James, the Zebedee brother of John, and seeing that it made a hit with the Jews, went after Peter and put him in prison. An angel got Peter out the same night (Acts 12:1-11).

Herod Agrippa II — a good friend of Josephus, as it turns out —

continued the tradition. The revolutionary violence accelerated: violence against the Romans, violence against the Sadducees, and now violence against the Christians — and the Romans responded with violence on all fronts. A culture of violence.

But here is the remarkable thing: the Jesus movement did not participate in the violence. There is not a single instance of violence in those years by anyone in the company of Jesus' followers. The closest thing was in Gethsemane on the night of Jesus' arrest when Peter pulled his sword and cut off the ear of the high priest's slave, Malchus. Jesus told him to quit it, and then healed the man's ear (Luke 22:51). And that was the end of that.

The reason this is so remarkable is that most of the revolutionary violence going on in Palestine in those years, at least from the Jewish side, was fueled by religion — a concern for the freedom of God's people, a zealous resistance to the corrupting pagan presence of Rome, a furious and adamant "No!" to the contaminating secularism of Hellenism, a conviction that God and no other was Lord. The Jews served a jealous God and they were jealous on his behalf. They were part of a long tradition of Holy Wars: Abraham freeing Lot, Moses leading the Exodus out of Egypt, Joshua conquering Canaan, David killing Philistines, the Maccabees in guerrilla warfare against the Greek Seleucids, and now out-of-control zealotry sweeping through the Roman-occupied countryside — an epidemic of violence. This was the milieu in which the fragile, embryonic resurrection community was being formed.

This was all *religious* fighting, fighting on God's behalf against the Romans and the false gods and the loose morals invading their country, fighting to uphold the purity of their law and the sanctity of the Sabbath and the freedom to worship.

As it turned out, Josephus was a master at using the war motif to further his own ambitions. Growing up in a culture of war was a sheer gift to Josephus. War and violence are powerful motivators. The energies fueled by warlike causes are the easiest to whip up and the easiest for a charismatic leader — if he or she is unscrupulous enough — to use in the exercise of personal power. Under the intoxicating spell of killing, the rational mind is drugged, and emotions of the people around you can be exploited for almost anything. Josephus grasped that culture of violence with both hands and skillfully used it to achieve first of all celebrity as a Jew and then a pampered life of luxury as a Roman literary icon. Josephus was not a religious career man like Caiaphas — his religious passion didn't seem to have survived his adolescence — but there was a residue of religion there. He put what was left of his early dabbling in the spiritual into becoming a master religious propagandist. Religious propaganda is religion without morals, without truth (theology), without relationships — it is unadulterated *means*. For Josephus it was religion individualized and customized to augment his natural charisma. It was a bastard religion in the service of a cause, the cause justifying any means that promised success. The culture of war was conveniently at hand for Josephus. He used it skillfully to achieve fame and fortune. Killing the opposition, for Josephus, was not a cause, it was a means. For Josephus the cause was Josephus.

But these first followers of Jesus didn't kill, didn't use violence, even though in the religious atmosphere of the day it was the most natural thing in the world to do. Why didn't they? The simple answer is that they were following the resurrected Jesus, and the Jesus who was now living in them wasn't killing anyone.

The Zealots

It is important to observe at this juncture that Josephus was not a Zealot. Josephus was active in a world full of Zealots, and he was a general in a war in Galilee in which many of his soldiers were Zealots. But Zealots *believed*. They were committed to a cause, which they believed was God's cause. And they were committed to the death. A Zealot was a person whose entire identity was shaped by the conviction that God and only God demanded allegiance, and that violence was legitimate, even required, against the oppressor, the Evil.

Zealots were passionate for justice and fairness. They cared about people who were knocked around and exploited, the victims and the persecuted. They had a vision of a better world and they were ready to die for it. Their behavior was rooted in a conviction that God wanted justice, that God wanted a better life for his people than the Romans could ever give them, a life of freedom and especially the freedom to worship God, freedom to keep the Sabbath and be circumcised, freedom to maintain their core identity as God's people, not Rome's people.

Despite his youthful ventures into religion, none of Josephus' spiritual inclinations developed into convictions. Josephus was out for himself. He had no loyalties and no principles. He changed sides so that he could be with the winners, changed his name when that was expedient, changed his god when it was opportune, changed wives when that was advantageous. He sacrificed anyone who might be handy for the sacrifice — those forty men in the cave with him at Jotapata! — in order to survive and succeed in the world.

We must remember that Zealots were popular heroes among the Jews. Zealots were ready to give their lives for their country and many of them did. The glamour of heroism, of valor, of fighting for the underdog — all that attached to the Zealot. The various sects were sometimes rivals, other times allies for strategic reasons. But they had a common enemy: Evil.

Josephus summarizes zealotry under five revolutionary groups. First were the Sicarri, descendants of Judas the Galilean, who protested the imposition of taxes by the Roman governor of Syria, Quirinius, in A.D. 6. (This Judas is referred to by Gamaliel in his defense of the early church leaders in Acts 5:37.) Then there were the Zealots proper, led by Eleazar, a priest. In the course of cleansing the temple of Gentile influence in A.D. 67 to 68, Eleazar kicked off the all-out Jewish war with Rome. Third was John of Gischala, a Galilean who attracted many followers, who were more like a band of roving bandits. (John hated Josephus because he sensed that even though Josephus was clever and brilliant and charismatic, he had no principles — there was no steel in his backbone. And, of course, it wasn't long before the whole country knew that there wasn't. John despised Josephus; Josephus returned the compliment.) Fourth was Simon bar Giora, a champion of the lower classes who led the largest force in the defense of Jerusalem. The fifth group was made up of the Idumeans, who played a major part in the Jerusalem war. Two other Zealot-like groups are referred to in the Acts: a group led by Theudas, a revolutionary referred to by Gamaliel (Acts 5:36); and four thousand assassins (sicarii) led by an unnamed Egyptian out in the wilderness (Acts 21:38).

We get the picture. The country was overrun with Zealots of one stripe or another, sometimes fighting with one another, sometimes coming together to fight the Romans and Rome sympathizers, but always fighting in God's name.

*   *   *

Zealotry in Judaism had a noble heritage. The Maccabean revolt in 163 B.C. set the stage for the Jewish movement that eventually acquired the name "Zealot." We have already made reference to Mattathias, the old priest at Modein. With his five sons he set off the revolt against the foreign oppressor, the vile Antiochus IV Epiphanes who had set up the infamous "abomination that desolates" in the Holy of Holies of the Jerusalem temple. Judas Maccabeus scoured the temple of the sacrilege, rededicated it to the worship of God, and went on to clean up the country of pagan influence. He and his brothers ended up achieving a nation free of foreign domination — Judah, a free nation once more! The stories of daring and risk and courage that came out of those Maccabean years make for high drama still. The great winter feast of Hanukkah ("Dedication") referred to in St. John's Gospel (10:22) is the annual feast that remembers the Maccabean triumph and the rededication of the temple, still celebrated among Jews today.

An interesting aside here: one day when Jesus was in the Jerusalem temple teaching, he was asked by some there if he was the Christ. When his answer didn't please them, they made a good Maccabean response — they picked up stones to kill him (John 10:22-39). Violence in the cause of God. Apparently many of Jesus' contemporaries who cared about God had a good dose of Maccabean blood in their veins.

After a hundred years of rule by Maccabean kings, the Romans came in and put a stop to it. The freedom movement had lasted a single century. Then the Romans took over the country. A few years later (it was 37 B.C.) the Romans appointed Herod as king. Soon the people were again faced with the contaminating effects of idolatrous religion and pagan morals. Several years after Jesus was born, Judas the Galilean started a revolt (the year was A.D. 6) against oppressive Roman taxation. The revolt soon galvanized into the Zealot party. The old Maccabean spirit was still smoldering in the national psyche. The zealotry ignited by Judas the Galilean had its fundamental impetus from a nationalism that in the Maccabean period reached heights never attained before or since by the Jews.[8] At the time, the Roman presence was too strong to fight head-on. But the Zealot spirit persisted and spread. Sixty years later, Eleazar, son of Judas the Galilean, ignited the hostilities that resulted in the great war with the Romans that ended in the destruction of Jerusalem.

*   *   *

If we are to understand how radical the way of Jesus would have seemed to that generation, we need to keep reminding ourselves that by and large Zealots were admired. Zealots had a reputation for courage. They were continuing the God-blessed (they assumed) heritage of the Maccabees. A Zealot would give his life in a minute for God and for God's people.

The most dramatic story coming out of the Zealot movement, contemporary with but in contrast to Jesus' resurrection community, took place at Masada, a massive fortress built earlier by Herod the Great. Toward the end of the Jewish War, at about the time Josephus defected to the Romans, the Zealots retreated to Masada on the western shore of the Dead Sea (about thirty miles south of the Qumran community). It was virtually impregnable, but the Roman general Silva patiently and determinedly made his way, and finally got in. When he en-

---

8. See William Farmer, *Maccabees, Zealots, and Josephus* (New York: Columbia University Press, 1956).

tered the fortress he found 960 Zealots dead, all suicides. They chose to live not even one minute under godless, pagan Roman rule. As the Romans walked around among the corpses, they came upon a couple of women hiding in a cave who told them what had happened.

The Zealots understood themselves as a continuation of biblical tradition. They saw themselves as heirs of Phinehas, who killed Zimri and his Midianite girlfriend Cozbi (Num. 25). They saw themselves as part of the tradition of Elijah, who killed 450 prophets of Baal on Mount Carmel. They saw themselves fighting as the descendants of Joshua and Samuel and David. They were zealous for God, fighting on God's side.

That same spirit of violence was just below the surface still, even as the disciples were following Jesus. On Jesus' final trip to Jerusalem, when his disciples were getting unfriendly treatment in Samaritan country, the hot-headed Zebedee brothers, James and John, said to Jesus, "do you want us to command fire to come down from heaven and consume them?" (Luke 9:54). They had good biblical precedent for their question. They were in the very Samaritan country in which Elijah had done just that, called fire down from heaven, incinerating in turn three companies of fifty soldiers each (2 Kings 1). And of course the disciples had plenty of Zealot encouragement in the culture.

Jesus simply "rebuked" James and John (Luke 9:55). No rhetoric. No arguments. A simple no. There is to be no violence in the cause of God. None. End of discussion.

The rebuke holds.

*   *   *

Zealotry continues. It continues to be admired by many. It is hard to eradicate it from the human spirit, especially the religious human spirit. When we believe that God is on our side, that we have a mission to perform sanctioned by God, it is easy to do anything that we think will be effective — using force, pushing, bullying, manipulating, and, yes, killing — to bring victory to God. It is virtually irresistible when the opposition is identified as Evil.

Thomas Merton is blunt and uncompromising in his warning:

We must be on our guard against a kind of blind and immature zeal — the zeal of the enthusiast or the zealot — which represents precisely a frantic compensation for the deeply personal qualities which are lacking to us. The zealot is man who "loses himself" in his cause in such a way that he can no longer "find himself" at all. Yet paradoxically this "loss" of himself is not the salutary self-forgetfulness commanded by Christ. It is rather an immersion in his own willfulness conceived of as the will of an abstract, non-personal force: the force of a project or program.[9]

The Christian church has a long and sorry track record in this: the Crusades in Europe, the inquisition in Spain, the witch burnings in New England, Cromwell's revolution in England, the conquistadors in Central and South America.

Men and women in our Christian nation are still killing others in the name of Jesus, sometimes with guns, sometimes with words. Do we forget so easily that Jesus equated word-killing and sword-killing (Matt. 5:21-22)? There is plenty of Zealot spirit around still, with "religious" people using words or images or weapons to manipulate or interfere with a free response to God.

But the rebuke has, as yet, not been rescinded. As one early-church pastor put it, "force is no attribute of God."[10]

Jesus and the Zealots

Is there any way to retain the energy and focus and zeal of the Zealots without the violence? I think there is. The evidence is in this early

9. Thomas Merton, *Seasons of Celebration* (New York: Farrar, Straus and Giroux, Noonday paperback, 1977), p. 18.

10. *The Epistle of Diognetus*, quoted by Douglas Steere, *Dimensions of Prayer* (New York: Harper and Row, 1962), p. 19.

Christian community that was learning how to follow Jesus in a culture of violence (not unlike our culture of violence) without becoming violent. But also without being intimidated or silenced by the violence. They could have withdrawn into secure ghettos but they didn't. They stayed public, as public as the Zealots did. But unlike the Zealots, they were consistently nonviolent.

There is an important word that manages to convey both what zealotry without violence looks like and what it consists of. The word is *homothumadon*. Some words resist translation. We don't translate "Amen." We don't translate "Hallelujah." We don't translate "Hosanna." These words accumulate layers of meanings through the centuries and radiate rich associations and connections. When we translate them they fall flat. *Homothumadon* is one of these words. It is too bad that it wasn't included in the list of "untranslatables." We have to do the best we can by taking the word apart and then putting it back together again.

The word is used twelve times by Luke as he narrates the story of the resurrection community in the Acts of the Apostles, and once by Paul in Romans. It is usually translated "of one accord" or "of one mind" or simply "together."

When the 120 were gathered in the upper room praying and waiting for the gift of the Holy Spirit, they were *homothumadon* (with one accord; RSV) (Acts 1:14).

After that great Pentecost gathering when the Holy Spirit descended on them the Christians continued to be daily *homothumadon* (together), in the temple, praying and breaking bread in their homes (2:46).

After Peter and John had been delivered from prison by an angel and gave their report to their friends, they all "raised their voices *homothumadon* [together]" and prayed (4:24).

In the middle of the signs and wonders of those early days they were *homothumadon* (all together) in Solomon's Portico as people brought their sick friends and family members to be healed (5:12).

When Philip went into Samaria on a preaching mission, "The crowds *homothumadon* [with one accord] listened eagerly to what was said by Philip. . . . So there was much joy in that city" (8:6, 8).

At the Council of Jerusalem, as the apostles hammered out the policy that would keep converted Jews and Gentiles together, they sent the results of their work to Antioch, saying, "it has seemed good to us, *homothumodon* [having come to one accord; RSV]" (15:25).

Paul provides the final entry of the word in the New Testament near the end of his great letter to the Romans, praying "that *homo-thumadon* [together] you may with one voice glorify the God and Father of our Lord Jesus Christ" (Rom. 15:6). I wonder who used the word first, Luke or Paul, companions in missionary travel. Who was the first to come up with the lilting polysyllabic adverb that marked the way our early ancestors responded and were present to what God was doing, totally engaged but without a trace of violence?

"Of one mind" or "together" or "of one accord" all seem too tame to me. *Homothumadon* is a compound word: *homo* means "the same"; *thumas* means a strong emotion of anger; and the final syllable *don* signals that the word is adverbial. It is the middle component, *thumas,* that won't translate. *Thumas* is a fiery word, surging with energy — flying off the handle, losing your temper, lashing out. Except that in the context of the resurrection community there is nothing negative in it, no meanness, no violence. How do we get that intensity, that fire, that focused and controlled energy into a single English word that is energetic in love and peace and congenial community? I can't find one. That's why I just want to say *homothumadon.*

There was something burning within those followers of Jesus, drawing them together in the same mind and spirit, something akin to the energy of anger, but without anger. Something as fiery as the Zealots but without the Zealot violence.

Usually when we talk about unanimity we are describing what takes place in a meeting late at night when half the people have gone home and the rest are exhausted and nodding off, and the nods are interpreted as yeses and so there is a unanimous vote. That is not *homothumadon. Homothumadon* has fire in it. It is the passion of a consensual, unanimous response to something God does. We don't work it up. It is always dependent on something God has just done, or is about to do, or we are participating in. It is not something we bring about by conflict resolution or arbitration. It is fire. And it marks the church as it is formed by the Holy Spirit.

To get this right it is important to observe that *homothumadon* is not a theological or spiritual word as such. I gave seven citations in which it describes our response to God; but there are four other uses in Acts when it is used of negative, mean, or simply neutral emotions (Acts 7:57; 12:20; 18:12; 19:29). So there is no virtue in *homothumadon* as a thing in itself. We find the Zealot fire without the Zealot violence in this word only by staying close to the actual resurrection context of the stories in Acts. Apart from a resurrection context, the word can turn ugly. Fans at a football game experience *homothumadon* when their team scores, which sometimes leads to rioting. On the other hand, everybody in the room when a baby is born experiences *homothumadon* in the fresh beauty of new life that prefigures resurrection life, in awe before the mystery.

But the distinctive thing in the early church is that they were following the resurrected Jesus, with a compelling sense that something had happened out there which was now active in here among them. The Holy Spirit did something in Jesus and then he did it in them. The primary action takes place in Jesus and only then in us. It is beyond us but then gets into us. We are following and believing and worshiping — and then, there it is: *homothumadon*.

This is not whipping up enthusiasm for Jesus. This is not arguing or persuading people into agreement. This is not managing various self-interests into a workable program or plan. This is not contrived by us.

But it must be recognized by us. The conviction behind the possibility of this uniquely Christian *homothumadon* is that the resurrected Jesus is still doing what he has always done, and he is doing it in our world, in our neighborhood.

The difficulty of experiencing *homothumadon* is that typically we aren't paying any attention to the resurrected Jesus, or don't know what to look for, or are impatient in the waiting, or are distracted by more glamorous and riveting events and circumstances that promise shortcuts.

There was no lack of *homothumadon* in the world of Josephus. War is probably the most powerful action in human experience for getting us to feel and think and act together, as one, *homothumadon*. And wars, both big and small, neighborhood skirmishes and full-scale battles, were breaking out daily as the early church was in formation. How did the Christian community maintain its fire without getting caught up in the violence, whether with words or swords? How did the Christians stay on track, on the path of following Jesus?

Praying on the Way with the Resurrection Christians

Amid much talk to the contrary, the fact is that there are no secrets to living out the Christian life. No prerequisite attitudes. No conditions more or less favorable to pursuing the Way. Anyone can do this, from any place, starting at any time.

But it never takes place without prayer. Prayer is basic. Prayer is basic because it provides the primary language for everything that takes place on the way of Jesus. If we go to a shopping mall in North America, we speak English to get what we want. If we go to a restaurant in France, we speak French to order our meal. If we travel in Greece, we speak Greek to find our way to the Acropolis. And if we decide to become Christians and follow Jesus, we pray. We pray because it is the only language we have for speaking to the God revealed in Jesus. It is also the only language we have for listening to the commands and blessings and guidance that God provides through Jesus. God is nothing if not personal. Both God and we humans are most personal, most characteristically our unique selves, in our use of language. When language has to do with God and us, us and God, we call it prayer.

What I want to insist on is that prayer is not something added on to the Christian life (or any life for that matter). It is the language in which that life is lived out, nurtured, developed, revealed, informed; the language in which it believes, loves, explores, seeks, and finds. There are no shortcuts or detours. Prayer is the cradle language among those who are "born anew" and then the intimate, familiar, developing language of growing up to follow the way of Jesus.

But because in our secularized society prayer is often associated with what people of "spiritual" interests pursue or with formal acts conducted by professional leaders, it is necessary from time to time to call attention to the fact that prayer is the street language that we use with Jesus, who walks the streets with us. We can't put off prayer until we "get good at it." It is the only language available to us as we bring our unique and particular selves, "just as we are without one plea," into the daily, hourly speaking and listening to God who comes "just as he is" in Jesus.

$$*\quad*\quad*$$

This is what the early resurrection-formed Christians did in the world of Josephus and the Zealots. It is what put the kind of fire in their lives that was nonviolent, enlivening rather than killing. It is not enough to be warned of the opportunism of Josephus and the violence of the Zealots. Both the opportunism and the violence are so much a part of our society and culture still that we take them in with our mother's milk. In the midst of all the stimulus and attraction and pressure and precedent to take things into their own hands and accomplish a victory, whether through conniving Josephan manipulations or using Zealot daggers, some men and women managed to keep their attention on Jesus, managed to follow the risen Jesus. It is possible still.

But it is possible only through prayer. We can only *pray* our lives into the way of following Jesus. This praying is, in large part, the Spirit praying in us. The way we follow must be internalized and embodied — prayer both internalizes and embodies Jesus; there is no other way into the Way. Judas followed Jesus with his feet all over Palestine, but it never got inside him; he was an opportunist to the end. Peter followed Jesus all over Palestine, but at the crisis in the garden he turned unaccountably into a zealot, swinging his sword with the best of them. Prayer is the way we get the following (not just the feeling!) inside us. Or, as that wonderful phrase in Psalm 84 has it, we become the person "in whose heart are the highways to Zion" (Ps. 84:5).

$$*\quad*\quad*$$

The first prayer recorded after the church came into being on the day of Pentecost (there is a pre-Pentecost prayer at Acts 1:24-25) is prayed by the early Christians. Peter and John had just been let out of prison by Caiaphas, had rejoined their friends and given their report. The spontaneous response was prayer, a prayer that seems to me to be particularly well-suited for our use as we follow this narrow path, flanked by the broad roads of Josephus on one side and the Zealots on the other. Here's the prayer:

> Hearing the report, they lifted their voices in a wonderful harmony [*homothumadon!*] in prayer: "Strong God, you made heaven and earth and sea and everything in them. By the Holy Spirit you spoke through the mouth of your servant and our father, David:
>
>> Why the big noise, nations?
>> Why the mean plots, peoples?
>> Earth's leaders push for position,
>> Potentates meet for summit talks,
>> The God-deniers, the Messiah-defiers!
>
> "For in fact they did meet — Herod and Pontius Pilate with nations and people, even Israel itself! — met in this very city to plot against your holy Son Jesus, the One you made Messiah, to carry out the plans you long ago set in motion.
>
> "And now they're at it again! Take care of their threats and give your servants fearless confidence in preaching your Message, as you stretch out your hand to us in healings and miracles and wonders done in the name of your holy servant Jesus." (Acts 4:24-30, *The Message*)

This can stand as the signature prayer of the resurrection community, who were filled with the fire of the Holy Spirit that raised Jesus from the dead, but without raising their arms in violence. They refused the violence so widespread in both world and church that leads people away from God down all kinds of blind alleys and dead ends on life-wasting detours — damning, bullying, rejecting, and killing the opposition.

The most conspicuous element in this prayer is its sense that God rules. The people in a wonderful vital harmony, *homothumadon,* address their all-powerful, all encompassing "Strong God" *(Despota).*

Strong God. Confidence coupled with humility develops out of this kind of praying. If God is in charge, then I'm not. I live in the confidence that God is either doing or allowing whatever is going on, and also in the confidence that I am included in his rule. My participation is part of it. Didn't my early Christian friends also pray for boldness to continue to speak God's word, participating significantly in his Lordship? Everything that I am and feel and think and pray is part of his rule. That God's "throne is in heaven" (Ps. 11:4) has never meant — in our Scriptures, in the revelation in Jesus, in our best pastors and theologians, or in our many daily friends and companions in the way — that God is saying, "You just go about your business and leave the running of the universe and history to me." Not at all. This prayer was offered in a world in which Rome and Rome's Palestinian henchmen, the Herod boys, called all the shots, in which the religious temple establishment dominated by the high priestly family of Caiaphas had the final say-so on all matters regarding Israel's religion, and in which Josephus carried off all the honors and the Zealots were at the center of the action. But this prayer bypassed the politics of Rome, establishment religion, and the newspaper headlines, confident that the Strong God was, in fact, still in the ruling business.

These first-generation Christians, no more privileged than we are in these matters, were confident that they were, part and parcel, participants in that rule, that God included them in his rule and his ruling. And they prayed for the boldness that would reflect that confidence, would prevent them from sinking into a passivity that used God's rule as an excuse to be spectators to history. How do we develop humility — which means staying human and not developing god-pretensions — without becoming a doormat? How do we develop humility — which means working within the bounds of morality and wisdom — without becoming small-minded and provincial and domesticated? How do we develop humility — which means being just who we are, no more and no less — brimming with energy, risking life, a person who runs, not plods, in the way of God's commandments?

When we follow Jesus, that's what we do — and pray prayers like this prayer, which gradually and steadily internalizes and embodies a robust confidence in God's rule and a relaxed acceptance of our humanity.

This prayer developed out of long meditation and much praying of Psalm 2, which is a favorite psalm of New Testament writers. It is quoted or alluded to nine times (Matt. 3:17; Acts 4:25-26; 13:33; Heb. 1:5; 5:5; 2 Peter 1:17; Rev. 2:26-27; 12:5; 19:15). It shares honors with Psalm 110 as the most quoted psalm in the New Testament. The contrast with our times is significant. What are our favorite psalms? What psalms have we memorized? Psalm 23 tops the charts. Psalms 1 and 100 and 121 are runners-up. But Psalm 2?

Psalm 2 provides a text-prayer for personally realizing and internalizing, feeling in our gut and in our muscles, the unbridgeable abyss fixed between the ways of this world — its Herod and Caiaphas and Josephus ways, and also the counter ways pursued by the Pharisee and Essene and Zealot sects — and the Strong God and his Messiah: "Don't you know there's a King in Zion?" (Ps. 2:6 *The Message*).

The first generation of Christians took Jesus at his word when he announced that his kingdom was at hand — a real (not ideal) kingdom with a real king, King Jesus. The words and sentences of Psalm 2 dismissed the pretensions of all these other ways and let Christ the King permeate their preaching and prayers and following. They followed the resurrected Jesus with an air of triumph and praise. The gospel was not something private that they cultivated in the cozy security of their homes and hearts; it was public, the most powerful force in human history, shaping the destiny of nations as well as the souls of men and women.

And there is this: the prayer is Trinitarian. It is addressed to God the Creator: "Strong God, you made heaven and earth and sea and everything in them" (Acts 4:24). It uses as its text the inspired words of David that God spoke "by the Holy Spirit" (v. 25); and all the action is centered in "your holy Son Jesus . . . Messiah" (v. 27).

A unique thing was taking place in the Christian church as our early ancestors were saying and praying what they believed — a formulation of God as Holy Trinity. This prayer is laying groundwork for that formulation. Two thousand years later Trinity continues to serve as both the most succinct and the most comprehensive way to maintain our bearings as we follow Jesus and stay alert to the uniqueness of what it means to follow him in a world that is dominated by the powerful and popular anti-Trinitarian ways of Herod, Caiaphas, and Josephus.

By insisting that God is three-personed — Father, Son, and Holy Spirit; God-in-community — we are given an understanding of God that is emphatically personal. The only way he reveals himself or works among us is personally. God is personal under the personal designations of Father, Son, and Holy Spirit, and never in any other way. Never impersonally as Force or Influence. Never impersonally as Idea or Cause.

It is the easiest thing in the world for us to use words as a kind of abstract truth or principle, to distribute the good news in tabloids of information. Trinity prevents us from doing this. We can never get away with depersonalizing either the gospel or God to make things easier, simpler, or more convenient.

And Trinity is a perpetual reminder that the only way that we can follow in the way of Jesus is by being personal participants — not just by thinking right thoughts or carrying out assigned tasks, but prayerfully and believingly involved in the very lives with whom, name by name, face by face, God is involved.

*   *   *

I readily admit that I don't get it. I have no hard empirical evidence to support this psalm and to confirm this prayer of the first Christians. Nothing on the news, nothing in the headlines, nothing in the history books, nothing in the financial world, and nothing in massacres and floods and hurricanes and starvation and hijackings that keep being reported from all over the world establishes the believability of this psalm.

But here's the thing: the first Christians had no better documentation. By the end of the first century, with Josephus going to a comfortable death under the patronage of the Roman Empire and the stories of the Zealot patriots on Masada instilling pride in every Jewish boy and girl, the people of the Christian church were still living furtively at the margins of society. They had no empirical evidence that their sovereign God was any match for any of the leaders in Palestine or Greece or Rome. And if they wanted to do something about what was wrong with the world, which they certainly did, they had prominent models of successful leaders at hand, represented in Herod and Caiaphas and Josephus, along with counter models in the Pharisees, Essenes, and Zealots.

Nobody seems to have argued that although Jesus had got them started in the new and right way, now that they were plunged into the so-called "real world" and getting down to the business of building this kingdom of Jesus, it would only be prudent to examine how Herod and Caiaphas and Josephus did it and employ their skills and strategies, or go looking for allies among the Pharisees, Essenes, and Zealots. They didn't do it.

What stands out as we consider all these dismissed options is that following Jesus is a unique way of life. It is like nothing else. There is nothing and no one comparable. Following Jesus gets us little or nothing of what we commonly think we need or want or hope for. Following Jesus accomplishes nothing on the world's agenda. Following Jesus takes us right out of this world's assumptions and goals to a place where a lever can be inserted that turns the world upside down and inside out. Following Jesus has everything to do with this world, but almost nothing in common with this world.

*   *   *

At the end of the first century, in A.D. 100, Josephus died in Rome in comfortable luxury, a successful diplomat, military leader, and writer. It was seventy years after Jesus' resurrection and as yet the followers of Jesus hadn't made an observable dent anywhere: not in Judaism, not in

Hellenism, not in the Zealot movement, not among the Pharisees, not in Roman rule.

And yet they kept at it. We are keeping at it still. And why? Because in following Jesus we have learned something about kingdom that Herod didn't know, and about God that Caiaphas didn't know, and about the soul that Josephus didn't know. And we are convinced that this kingdom in which God rules, and this God who is revealed in Jesus, and this soul that is sanctified by the Holy Spirit are real and eternal and true. They hold the world as we know it together. And nothing else does.

The most powerful biblical witness to this is the final book of the Bible, St. John's Revelation, a rousing, noisy, praising, colorful witness to the present reality of Jesus' kingdom of salvation at work, using the lives of obscure Christians in a world that doesn't even know they exist. The prayer of those first resurrection Christians in Jerusalem, reported in Acts 4, over the course of the next seventy years of the first century expanded into the grand worship that is on display in the Revelation.

When that prayer was finished, Luke tells us, "they were all filled with the Holy Spirit and spoke the word of God with boldness" (v. 31). They had become the prayer they prayed.

*   *   *

Herod, Caiaphas, and Josephus, all three in their lifetimes, were more influential and more effective than Jesus. The three protest movements prominent during the years when Jesus was announcing the presence of God's kingdom and when his resurrection church was in formation — Pharisees, Essenes, and Zealots — all attracted far more followers than did Jesus.

And here's the sobering thing: they still do. We are faced with this wonderful, or not-so-wonderful, irony: Jesus — most admired, most worshiped (kind of), most written about. And least followed.

But in every generation a few do follow Jesus. They deny themselves, they take up their cross, and they follow him. They lose their lives and save them — and along with their own, the lives of many, many others.

Some Writers on Discerning the Way

It is evident by now, I would think, that there is far more to following the way of Jesus than knowing right from wrong — the Ten Commandments sort of thing. And there is more to it than believing rightly, as outlined in the Apostles' Creed. Discernments need to be made continuously between this and that, when and how. Conditions on the road are constantly changing, companions and friends are a movable feast, the devil's seductions come in a bewildering variety, the weather can shift unannounced from quiet sunshine to noisy thunder and dangerous lightning. Even though I have the map I need and the basic survival essentials, circumstances arise and people show up that baffle me. To add to the confusion, I find that I live in a culture that is overrun with advice-givers. I am first pleased but then alarmed that there are so many people out there who are eager to help me. Who do I listen to? Who do I trust?

I am wary of experts who are quick to offer advice. I have been warned that the devil often appears as an angel of light. I also know that the way of Jesus is under perpetual attack but that the attack rarely looks or feels like an attack. There is a good deal of sleight of hand involved. As Amos Wilder wisely comments, "The Spirit is not to be quenched, yet the spirits should be tested."[1]

1. Amos Niven Wilder, *Theopoetic* (Philadelphia: Fortress, 1976), p. 22.

The fact is that I need wise and alert Christian friends, vigilant for dangers that I don't recognize as dangers, in order to discern the ways of Jesus. I need friends who are not naive concerning the complexities involved in following Jesus on roads heavily trafficked with blind guides and false prophets, but who are at the same time wide-awake to beauty and wonder, capable of being astonished and responsive to the richness of life all around me. I need friends who can be trusted to know something about discerning the ways that I follow the Way.

Such friends are not always at hand when I need them. But with their books I can maintain a running conversation with them. They keep me alert to the discernments required on the way. Here are seven who have served and continue to serve me well.

Albert Borgmann, *Technology and the Character of Contemporary Life*

The proliferation of technology is a major factor, maybe *the* major factor, in the way we live our lives these days. Borgmann, a philosophy professor at the University of Montana, is our most incisive analyst of the hidden ways in which technology disengages us from firsthand, personal engagement with things and people and thereby subverts the ways in which we "take up with the world" (his phrase). He doesn't propose that we eliminate or even reduce technology. He wants us to understand how it works. He diagnoses the nature of the technological world in which we are immersed, so that we can make prayerful and wise discernments in the ways we live. His counsel and wisdom have enormous implications for those of us who are determined to stay personal and present to Jesus and one another on this way. (Chicago: University of Chicago Press, 1984)

John Muir, *The Wilderness World of John Muir*

Way is first of all a word that designates a feature of the landscape: a road, a path. Whatever else the way involves, it begins by putting our feet on the ground so we can walk to some place — and pay attention while walking to what is beneath and around us. Spirituality begins in place. All love, all worship, all believing, all obedience occurs in place. The life of the spirit is as much about geology and geography as it is about theology and prayer. John Muir came to America from Scotland with his father in 1849. He was eleven years old. For the next sixty-five years he treated the North American continent as a sanctuary for the worship of God. For me he is the first in an illustrious company of men and women who have guided me in discovering and exploring the spirituality of the land — mountains and streams, lakes and plains, flowers and forests and glaciers. These keep my feet on the ground, *ground* me, even as I pursue the ways of prayer and sacrifice, worship and obedience in this creation that Calvin designated the "theater of God's glory." (Boston: Houghton Mifflin Company, 1954. Edited and with comments by Edwin Way Teale.)

Marva Dawn, *Powers, Weakness, and the Tabernacling of God*
Every attempt we make to use the ways of the world, the flesh, and the devil to accomplish the agenda of the kingdom of God, weakens the church and enervates faith. But the gospel is absolutely unique, and its "ways" are absolutely unique. Marva Dawn tightens the focus on what is unique in what we are doing, especially as that uniqueness is expressed in worship. She is insistent and relentless in exposing the fraudulence involved in marketing the gospel by employing the strategies of a consumerist culture. I read her books to keep from being duped by the "deceitful tongue" of slick contemporaneity. Careful and honest exegetical work are combined with years of frontline experience in dealing with the lies and illusions of our culture that are corrupting our churches and our culture. As she confronts the flabbiness of soul promoted by "the powers," her prophetic voice is trenchant. (Grand Rapids: Eerdmans, 2001)

Dorothy Day, *The Long Loneliness*
As we follow Jesus we listen to him tell the parables of the Sheep and Goats at the last judgment and the Good Samaritan on the Jericho Road. His stories make it clear that if we choose to follow him we are necessarily involved in social responsibilities on the road. People are in trouble and need help. Poverty, social unrest, class conflict, unemployment, homelessness, and war are complex issues that defy simplifica-

tion, solution by slogan. Jesus doesn't give us step-by-step instruction: how to give the cup of water, how to bind up the wounds, how to do any of this. He only tells us that we must. The social ills that converged in the 1930s in America provoked a major crisis in American life. American democracy and the American church were put to the test. They both survived, but neither survived unscathed. The ways in which American Christians lived through that time brought out the best among some and the worst among others. It brought the best out of Dorothy Day. Her autobiography is an honest account of the way of Jesus lived out on the American road: devoutly and openly Christian, passionate for the poor, working tirelessly in the cities among the homeless and unemployed. She demonstrates a rare and marvelous integration of soul and body, social needs and personal salvation, self-survival and self-sacrifice. She is an icon of the Christ-centered life lived out among the poor, whom Christ so unequivocally blessed. (San Francisco: Harper and Row, 1952)

Georges Bernanos, *Diary of a Country Priest*

I bought this book forty years ago in paperback in an airport bookstall to while away a transcontinental flight. I had never heard of the author — I purchased it on the strength of its title. I was gripped by the story. I was learning how to follow Jesus in a religious world in which I was finding myself consistently at odds with the prevailing values and practices. I assumed I was reading an autobiography since it was written in the form of a diary. The discernments involved in following Jesus, worked out in conditions of poverty and humiliation, struck me with a depth of authenticity and gospel obedience that I hardly imagined possible. I later learned that the book was a novel. I read it again. It may have been fiction, but there was not a false note in it — every sentence rang true. Through numerous re-readings it has permeated my imagination. For me it is a major witness to the nuances and subtleties involved in following the actual, revealed Jesus in a culture that has installed religious conventions and fantasies in place of the real thing. (Garden City, N.Y.: Image Books, a division of Doubleday, 1954 [first printing, 1937])

Stanley Hauerwas, *Vision and Virtue*

For forty years my theologian of choice as a conversation partner in discerning the ways appropriate to following the way of Jesus has been Stanley Hauerwas. He is a prolific writer and courageously takes up questions that arise in virtually every area in which Americans have to work out our salvation in either a society or a church that provides no consensus. He does not offer "solutions" or "answers" that the rest of us can carry around with us and apply when the circumstances require them. Rather, he immerses us in a narrative world in which every detail of our lives is embodied in personal relationships that are faithful to the way of Jesus. (Notre Dame, Ind.: University of Notre Dame Press, 1981)

Czeslaw Milosz, *A Treatise on Poetry*

This Polish poet — modestly self-identified simply as a witness — provides a rich array of discernments for living truthfully in uncongenial circumstances. His poems are field notes written as he picked his way, making survival discernments as he went, through the successive minefields through which he lived — German nazism, Soviet communism, French secularism, American consumerism — decade after decade across most of the twentieth century. The bottomless pit of evil in which he began and the subsequent exilic conditions of his maturity galvanized his art in discerning God's truth and beauty in the particulars of his life and times. When he was awarded the Nobel Prize in 1980 he said, "My presence here on this tribune should be an argument for all those who praise life's God-given, marvelously complex unpredictability." His poetry, steeped as it is in personal, cultural, and political conditions, repeatedly strengthens my resolve to keep the ways of Jesus undiluted by compromise with the ways of the world. His poetry documents his conviction that "One clear stanza can take more weight / Than a whole wagon of elaborate prose." (New York: Ecco, 2001. Translated by Robert Hass.)

Index of Subjects and Names

Index of Scripture References